Disappearing Traces

THE STEPHEN S. WEINSTEIN SERIES
IN POST-HOLOCAUST STUDIES

The Stephen S. Weinstein Series in Post-Holocaust Studies carries on the work and publications of the Pastora Goldner Series (2004–2007), exploring questions that continue to haunt humanity in the aftermath of Nazi Germany's attempt to destroy Jewish life and culture. Books in this series address the most current and pressing issues of our post-Holocaust world. They are grounded in scholarship undertaken by the Stephen S. Weinstein Holocaust Symposium, whose membership—international, interdisciplinary, interfaith, and intergenerational—is committed to dialogue as a fundamental form of inquiry and understanding. The symposium and the series are generously supported by Stephen S. Weinstein, who, with his wife, Nancy, is dedicated to the work of *tikkun olam*, the healing of the world, and whose commitment to combating present-day evils in our world has inspired the participants in the symposium who contribute to this series.

SERIES EDITORS

DAVID PATTERSON, *University of Texas*
JOHN K. ROTH, *Claremont McKenna College*

EDITORIAL BOARD

MARGARET BREARLEY, *London, England*
MYRNA GOLDENBERG, *Bethesda, Maryland*
HUBERT G. LOCKE, *University of Washington*
ROCHELLE L. MILLEN, *Wittenberg University*

Disappearing Traces

HOLOCAUST TESTIMONIALS, ETHICS, AND AESTHETICS

Dorota Glowacka

UNIVERSITY OF WASHINGTON PRESS   *Seattle and London*

THIS BOOK IS MADE POSSIBLE BY A COLLABORATIVE GRANT
FROM THE ANDREW W. MELLON FOUNDATION.

Publication of this book has also been aided by
generous grants from the Millard Meiss Publication
Fund of the College Art Association; the James P.
Geiss Foundation; and the China Studies Program,
a division of the Henry M. Jackson School of
International Studies at the University of Washington.

University of Washington Press
P.O. Box 50096, Seattle, WA 98145 U.S.A.
www.washington.edu/uwpress

Library of Congress Cataloging-in-Publication Data
Glowacka, Dorota, 1960–
Disappearing traces : Holocaust testimonials, ethics,
and aesthetics / Dorota Glowacka.
p. cm.—(Stephen S. Weinstein series in post-
Holocaust studies)
Includes bibliographical references and index.
ISBN 978-0-295-99169-6 (pbk. : alk. paper)
ISBN 978-0-295-99168-9 (hardcover : alk. paper)
1. Holocaust, Jewish (1939–1945)—Personal
narratives—History and criticism. 2. Holocaust,
Jewish (1939–1945)—Moral and ethical aspects.
3. Art—Moral and ethical aspects. I. Title.
D804.348.G56 2012
940.53'18—dc23   2011051659

For Tato, Wiktor Jassem,
and in memory of Mama, Grażyna Jassem

I wanted some trace of them to be left behind.

—IDA FINK

CONTENTS

ACKNOWLEDGMENTS

This book has been many years in the making, and most of the ideas that finally found their way onto its pages probably first raced through my head in the classroom, in response to tough, clever questions asked by my students. Their love of books, curiosity, and unrelenting passion for new ideas have inspired me over the years and kept me going, and I would like to thank them all. The University of King's College, where I have been allowed to teach "whatever I want," has been a wonderfully supportive environment, and I cannot give enough thanks to my colleagues, the administration, and the support staff for never turning down a request—whether for a little extra funding, help with the new computer software, or a little break and a good word when things seemed too busy to manage. Thank you also to two gifted student assistants, Martin McCallum and Melinda Robb, for stepping in to help me with the nitty-gritty editorial tasks.

Some of the research, the funds to offset the costs, and the time afforded for writing were made possible by a grant from the Social Sciences and Humanities Research Council of Canada for which I am grateful.

I have drawn sustenance for this project from an association with a very special group of friends at the Stephen Weinstein Wroxton Holocaust Symposium. Being invited to join that community of minds and to discuss ideas together has been a true blessing in my professional life, although engaging with these exceptional, inspiring individuals has also enriched me as a person. My admiration and gratitude to Skippy and Nancy never ceases to grow, not only for making "Wroxton" possible but also for having very big hearts.

|||

Putting this book together has been beneficial in unexpected ways: getting to know, via e-mail, some of the amazing artists whose images are included in the book has been a privilege. I would like to thank Gerson Leiber, Herzl Kashetsky, Mindy Weisel, Lily Markiewicz, Bracha Ettinger, and Ewa Kuryluk for their exceptional generosity, patience, and, on occasion, helpful explanations of the details of their work. Many thanks as well to Mrs. Ora Ardon for being so gracious with my request for a permission to reproduce Mordecai Ardon's work, and to Professor Jan Jagielski, for providing me with the photographs from his book *The Last Remnants of the Warsaw Ghetto*. The editors at the Washington University Press have been most encouraging, professional, and patient, and I am grateful for that extra help and a human touch, so much appreciated in the cold, big world of publishing. I am grateful to the reviewers for the Press for being extraordinarily careful readers. Their comments helped me fill in at least some of the gaps in the text.

Disappearing Traces is dedicated to my Tato, Wiktor Jassem, who "gave me my Holocaust." For all their horror and tragedy, the stories of his survival and courage have also been a precious gift that continues to give. This book is also a tribute to my Mama, who was a true Levinasian in spirit, although she never read a page of the French philosopher's work. But there are so many people to whom I have a debt of gratitude beyond repayment. I would like to thank Piotra for always giving more than anyone can give and without whose generosity nothing would have been possible. Thank you to my daughter Maga, for whom visiting the United States Holocaust Memorial Museum in Washington was too much because she knows exactly where she comes from. She has even taught me a thing a two, which goes to show that the transmission of memory and wisdom between generations is a two-way street. And thank you to my son Jerome, who always wants to know things because "they are interesting" and because he always cares. My endless, loving, and very guilty thank you's to my husband Zbyszek: I know it has not been easy to put up with "that."

Disappearing Traces

Figure 0.1.   A family of Holocaust survivors in Kraków, Poland, 1947. From left to right: Marek Jassem, Wiktor Jassem, Felicja Jassem, and Arnold Jassem. Photo courtesy of the author.

Introduction

Disappearing Traces: Holocaust
Testimonials between Ethics and Aesthetics

It is not an event. It is not an event. It is something horrible.

—HELENA JOCKEL, a Holocaust survivor

The truth doesn't kill the possibility of art.

—SHOSHANA FELMAN, "The Return of the Voice"

During the ceremonies inaugurating the Montreal Holocaust Memorial Center in 2003, Aba Beer, a Holocaust survivor, was asked to reminisce about his experiences during the war. At a loss for words as to how to describe the horrors he had undergone, he remarked, "It takes a poet to describe it. I don't have the words" (MacAfee, 2003). What does it mean when an eyewitness to the events, on whom we rely absolutely for knowledge about the past, summons the imaginary powers of a poet to convey the truth about his Holocaust ordeal? When Beer admits his linguistic powerlessness vis-à-vis the experience he has tried—and failed—to describe, his plea that a poet come to his aid is underwritten by the ethical imperative (Remember!). Beer's remark thus reveals a paradox inherent in the majority of Holocaust testimonies: the obligation to remember, which derives its ethical force from the horror of the victims' experiences, requires aesthetic prowess and the imaginative tools of a poet so it can be carried out.

This conflict between the ethical imperative to remember the catastrophic past and the iconoclastic impetus of art called upon to convey that memory is even more pronounced in literary and artistic works about the Holocaust, as Theodor Adorno already knew when he proclaimed, in 1949, an injunction against "writing poetry after Auschwitz."[1] As I argue throughout this book, Holocaust testimonials provide a locus where received notions of ethics and aesthetics, their foundational categories and concepts, and traditional distinctions between their proper domains are continuously contested and transformed. The goal, then, is not to find out what constitutes ethically responsible representations, as opposed to irreverent, merely aesthetic productions. In the last two decades, such distinctions have become increasingly fluid, as witnessed in discussions about Art Spiegelman's comic book *Maus*, Binjamin Wilkomirski *alias* Bruno Doesseker's fake Holocaust memoir *Fragments: Memories of a Wartime Childhood* (1995),[2] Norman Finkelstein's polemical study *The Holocaust Industry* (2000),[3] Roberto Benigni's Oscar-winning film *Life Is Beautiful* (1997), Peter Eisenmann's *Memorial to the Murdered Jews of Europe* in Berlin (inaugurated in 2005), the exhibition *Mirroring Evil: Nazi Imagery/Recent Art* at the Jewish Museum in New York (2001),[4] Quentin Tarantino's revenge fantasy *Inglourious Basterds* (2009), and other contentious Holocaust productions. Instead, the book explores an aporetic relation between ethics and aesthetics in works about the Holocaust, revealing this tension to be a fundamental component of the labor of memory, the task of which is to bring the traumatic past into the fold of the present and carry it toward the future. This constitutive tension between ethical and aesthetic imperatives animates the search for new means of expressing their intertwined, yet contradictory, claims. The resulting new literary and artistic idioms come to the aid of the Holocaust survivor as well as his listeners—potential future rememberers, whom his words, aided by "a poet," bring into existence. In works of literature and art, these new languages of testimony make it possible for us to describe, to understand, to imagine, and to remember.

Beer's remark also draws attention to a relatively recent shift in the dominant modalities of representing traumatic history. As French historian Annette Wieviorka noted in 1998, although literature and art initially were considered inferior to historical research and documentation, and inadequate to the task of depicting atrocities, increasingly they became accepted as legitimate forms of testimony. As Ernst van Alphen (1997) writes in his study of Holocaust art, "Whereas the education I received failed to make the event of the Holocaust a meaningful event to me, Holocaust literature and art finally succeeded in calling my attention to this apocalyptic moment in human history" (3). The elevation, and even privileging, of imaginative representations as forms of engagement with the past allows us to interpret them as memory sites in their own right. They can even be considered unique because of their capacity for conveying the mnesic trace of that which falls outside traditional techniques of preserving the past. As Brett Ashley Kaplan (2007) argues in *Unwanted Beauty*, the indisputable beauty of many depictions of the Holocaust "encourages us to see the complexity of the Shoah in ways that conventional works fail to achieve" (3).

The term "Holocaust testimonials" is used here to designate this wide range of literary and artistic works inspired by the memory of the Holocaust. My intention is to indicate their common focus on the testimonial imperative and yet to situate them in a larger context, beyond eyewitness testimony as such, even though the majority of texts discussed here were indeed written by firsthand witnesses to the events. However, the word "testimonial" also alludes to an expression of gratitude when awarding an exceptional person in recognition of his or her service or unique deed. This connotation of the word "testimonial" brings out the fact that all of these works have been circumspectly produced as gifts. They are offered as an homage to the dead, to whom a debt of memory is owed, but also as a recognition of those in the present—the community of readers or viewers that the work hopes to bring together—and of those in the future who will continue to remember because of their deep need to do so. In choosing the term "Holocaust testimonials," I am also guided by literary theorist Robert Eaglestone's (2004) insight that Holocaust testimonies, whether diaries, memoirs, or oral testimonies, constitute a genre in their own right (8). This genre, moreover, has gained a prominent place in the last four decades, to which Wieviorka refers as "the era of the witness." According to Wieviorka (2006), this new epoch of historical consciousness dawned in the wake of the Eichmann trial in 1961, when, for the first time, testimonies of Holocaust survivors became central to our understanding of recent history and thus gained legitimacy as ways of relating to the past. Wieviorka writes, "The Eichmann trial freed the victims to speak. It created a social demand for testimonies. . . . With the Eichmann trial, the witness became an embodiment of memory [*un homme-mémoire*]" (87–89).

What does it mean, however, for Holocaust testimonials to be "embodiments of memory"? What is their status and their modus operandi as "witnesses" to the events in the past that they recreate imaginatively? Further, what transformations in the existing conceptions of language, truth, experience, and the human subject does the

recognition of the primacy of testimony bring about? In order to pursue these questions, I bring literary and artistic works into philosophical contexts, drawing especially on French philosopher and Holocaust survivor Emmanuel Levinas's message of ethical responsibility
to the other, in conjunction with theoretical reflections on language
and the problematic of representation in general (by Jean-François
Lyotard, Jacques Derrida, Hannah Arendt, Walter Benjamin, Giorgio Agamben, and others). Admittedly, many Holocaust scholars
find theoretical concepts too abstract and distancing to be applied to
events fraught with human suffering. Some historians, for instance,
view poststructuralist theory as advocating relativism, which, as Deborah Lipstadt fears, plays into the hands of Holocaust deniers. Jewish theologian David Patterson (2006b) maintains that modernist and
postmodern philosophies are responsible for the general "bankruptcy
of [Western] thought" (32). Patterson sees in postmodernism the culmination of self-centered thinking, which disregards the radical alterity of another human being. As such, it bears the stigma of radical evil
that found its most gruesome expression in National Socialism. Other
critics, such as David Hirsch, Elizabeth Bellamy, and Richard Wolin,
object to integrating Holocaust remembrance with theoretical works
whose authors have been influenced by Martin Heidegger, while dis-
regarding the German philosopher's wartime association with National Socialism, and by Paul de Man, despite his prewar anti-Semitic
writings.[5] Although these objections still persist, theoretical perspectives have also been gradually accepted among many Holocaust scholars. This growing tolerance most likely is related to critical theory's
"ethical turn" in the 1990s (largely brought about by theorists' responses to the Heidegger and de Man "affairs"), and the ensuing recognition of theory's political and ethical ramifications. The increasing
centrality of Levinas's ethics in contemporary thought has been another factor, and philosophers such as Lyotard and Derrida have acknowledged its influence on their work. Further, as Robert Eaglestone
has shown, a number of contemporary theorists are deeply committed
to the memory of the Holocaust, and the necessity to respond to "Remember!" animates their work, even if some of them acknowledge the
impact of that legacy only indirectly.

More broadly, many Holocaust scholars now recognize that the
radical challenge of critical theory to Western politics of representation, especially in light of its ethical turn, allows us to ask important
questions about the past and to interpret Holocaust testimonials in a

more discerning and multifaceted way. The argument that theoretical knowledge can deepen significantly our understanding of the Nazi genocide is the premise of Neil Levi and Michael Rothberg's groundbreaking collection *The Holocaust: Theoretical Readings* (2003). According to the editors, theoretical comprehension is indispensable if we are to heed Adorno's prescription that, "after Auschwitz," true thinking must be "thinking against itself" (5). Since the events of the Holocaust exceeded the framework of traditional categories of thought, it is imperative to reflect on their implications for every domain of thought, be it history, memory, aesthetics, or ethics. Moreover, as Levi and Rothberg contend, a number of concerns that are vital to contemporary theorists, such as questions of representation and language, or the construction of identity, especially in terms of gender and race, correspond to issues central to Holocaust studies. It is unsurprising, then, that Levinas's work, which has been so influential for a number of theorists, has been applied recently in various interpretations of Holocaust literature.[6]

Theorists representing different disciplines, such as, for instance, intellectual historian Dominick LaCapra, literary theorist Cathy Caruth, social anthropologist Joanna Tokarska-Bakir,[7] philosopher John Roth, and art theorist Griselda Pollock, have convincingly employed theoretical frameworks to examine Holocaust testimonials. In turn, such "applications" of theory in Holocaust contexts have revealed the need to question and revise existing theoretical constructs. As Pollock (2001a) observes, "Many of the dilemmas and dislocations of the [postmodern theory] are at a profound and, I would argue, generalizable level, in effect, 'after Auschwitz'" (4).[8] In addition, theoretical considerations developed in Holocaust contexts have been instrumental in wide-ranging discussion about disciplinary boundaries. In his influential essay "Resisting Apocalypse, Rethinking History" (2007a), LaCapra draws on these contexts in order to argue that history can no longer hold onto the illusion that it is a self-sufficient discipline whose task is to produce truth claims based on evidence; instead, it must welcome interventions from other disciplines. A constructive interchange between history and theory allows historians to question the limitations of their discipline (its ethnocentrism, for instance), to redefine their understanding of historiography and historicity, and to rethink the function of the archive. LaCapra cautions against radical constructivist positions in historiography that blur the distinction between historical knowledge and fiction and undermine the role of evidence-based archival research. He insists, nevertheless, that "historians should read demanding, often difficult to understand theoretical texts" (161). German studies scholar Eric L. Santner (1990), however, whose work combines historiography, psychoanalysis, literature, and philosophy, emphasizes that interdisciplinary, postmodern discourses are committed to a radical critique of the project of modernity, founded on the Enlightenment faith in progress. It is imperative to question such nostalgic constructs, which continue to influence today's political and cultural consciousness, since they are inseparable from the fantasies of totality, unity, mastery, and purity that informed Nazi ideology. Against the totalizing, fundamentalist project of modernity, postmodern approaches allow us to envisage alternative forms of social coexistence, based on the tolerance of difference. Focused specifically on the phenomenon of "the refusal to mourn" in postwar Germany, Santner's engagement with trauma theory to diagnose the malaise of German Holocaust remembrance leads him to conclude that theoretical strategies can be instrumental in undoing a certain "repetition compulsion" of modern European history, which, in his view, has been based on the disavowal of difference. Conversely, "the ethical and intellectual imperatives of life after Auschwitz" must remain in the forefront of the inquiries into changing fundamental cultural norms and definitions, especially those concerning self-identity and community (xiv). Although I apply theoretical insights to speak of literary and artistic works, I also question the rigid distinction between "theory" and literature or art that prevails in the works mentioned above. I acknowledge the boundaries between these very different genres of writing and thinking about the Holocaust, yet my own readings straddle these distinctions, revealing, for instance, how philosophical works (Levinas's in particular) are structured by the exigencies of testimony while, conversely, literary or artistic works are framed as theoretical reflections (and not only in the cases when the writer or artist actually has philosophical training, as in the case of novelist Jorge Semprún or artist Bracha Ettinger).[9]

The readings in this book draw on a wide range of discourses and disciplines, bringing into conversation very different genres of writing and artistic production, such as, for instance, Walter Benjamin's theory of translation and Isabella Leitner's memoir; or Levinas's ethical philosophy and Mindy Weisel's abstract canvases.[10] Bringing together works that are strikingly different in terms of genre, language, and attitude to the task of remembering goes against the common practice of discussing them in separate monographs or at least in separate chapters of a book. One of my objectives, however, is to traverse the boundaries between various modes of encountering traumatic past and thus to explore more fully the interplay between them. I hope to create spaces for those different representational forms to comment on one another and to inform one another's complexly rich, very different forms of textuality.[11] The encounters between Levinas's ethical thought, literary texts, and works of art, for instance, provide a corrective to the philosopher's relative inattention to the performative function of representation in the constitution of the witnessing subject. As a matter of fact, Holocaust writers and artists themselves make a case for such dynamic interplay of apparently disparate voices. Since they have to confront the dissolution of language as a means of communication during the Holocaust and write themselves out of that impasse, the authors of Holocaust testimonials are impelled by a strong dialogic imperative and a desire to forge new communicational strategies. This can be accomplished only by forming alliances that are innovative in themselves and that transcend and transform existing paradigms. As art curator Jill Snyder (1994) observes, "The stories, memories and histories call for reconfigured approaches to the incisions and traces of the incommensurable" (11). There is a danger, of course, that orchestrating such diverse encounters will blur the boundaries between disciplines and discursive territories. I believe this risk is worth taking. Testimonial works cut across generic and disciplinary distinctions, and reading them requires complementary innovation in the modes of interpretation. Just as each of these works looks for new idioms that would allow the author to work through the past and to remember it for the sake of the future, so do unexpected encounters between them create unique "memory events," communicating across what may at first seem to be impassable boundaries.

What these various encounters have in common, however, is a critical examination of the boundaries between ethics and aesthetics. In recent decades, poststructuralist thinkers (Jean-Luc Nancy, Philippe Lacoue-Labarthe, Lyotard, Luce Irigaray, Derrida, and others) have questioned the separation between ethics and aesthetics and their established definitions.[12] In this context, Levinas's work might appear to champion a more traditional conception of the relation between the two domains. Levinas argues that art is subordinate to the ethical sphere, and, in his earlier writings, he refers to ethics as "waking up" from aesthetics, that is, as opposed to free poetic or artistic imagining, the goal of which is aesthetic pleasure. For Levinas, aesthetics is the corollary of epistemology's conquest of the other: like the theory of knowledge, aesthetics relies on the paradigm of representation, which subsumes radical otherness. Since aesthetic representations correspond to the totalizing nature of Western knowledge, they are inherently violent and appropriative. Hence the philosopher argues for a need to reclaim radical alterity from the egotistic "games of art," so that the other can come forth, unhindered by the absorptive claims of representation. It is important to note that, in these statements, Levinas relies on traditional formulations of aesthetics, while his conception of ethics, in light of which he performs this critique, is radically novel. Levinas departs from both the Aristotelian notion of ethics, based on virtuous life, and Kant's definition of ethics as man's fundamental freedom to act.[13] He questions the primacy of the self that underlies both of these definitions, instead grounding ethics in the other's ascendancy over the self, that is, in the self's unconditional responsibility for another. It is therefore unsurprising that a different conception of aesthetics gradually emerges in Levinas's own writings, although it remains largely unthematized. In his readings of contemporary writers such as Maurice Blanchot, Shmuel Agnon, Paul Célan, or Michel Leiris (especially in the volume *Proper Names* [1976]), Levinas acknowledges literature's capacity to transcend totality and to become a vehicle through which the ethical relation with the other can be expressed. Certain kinds of art and literature may indeed have an ethical import, or, as Levinas (1996) writes in one of his texts on Blanchot, "The authenticity of art must herald an order of justice" (137).[14]

Although the engagements with Holocaust literature and art in this book have been fundamentally inspired by Levinas's ethical thought, my objective is to show that the philosopher's indictment of traditional aesthetics opens up the possibility of thinking about aesthetics "otherwise." I refer to this alternative aesthetics, if it is still to be called "aesthetics," as "poethics of disappearing traces." The neologism "poethics" is borrowed from Michel Deguy: the French poet coined the term in a collection of poems titled *Jumelage* (1978) to describe the movement of *poiesis*, or imaginative fashioning of the world, as an always already ethical gesture.[15] The phrase "disappearing traces" alludes to Levinas's notion of the "trace of the other," which is a nonphenomenal mark of alterity that always interrupts and questions the parameters of my world and unconditionally consigns me to the other. Disrupting mimetic paradigms of representation, "poethics of disappearing traces" roots literature and art in ethical responsibility. At the same time, it foregrounds the necessity of producing words and images, since it is only in such representations that the other can leave a trace of his or her existence. Thus, as Richard Kearny (2002) argues, Levinas's indictment of images "is not directed against the poetic power of imagination *per se* but against the use of such power to incarcerate the self in a blind alley of self-reflecting mirrors" (87–88). This alternative aesthetics, implicit in Levinas's writings, harbors a potential to "form an alliance between an ethics of responsibility and a poetics of imagination" (89).

However, to argue, with Levinas, for a poetics unconditionally committed to an ethics of responsibility is to still subsume aesthetics under the ethical imperative, even though both realms are now no longer understood in a conventional way. Such subordination of aesthetics to ethics seems consistent with the central claim placed upon Holocaust representations that they bear witness to death and suffering, and hence with the belief that, in the last instance, "art pales before the horror." This is a powerful demand, one that derives its authority from an obligation to remember. Yet to obey it unconditionally is to deny, in Kearney's words, "the right of art as art to explore a realm of imagination" (94). In light of Aba Beer's appeal to a poet's talents in order to describe his Holocaust experience, it seems that Kearny's reservations about Levinas's relative inattention to the demands of artistic imagination have to be taken as more than an affirmation of the right to artistic license. In my view, Holocaust testimonials reveal that the freedom to imagine should not only be "allowed" in order to produce unique and compelling representations but must be recognized as the necessary condition for the ethical task of giving testimony to be fulfilled.

A similar insight underlies Kaplan's important study of Holocaust representations, in which she argues that the beauty of many literary and artistic works dealing with the subject "transforms Holocaust memory in important, enlivening and indeed beneficial ways" and helps to bring it to the forefront of cultural consciousness (1, 13). In foregrounding the power of aesthetic representations to deepen our understanding of traumatic events, Kaplan argues against the "demonization" of beauty in Holocaust literature, art, and memorials, and she questions the opposition between "aesthetics and history" in critical literature about Holocaust representations (1). Kaplan substantiates her defense of beauty in contemporary depictions of the Holocaust by showing that, during the Holocaust, aesthetic pleasure was often a means of survival and of coping with horror. Although she fruitfully explores the conflictual relation between historical and aesthetic representations of the Holocaust, Kaplan does not address what I see as a more fundamental tension between aesthetic and ethical imperatives, in which, it seems, her own claims about "unwanted beauty" are grounded.

The need to probe this tension further in relation to the dilemmas of "the aesthetics of remembrance"[16] has led me to supplement a Levinasian reading of Holocaust testimonials with the insights gleaned from the work of Lyotard, a student of Levinas, for whom the questions of aesthetics are foundational in practicing philosophy that is ethically and politically engaged. This fundamental conjunction between aesthetics and ethics is reflected in Lyotard's use of the category of the sublime to both characterize the spirit of "the postmodern" and forge new ethicopolitical categories. Lyotard departs from Kant, who described the sublime as a negative presentation of the unpresentable, resulting in a feeling of simultaneous pleasure and pain. The French philosopher argues that what primarily eludes representation is the very *event* of presentation, its happening in the *here and now* (for instance, in one's experience of a work of art). Thus Lyotard argues for the unbridled power of imagination to invent new idioms through which to express this event, a view that contrasts with Levinas's distrustful probing of the limits of imagination and of its ethical potential.

In the context of debates about Holocaust representations, Lyotard has been criticized for his emphasis on the unpresentability and unspeakability of "Auschwitz" (the same criticisms that have also been leveled at George Steiner, Elie Wiesel, and Claude Lanzmann). For decades the claim of the Holocaust's inexpressibility went largely uncontested. It was central to survivor testimonies, and it informed theoretical debates about the possibility of representing atrocity.[17] The last fifteen years, however, have seen a backlash against what formerly seemed to be an uncontroversial view. This criticism is reflected, for instance, in Kaplan's defense of unwanted beauty and her rejection of the sublime as a category viable for post-Holocaust aesthetics. She writes, "The sublime and the beautiful often blur into each other. . . . There is one important distinction that seems to hold fast: the sublime is often associated with the unpresentable whereas the beautiful is not. It is for this reason that I use the term beauty" (8). Because the sublime is tantamount with "the chilly terror of the rigorous impossibility of understanding," it is politically and ethically retrograde (9). Kaplan's indictment of the sublime is informed by Giorgio Agamben's accusation, in *Remnants of Auschwitz*, that, in the context of Holocaust remembrance, Lyotard's notion of the unrepresentable, or, as Agamben prefers, the unsayable, amounts to "adoring in silence, as one does with a god. Regardless of one's intentions, this contributes to its [the atrocity's] glory" (199, 32–33). Instead, Agamben insists on the duty to know and to comprehend the juridicopolitical mechanisms that led to Nazi extermination camps; for Agamben, enshrining the Holocaust in the idiom of the unspeakable detracts from that primary task.[18] Although Agamben does not elucidate the ethical stakes of his protestations against the dogma of unspeakability, they are grounded in the idiom of an ethical demand that the thinker not contribute to the sacralization of horror. In that way, Agamben seems to blur cognitive, juridicopolitical, and ethical senses of the notion of the unspeakable. This is why Thomas Trezise, for instance, in "Unspeakable" insists that we must carefully distinguish between the different senses of the term: linguistic, cognitive, aesthetic, and ethical (and, I would also add, psychoanalytic). Yet Trezise's only reference to aesthetics is a generalized sense of the unspeakable as a matter of judging something to be in "bad taste" and thus objectionable or hateful (2001, 41). This conspicuous lack of engagement with the problematic of the sublime, despite his attention to the issues of artistic representation, prevents Trezise from exploring the complexities of the paradigm of unpresentability or noting the centrality of the problematic of presentation in Lyotard's work, which he cites at length in support of his argument. In *Against the Unspeakable*, Naomi Mandel also argues that we must distinguish between the different senses of the unspeakable, especially between the conceptual limits of language, representation, and knowledge, and the rhetorical invocations of such limits that in fact facilitate distance from the experience of suffering on the grounds of ethical deference to atrocity and trauma. In Mandel's view, the elevation of the Holocaust to the unsurpassable and unique emblem of historical trauma that this conflation enables is tantamount to the abdication of moral and historical responsibility, including the responsibility to acknowledge the atrocities that do not normally come under the radar of Eurocentric, Western paradigms of knowledge and culture. Through a parallel interrogation of Jewish American and African American accounts of histories of suffering, Mandel draws attention to appropriations of the rhetoric of unspeakability in the service of identity politics. Further, in Mandel's view, reifying traumatic history as inaccessible reinforces the distance between the critic and her object of study, while at the same time divesting attention from her own representational practices and "act of articulation" (2006, 13). This leads Mandel to call for the "eschewal of the unspeakable" (17) in favor of recognizing and implementing what she terms "complicity" as a responsible critical practice. Grounded in the recognition of one's implication in the discursive and ideological conditions of representing history, "complicity," as distinct from "collaboration" or "culpability" (in the judicial sense), is thus "the condition of possibility for ethical engagement" with the violence inherent in the very act of representation (24). Mandel's nuanced analysis, which leads her to propose that we substitute the rhetoric of the unspeakable with the idiom of complicity, suffers from her unwillingness to situate her central concept of complicity in the context of Levinas's ethics of unconditional responsibility (though she references Levinas's notion of the "face" elsewhere in the book). Considering that, for Levinas, the other, the one who obligates me and always renders me "complicit," is always troped as inaccessible in representation, an engagement with Levinas would render problematic Mandel's setting up of the unspeakable and "complicity" as oppositional terms. Similarly, her lack of engagement with the complexities of the notion of presentation in Lyotard, as it is informed by the ethical imperative (of Levinasian provenance) renders problematic her charge that Lyotard's idiom of unpresentability leads him to avoid complicity. In fact, one can argue that "complicity," in the positive critical sense elaborated by Mandel, is central to Lyotard's articulation of the postmodern "unspeakable" (the sublime), insofar as it is a challenge to thinking to constantly scrutinize its own discursive practices, the challenge expressed in the philosopher's epigraphic call to "save the honor of thinking."[19] In Rodolphe Gasché's words, the task that Lyotard sets for himself is "to thinkingly address the evils of thinking while allowing that no enlightening critique can ever hope to completely free thinking from its potential for the worst" (2007, 294).

German scholar Georges Didi-Huberman, in his book *Images in Spite of All*, in which he discusses four clandestine photographs of the

Sonderkommando burning corpses on a pyre in Auschwitz-Birkenau, sets out to argue that to consign traumatic experience to the realm of the unimaginable means to perpetuate the injustice that was inflicted both on those who died and on the survivors who have struggled for decades to convince the world that their stories are true. He insists that "*We are obliged* to that oppressive imaginable. . . . So let us not invoke the unimaginable" (2008, 3; emphasis in the original). He also points out that the "closed notion of the unsayable" is untenable since it has been refuted over and over again by the very existence of testimony (25).[20] Also drawing on Agamben's scathing critique of "the unsayable," Didi-Huberman repudiates the "negative aesthetics" that Lyotard's sublime is said to exemplify. "To remember, we must imagine," he concludes (25). Yet this imperative coincides with Lyotard's own argument for the use of imagination, which the French philosopher defines as "the power to invent criteria" that allow us to pursue new means of expression (Lyotard 1989, 17). Hence, I challenge the readings of Lyotard's sublime primarily in terms of the quasitranscendental unrepresentable that either erases the historical specificity of the referent (Agamben) or occludes the secondary witness's corporeal and ideological implication in the processes of representation (Mandel). On the contrary, I see this category as a helpful conceptual tool to explore and render problematic the very opposition between the former paradigm of the "inexpressibility" of the Holocaust and the recent vociferous arguments against it. Granted, to be effective as an innovative concept, Lyotard's "unpresentable" must be brought out of the rather narrow and abstract scope of his engagement with "Auschwitz," the term that, as both Mandel and Karyn Ball note, he uses as an overarching metonym, in danger of disarticulating any meaningful content.

Besides the Holocaust's gradual receding into history, the proliferation and increasing acceptance of literary and artistic interpretations of the Holocaust, even if some of them fail to meet historians' standards of verisimilitude, likely have contributed to the shift of critical emphasis from "the unsayble" to the "sayable," described above. After all, the authors of these imaginative explorations search for new ways of expression, discovering territories where the new idioms to speak about the "unspeakable" can be instantiated. In light of Didi-Huberman's (and Lyotard's!) demand that we continue to "imagine," we should continue to ask what the witness means when he or she invokes the unspeakable, rather than prohibit such evocations. Instead of simply rejecting the "unpresentable" in favor of "speakability" and

understanding, we must also consider "the unpresentable" as a powerful rhetorical figure that designates the tensions between the aesthetic,
cognitive, ethical, and political demands inherent in Holocaust representations.[21] According to Mandel, the figure of the unspeakable maintains the gulf between the actual experience of the event and its representations, upon which it imposes limits. This is undoubtedly true of
a number of literary and philosophical evocations of the Holocaust's
sanctity and untouchability (such as Elie Wiesel's or George Steiner's).
A rigorous rethinking, via Lyotard, of the sedimented notions of presentation and presentability in the relations between traumatic past
and the present in which it is evoked, represented, and worked through
allows for more nuanced explorations of the conflict between the impossibility of describing what happened (or, in some cases, the interdiction against putting it into words) and the necessity to imagine the
atrocity and to capture it in words and images. Although Holocaust
testimonials are committed to the past, they search for ways to locate
that past in the present, and they do so by breaking away from sanc-
tioned ways of narrating and understanding. In order to convey meanings that their authors describe as "unspeakable," they must find innovative ways of using language and forge alternative places of encounter
between the past and the present, between the experience of suffering
that will remain unknowable and its representations in the present
that make an ethical claim of bearing witness.

In the following chapters, I propose several formulations that reflect
my attempt to describe such interventions into sedimented modes of
representing the past. Apart from "poethics of disappearing traces,"
I refer to "subjectivity as the structure of witnessing," the "*differend*
between the ethical and the aesthetic phrase," "the translation *differend*," "memory phrase," and "memory event." Analogously to the
authors whose work I interpret, and mindful of the injunction to produce new idioms, I consider such a quest for different forms of expression to be an important task for scholars dedicated to post-Holocaust
thinking. Here, Adorno's admonition that, "after Auschwitz," "there
is no word tinged from on high, not even a theological one, that has
any right unless it underwent a transformation" (1983, 367) has not
lost its currency.

| | |

The first chapter, "'Like an Echo without a Source': Subjectivity as Witnessing and the Holocaust Narrative," elaborates the claim that redrawing the boundaries between ethics and aesthetics is related to the emergence of the genre of testimony in the wake of the historical trauma of the Holocaust. I show that the proliferation of Holocaust testimony has been a central factor in recent theoretical redefinitions of what it means to be a subject. A number of contemporary thinkers across a variety of disciplines—philosophers, intellectual historians, and literary and trauma theorists—have proposed ways of rethinking the subject in terms of witnessing, and it is no coincidence that each of them refers in their works to Holocaust testimonies. The term I use for this emergent concept is *subjectivity as the structure of witnessing*, which is derived from Levinas's ethical philosophy. For Levinas, the subject bears witness to the existence of the other prior to an intention to give such a witness; my life is first and foremost testimony to the life of another. Guided by Levinas, I argue that only because one is a witness in this preoriginal sense is one able to produce actual testimony in language. That is, articulating the ethical subject as the structure of witnessing enables us to trace a passage from the perceived impossibility of speech, as expressed in the figure of "the unspeakable," to actual speech in the form of testimony. I examine the performance of the witnessing subject in literary testimonials by Elie Wiesel and Imre Kertész, with references to other writers (such as Jorge Semprún, Isabella Leitner, and Ida Fink), although I also draw attention to the testimonial imperative in Levinas's own work. All of these texts reveal a convergence of repetition compulsion, as it is related to the return to the site of traumatic experience, and what Levinas calls "recurrence," in which the ethical subject is posited. By illuminating the notion of the witnessing subject through close encounters between Levinas's ethics and literary testimonials, I hope to suggest alternative modes of remembrance that are underwritten by an ethical exigency to remember yet also remain mindful of the performative power of aesthetic representation. Levinas often uses the metaphor of the echo to describe the ethical subject's indebtedness to the other. Perhaps this evocative figure of speech betrays the philosopher's own desire to search for alternative modes of representation, grounded in a hermeneutics of listening.

Chapter two, "The Tower of Babel: Holocaust Testimonials and the Ethics of Translation," explores the question of language as both the vehicle for transmitting traumatic memory and the medium in which this memory is constructed. Here, I focus specifically on the problem of translation, understood broadly as interactions and exchanges between languages as they take place in Holocaust testimonials. As writer Susan Rubin Suleiman notes, survivors' efforts to leave a record of the past have been affected by the necessity to give testimony in their second language, usually the language of their adopted country. We need to take into account, therefore, particular languages in which testimonials are written and to consider the impact of the mediation of the authors' language on the processes of memory and on their identity as witnessing subjects. Holocaust literature itself foregrounds the theme of translation. Primo Levi, for instance, describes the death camp as a "perpetual Babel," in which the inability to communicate, mainly due to the inmates' lack of knowledge of German and of one another's languages, was the true force of extermination. Under circumstances where the human capacity to communicate was annihilated, translation often became a life-saving strategy, as Levi and others have attested. Authors such as Levi and Ruth Kluger not only describe their use of that strategy during the war but also reenact it in their post-Holocaust writings. Yet various Holocaust literary testimonials foreground what I call "the translation *differend*," that is, the conflict between different languages presented in the text, which often results in the witness feeling betrayed by an act of mistranslation. Paradoxically, this sense of "betrayal" is experienced most strongly by authors who write in their mother tongue and who describe their alienation from their immediate linguistic community. Delving into these translatory tribulations has lead me to conclude that translation and witnessing are closely related. In fact, in the context of Holocaust testimony, we can think of translation as an instance of "bearing witness" in its own right and a unique "memory event." Further, translation is always an inscription of the trace of another language in one's native tongue, and it reveals the indebtedness of every national language to an exiled alterity that is inherent in its very structures. By facilitating passages between languages and positing the goal of communicability, translation thus has a potential to resist discriminatory forms of speech and encourage national languages to confront their own political investments and mechanisms of exclusion. Such vigilance is essential in post-Holocaust proclamations that we should remember for the sake of the future.

In the third chapter, "Lending an Ear to the Silence Phrase: Holocaust Writing of the *Differend*," I develop my engagement with Lyotard in order to explore the relation between ethics and aesthetics in Holocaust testimonials in more detail. Lyotard defines the *differend* as a conflict between radically incompatible claims. One or more parties in the conflict feel victimized because they have been deprived of a language in which they could express their sense of injustice: under the current rules of language, their case has become literally "unspeakable." Lyotard states that the *differend* thus marks "the unstable state and instant of language wherein something that must be able to be put into phrases cannot yet be" (1988, 53). The Holocaust context of Lyotard's argument is important since *The Differend* was written in response to Holocaust denier Robert Faurisson, who challenged survivors and historians to provide a scientific proof for the existence of gas chambers.[22] In Lyotard's view, by undercutting the truth claim of their testimony, Faurisson revictimized survivors and provoked a crisis in the realm of Holocaust memory. Lyotard therefore calls for new linguistic idioms, outside the current uses of language, in which the wrong perpetrated on the survivor's language can be articulated. It is in this context that I insist on the relevance of Lyotard's concept of the sublime, although I am mindful of the criticisms leveled against it by LaCapra, Agamben, and Kaplan. I thus explore literary and artistic representations of the Holocaust as powerful *memory events* whose aim is to search for new, unique idioms in which the injury perpetrated on the victim's language can be expressed. In proposing the term "memory event," I hope to supplement such well-known categories as James E. Young's "vicarious" memory or Marianna Hirsch's "post-memory." I stress the active modality of "eventing," of the occurring of memory in the "here and now," in this text, in this image, as the process that intertwines with the reenactment and construction of memory on the part of the testimonial subject. To engage in these reenactments, however, writers and artists must deploy imaginative strategies that often come into conflict with the ethical claims of Holocaust memory. I refer to this conflict as the *differend between the ethical and the aesthetic*, and I argue that in virtually all instances of Holocaust representations the call for justice and the imperative to remember must be considered in light of this tension. We must bear witness to this *differend* because it animates our desire and our ability to remember. Bringing out the genesis of Lyotard's ethicopolitical concept of the *differend* in the aesthetic category of the sublime,

I comment on the constitutive tension between ethics and aesthetics in a spectrum of works, including the Holocaust diaries of Dawid Rubinowicz and Petr Ginz, poems by Polish writer Jerzy Ficowski, memoirs by Elie Wiesel and Isabella Leitner, episodes in Claude Lanzmann's *Shoah* and in Polish director Andrzej Wajda's *Korczak*, and historian Pierre Vidal-Naquet's refutation of Faurisson in his book *The Assassins of Memory*.[23]

The fourth chapter, "Poethics of Disappearing Traces: Levinas, Literary Testimony, and Holocaust Art," develops the notion of the *poethics of disappearing traces*, which is an aesthetic realm of imagination, including philosophical imagination, as it has been always already inflected by the ethical. As mentioned above, this term integrates two concepts: Deguy's notion of *poéthique*, which he developed in the medium of poetry, and Levinas's "trace of the other," which is central to the philosopher's understanding of ethics as responsibility and which functions in his work on many levels. For Levinas, the trace is the invisible mark of the other's existence, which disturbs and displaces the self, and leaves a nonphenomenal imprint on its language. The witness's task is to recover these traces but also to pry open the strictures of one's own tongue in order to allow the other's voice to be heard through one's speech. My central literary example of the poethics of disappearing traces are short stories and dramatic pieces by Ida Fink, a writer who repeatedly relies on the metaphor of the trace to describe Holocaust witnesses' struggle to leave a record. Here, I also follow the figures of erased traces in several Holocaust art works (Mordecai Ardon's and Robert Morris's abstract art, and Herzl Kashetsky's photorealism). The emphasis on the poethics of traces also reveals implicit aesthetic claims of such documentary forms as the etchings left by the prisoners on the walls of cells in Auschwitz, in Joseph P. Czarnecki's *Last Traces: The Lost Art of Auschwitz*, and the photo album of the Warsaw Ghetto, titled *The Indelible Traces of the Warsaw Ghetto*. In order to reconceive Levinas's ethical notion of the trace in the context of visual art, I point to a remarkable similarity between Levinas's language of ethics and French philosopher Jean-Luc Nancy's conception of the sublime. As in Lyotard, the Nancean sublime signifies an impossibility of presenting a form that imagination is striving to put forth. Nancy, however, also emphasizes the syncopated movement of the figure being outlined and erased at the same time, to which he refers as the "infinite *tracing* of its own contour" (1993, 42; emphasis mine). The convergence between Levinas's language of ethics and the way Nancy defines the sublime leads me to consider Levinas's notion of the trace as a sublime figure in his own work, which he employs to describe the mode of giving testimony to the life of another that is unconditional and nonappropriative. As mentioned before, Didi-Huberman insists that we must imagine the events of the Holocaust in order to counter the Nazis' effort to obliterate the traces of the victims and thus to make the crime unimaginable. I propose that the notion of disappearing traces, in which Levinas's ethical concept of the trace is reconceived within the periphery of aesthetics, can be understood as that which *makes it possible to imagine* the events that, in their extreme impact on human lives, seem to defy existing representational strategies. As expressions of poethics of disappearing traces, works of Holocaust literature and art convert this potentiality to imagine into actual works of remembrance.

In the last chapter, "'Witnesses against Themselves': Encounters with Daughters of Absence," I look at artworks by four second-generation artists: Mindy Weisel, Lily Markiewicz, Bracha Ettinger, and Ewa Kuryluk, who are also daughters of Holocaust survivors. Considering these works as sites of traumatic recollection, I ask about their status as witnesses to the past and the way in which they function as memory events. For the most part, Levinas condemns visual art because it relies on gaze, in which the other's alterity is absorbed. In the art informed by the poethics of disappearing traces, however, the other is released from objectifying regimes of vision and allowed to "shine forth with his own light and speak for himself" (Levinas 1969, 14). The works discussed here reveal the witnessing subject that is embodied and emplaced by that experience. They also create physical spaces that allow for an affective engagement with the past during which an aesthetic representation is also experienced as an ethical commitment. While this art probes the stakes invested in collective memory, it also calls the stakes of art into question: it not only inscribes traumatic history into the present modes of existence but also discloses the traumatic kernel of representation itself—the fact that art primarily stems from the experience of loss, dispossession, and mourning. Similarly to the written works discussed in previous chapters, these artworks are inherently dialogic because they foreground their status as an address to another and present themselves as acts of witness. Engaging with the art of the second-generation female artists therefore allows me to polemically expand on the theories of Levinas and Lyotard, the two philosophers I mainly engage with in the book.

Moreover, these works reveal that the traditional conflict between the ethical and the aesthetic has always been couched in the idiom of gender (in so far as the ethical is aligned with the masculine while the aesthetic is the mark of feminine difference). My readings thus open up new venues for exploring the questions of the gender of memory at the intersections of ethics and aesthetics.

As the above synopses suggest, the concept of trauma underlies these engagements with the Holocaust representations at the intersections of ethics and aesthetics, just as it informs the work of writers, artists, and theorists discussed in the book. Both LaCapra and Eric Santner comment on the tendency, in Holocaust testimonies as well as in their interpretations, to fuse two very different understandings of trauma: the structural trauma, constitutive of every individual's psychic development and subjective self-construction, and the experience and memory of traumatic historical events. As Santner cautions, conflating the two senses of trauma risks *"displac[ing] and dispers[ing]* the particular, historical tasks of mourning" (1990, 29), and LaCapra admonishes Levinas especially for this slippage. I agree with both theorists that speaking of traumatic events in relation to a generalized notion of subjective trauma endangers the specificity of particular historical events. In the texts I analyze, however (especially in Levinas, Semprún, and Kertész, and in the artworks of the second-generation artists), it is exactly this intertwining of traumatic historical events with a sense of oneself as a traumatized subject that allows these witnesses to work through the past and to move toward new ways of envisioning the future. Indeed, the uneasy tension between the two senses of trauma lends a unique force to the authors' words or images, and it impels them to search for new idioms and means of expression.

Another difficulty that must be noted is the question of terminology as it pertains to the use of the word "Holocaust" (although I occasionally refer to the "Shoah" in the cases when this term is preferred by the author or artist I am discussing). Undoubtedly, as Derrida remarks, no name is worthy of describing what it has been summoned to signify. This is especially the case for the name that involved the "all-burning" of all other names, and Derrida himself avoids referring directly to the Holocaust as a historical event.[24] The use of the word "Holocaust" has been surrounded by controversies: in Agamben's view, for instance, it is "[entirely] incorrect" because of its religious connotations as a sacrificial "burnt offering" (1999, 28–31) and its etymological links with certain anti-Semitic motifs in

Christianity.[25] LaCapra disputes Agamben's total rejection of the term and casts doubt on the soundness of relying on etymological research, however erudite it might be. He argues instead that the current use of the "Holocaust" has largely "washed away" the sedimented association with the idea of sacrifice and its possible Christian connotations. Here I embrace LaCapra's view that one has to take into account the way the term has been widely circulated in various cultural fields, and, most importantly, its common acceptance among Holocaust survivors in relation to their experiences. As LaCapra puts it, this simply makes the usage of the term "Holocaust" "politically correct" (2004, 168). Ruth Kluger concludes, in her Holocaust memoir *Still Alive*, that "mass murder isn't a burnt offering to gods. . . . [but] I don't care particularly, as long as there is a word, any word, that unambiguously refers to what we are talking about without the need for a lengthy circumlocution to pinpoint a particular catastrophe and distinguish it from others" (2001, 189). This, of course, does not mean that we can allow ourselves to be careless in using such terminology; on the contrary, examining the intersections between ethics and aesthetics brings out more sharply the need for terminological vigilance.

Finally, considering the proliferation of Holocaust representations in recent decades, selecting texts for discussion from among the hundreds arranged on the shelves of every Holocaust scholar's library is a daunting task. My choices of texts are dictated by the themes I develop in each chapter, although I was also guided by strategic considerations. I decided to include some well-known authors, counting on the readers' familiarity with their work, such as Levi, Wiesel, Kertész, Célan, and Semprún (although, with the exception of Levi, lesser-known texts are included). In every chapter I also consider works that are less established within the Holocaust canon, such as those of Kluger, Leitner, Fink, or Weisel, or are very little known, such as Ficowski, Eta Wrobel, or Hanna Krall, in the hope of increasing their visibility. Although I rely on some highly acclaimed texts, my contention is that some of the stylistically simple texts (Leitner's, Krall's, or Wrobel's writings, for instance) and works of art (Weisel's or Kuryluk's) harbor the same transformative potential, not to mention that, at a closer look, that "simplicity" is deceiving. In my choices of texts, I have also been mindful of the fact that, for the most part, the authors whose work still awaits recognition are women. Despite the efforts of especially feminist scholars in the last twenty years, the Holocaust canon still remains dominated by works produced by men.

The larger objective of my readings, however, returns us to the question once asked by Griselda Pollock: "Faced with such a dire legacy of betrayal, can art [and, one must add, other representational forms] be made ethically without seeking a completely other foundation for its practice?" (2001a, 3). The following exploration of the boundaries between ethics and aesthetics in Holocaust testimonials—literary texts, philosophical commentaries and artworks—is a part of what I believe to be a vitally important, continuing quest for such a "foundation."

CHAPTER ONE

"Like an Echo without a Source"

Subjectivity as Witnessing
and the Holocaust Narrative

We are all witnesses and we are all messengers. He who listens to a
witness, he in turn becomes witness and messenger.

—ELIE WIESEL

All my life, I have never stopped making the journey to Auschwitz.

—CHILD SURVIVOR, a witness at the Papon trial in 1997

We have to remember that Echo produces the possibility of a cure against
the grain of her intention, and, even, finally, uncoupled from intention.

—GAYATRI SPIVAK

RETURNS TO THE SITE OF TRAUMA: HOLOCAUST "VARIATIONS ON A THEME"

In a short, poetic reflection, "Nocturnal Variation on a Theme," from
the volume *Traces*, Ida Fink (1998), an Israeli writer and Holocaust
survivor, describes a former camp inmate's recurrent nightmare of
returning to Auschwitz. In the first dream, "He was freed from the
camp and passed through the gate with the sign ARBEIT MACHT
FREI. He was overcome by a wave of happiness unlike any he had
ever known" (109). Like a refrain, this description of the longed-for
moment of liberation is repeated three times, at the beginning of each
dream. In each vignette, however, the prisoner's march toward a new
life turns out to be only a detour, a series of uncanny events that ultimately lead him back to Auschwitz. In the first episode, he forgets his
cigarettes on the cot in the barracks. Unless he turns back, he cannot
fulfill the request for a cigarette from the girl he loves and who has
been running to greet him, "her hair streaming in the wind" (109).
In the second dream, the prisoner runs away from the camp "with a

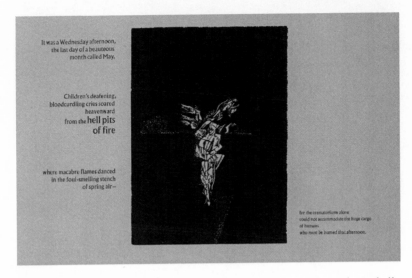

It was a Wednesday afternoon,
the last day of a beauteous
month called May.

Children's deafening,
bloodcurdling cries soared
heavenward
from the hell pits
of fire

where macabre flames danced
in the foul-smelling stench
of spring air—

for the crematorium alone
could not accommodate the huge cargo
of humans
who must be burned that afternoon.

Figure 1.1.   Gerson Leiber (American), "May 31, 1944; A Poem by Isabella Leitner," May 2000. Portfolio of linoleum block prints on Rives BFK paper, 8 pages and colophon. 14 in. x 22 ½ in. (35.56 cm x 57.15 cm) each. Edition of 40, 10AP (A-J). Courtesy of the Leiber Museum, East Hampton, New York. Photo credit: Gary Mamay.

light, almost winged step" (110), yet he mistakes the searchlight from the watchtower for the white glow of the moon, which he has followed in the belief that it is guiding him to freedom. In the last episode, he follows the white arrows that indicate the way around the turnstile that is blocking his path. However, the detour brings him back to the gate where stands an SS man, beckoning him over with a crooked finger.

Primo Levi recounts a similar nightmare. He repeatedly dreams of being seated at a dinner table with his family or friends, feeling an intense pleasure of being at home and "having so many things to recount." Suddenly he notices that the listeners become distracted and then leave him alone, and he feels a piercing, disconsolate grief. Levi (1993) mentions that, to his amazement, many of the inmates endure the same nightmare. He asks, "Why is the pain of everyday translated so constantly in our dreams, in the ever-repeated scene of unlistened-to story?" (60). In an epigraph of *The Drowned and the Saved*, Levi (1988) evokes the poetic figure of the Ancient Mariner, from Samuel Coleridge's poem, to convey the witness's sense of entrapment in a traumatic moment in the past:

Since then, at an uncertain hour,
That agony returns.
And till my ghastly tale is told,
The heart within me burns.

The Ancient Mariner is a paradigmatic figure of a traumatized witness, who compulsively repeats his story and reenacts the trauma in each retelling. Yet this pattern of repetition also attests to a truth specific to Holocaust testimonials: the survivor's story can never be told only once. The figure of the Ancient Mariner is the cipher of incessant, compulsive returns to the site of trauma through the performance of "the ghastly tale." The repeated act of storytelling is also imbued with an unspecified guilt that the storyteller is compelled to expiate, the task intertwined with the need to master the overwhelming impact of the past events.

If we peruse the canon of Holocaust literature, we notice that a number of writers, such as Primo Levi, Elie Wiesel, Imre Kertész, Isabella Leitner, and Jorge Semprún (to cite a few well known authors), performed such "variations on a theme," returning to the subject of the Holocaust directly or indirectly, after initially producing autobiographical accounts of their "survival in Auschwitz." Levi, for instance, first penned his Auschwitz memoir *If This Is a Man* in 1946, yet he felt compelled to return to it forty years later, in *The Drowned and the Saved*. Similarly, in his two-volume autobiography (*All Rivers Run to the Sea*, 1995, and *And the Sea Is Never Full*, 1999), Wiesel refashions the testimony he gave in *Night* (1958), although that account was already a rewriting of the narrative he first recorded in Yiddish immediately after the liberation (Wieviorka 2006, 33–47).

This literary "repetition compulsion" is especially striking in the Holocaust narratives of Jorge Semprún. A prolific writer, translator, and author of film scripts, Semprún often recalls his first attempt to write down his story immediately after his release from the camp, and his inexplicable failure to do so. It took him almost twenty years before he began to recount his experiences in Buchenwald, in different variations and told by different narrators, all of whom bear one of Semprún's noms de guerre. In the first account, *The Long Voyage* (1963), the narrative is framed as an imaginary conversation with another prisoner ("a pal from Seymour") during a long ride in the cattle wagon. The second "return," titled *What a Beautiful Sunday!* appears seventeen years later, and it includes more details about the camp life, as if the camp now had an even stronger grip on the survivor. Here the "acting out" of repetition compulsion is particularly notable. As in Fink's "variations," the narrative voice keeps circling back to one moment on a "beautiful" winter Sunday in December 1944, and it returns to the same place, where the narrator is standing, captivated by the beauty of a snow-covered tree. The tranquility and splendor of that recollection are remarkably incongruous with the background of the smoking crematoria chimneys and with the total collapse of the protagonist's attempts to make sense of his camp experience (the bitter irony reflected in the title of the novel). The forays back to the events that led him to the camp and forward to the events after the liberation do not restore linear time: the narrator is still standing as if rooted next to a tree in Buchenwald. As he says, "For my life is not like a river—above all not like an ever-changing river, never the same, in which one could never bathe twice. My life is always a matter of *déjà-vu* of *déjà-vécu*, of repetition, of sameness to the point of satiety" (Semprún 1982, 362). Semprún's account echoes Sigmund Freud's observation that traumatic experience "is as though these patients had not finished with the traumatic situation, as though they were still faced by it as an immediate task which has not been dealt with" (quoted in Ball 2008, 176). The most significant change between the retellings in the two novels pertains to Semprún's gradual disillusionment with the communist ideology to which he dedicated his youth (and for which he was imprisoned in Buchenwald). As a result, his later memory of Buchenwald begins to converge with a virtual memory of Stalin's Gulag, gleaned from Aleksandr Solzenitzyn's *One Day in the Life of Ivan Denisovitch*. While in *The Long Voyage* Semprún (2005) believed that his deportation was a comprehensible consequence of his actions as a communist resistance fighter ("I was free to get on this train"; 21), in *What a Beautiful Sunday!* he strips the narrator of idealism and youthful innocence. Perhaps as a result of this loss, the writer's alter egos in his subsequent narratives, *L'Algabie* (1981) and *La montagne blanche* (1986), end up taking their lives.

It is only in a much later retelling, *Literature or Life* , written in 1994, that the theme of a return to life cautiously emerges for Semprún, as if in a struggle with a ghost of Primo Levi, whose suicidal death is one of the leitmotifs of the narrative. Notably, the events take place on the day of liberation of Buchenwald. In the central episode, the narrator recalls how he and his comrade saved the life of a *Muselmann* whom they had pulled from under a pile of corpses in one of the barracks, a memory he has never divulged before. The insertion of a newly emerged memory is remarkable, considering that, as the narrator admits, he has already described all the other incidents numerous times.

Another striking example of repetition compulsion in Holocaust literature is the work of Isabella Leitner, a survivor from Hungary now living in the United States.[1] Immediately after the liberation, she started jotting down her recollections on scraps of paper, writing whenever she could not bear the pressure of the horrifying images that were stuck in her memory. As she later explained, she intended to discard the painful fragments and thus cleanse herself of the horror to which they bore witness, yet "a mysterious sense of history silently whispered in [her] heart" (Leitner 1994, 16), and she decided to keep those painful mementos. It was not until 1978, however, that she published *Fragments of Isabella*, in which, with the help of her American husband, Irving Leitner, she translated her notes into English. Later, Leitner revised her initial text several times, adding, rearranging, and editing her "fragments." *Saving the Fragments: From Auschwitz to New York* (1985) and *Isabella: From Auschwitz to Freedom* (1994) appeared as coauthored with her husband, and *The Big Lie: A True Story* (a book for children) was written in between (1992). The author also recorded her story on an audiotape and authorized its production on stage and as a motion picture.[2] As Karyn Ball (2008) notes, such imaginative traumatic repetition stems from the urge to "convene and fix once and for all images of an original wound" and thus to master what cannot be consciously contained, while at the same time, "keeping it alive" (179). While the other writers attempt fictional excursions beyond the landscape cordoned off by the barbed wire of the camp, Leitner's reimaginings of always the same story, albeit increasingly articulated in terms of educational goals, remain a potent instance of what LaCapra (2001) refers to as an all-consuming "fidelity to trauma" (22). In LaCapra's view, such committed keeping faith to the past through imaginative reenactment may prevent the survivor from "working through" trauma, resulting in its pathological sedimentation in the present.

As demonstrated in this chapter, however, this insistent movement of return establishes a recollecting subject as a witness, propelled by the need to tell it all, to explain it. Through the returns to the site of trauma, repetitive, changing literary excursions into the past draw attention to the continuous, open-ended nature of witnessing, and they foreground the very gesture of testifying rather than the task of archival safe-keeping of memory. In *Literature or Life*, Semprún (1997) dramatizes this manifold singularity of the witness's performance in language, during which he is simultaneously posited and destroyed: "You can tell all about this experience. . . . Even if you wind up repeating yourself. Even if you remain caught up in it, prolonging death, if necessary—reviving it endlessly in the nooks and crannies of the story. Even if you become no more than the language of this death, and live at its expense, fatally" (14). This subject also responds to the imperative "Remember!" which, as Leitner avows, was "whispered" into her heart. Numerous survivors of the Holocaust have testified that this imperative was their sole motivation to stay alive. One of the most compelling examples of survival by witnessing is the testimony of Filip Müller, a member of *Sondercommando* in Auschwitz, as it was captured on film by Claude Lanzmann (in *Shoah*). In one episode, Müller describes his encounter with a group of women from his hometown, who were among the victims he was delivering to the gas chamber. Suddenly realizing that his life "had become meaningless," he decided to die with them. Yet one of the women approached him, imploring him to save himself for the sake of telling their story. Müller recalls her words, "So you want to die. But that's senseless. Your death won't give us back our lives. That's no way. You must get out of here alive, you must bear witness to our suffering, and to the injustice done to us" (Lanzmann 1995, 152). In a chillingly literal sense, Müller owes his life to the necessity of becoming a witness.[3] Similarly, psychologist Dori Laub (Laub and Felman 1992) recalls one witness's testimony (from the Yale Video Archive): "We wanted to survive so as to stay alive one day after Hitler, in order to be able to tell our story" (78). Philosopher Giorgio Agamben opens his inquiry in *Remnants of Auschwitz* with a similar testimony from a camp inmate: "I firmly decided that despite everything that might happen to me, I would not take my own life . . . since I did not want to suppress the witness that I could become" (Langbein 1988, 186; quoted in Agamben 1999, 15).

In the context of Holocaust literary narratives, as they have been instigated by the testimonial imperative and driven by repetition compulsion, which we can call, after Primo Levi, the syndrome of the Ancient Mariner, I will turn to Emmanuel Levinas's ethical reformulation of subjectivity in terms of witnessing and of what the philosopher refers to as "substitution." Importantly, the idiom of traumatic repetition plays a central role in Levinas's own articulation of subjectivity. For Levinas, subjectivity is premised on "recurrence," a repeated movement of return to oneself, which is precipitated by traumatic encounters with alterity. Levinas (1998b) writes, "In the saying of responsibility, the one . . . denudes oneself in recurrence, substituting itself for another on the hither side of its own identity for another" (139). "Substitution," defined by Levinas as the nonappropriative putting oneself in place of the other, in turn, has to be elucidated in terms of bearing witness to the other: "Is not the ego a substitution in its solidarity as something identical, a solidarity that begins by bearing witness of itself to the other?" (119). In ethical terms, my life is primarily testimony to the existence of another.

In a way, Levinas's emphasis on bearing witness, articulated in his work in the medium of philosophy, is symptomatic of what Annette Wieviorka dubs "the era of the witness." Wieviorka draws attention to an unprecedented proliferation of testimonies that surfaced immediately after the war, following innumerable eyewitness accounts written during the escalating process of extermination. These postwar testimonials mostly served the function of commemorating the dead and trying to heal psychic wounds. According to Wieviorka, "the era of the witness" dawned only in the wake of the Eichmann trial, during which survival testimonies became central for the first time and thus gained legitimacy.[4] In the long run, however, they gave rise to an entirely new paradigm of memory construction and, subsequently, to new ways of understanding history.

Admittedly, Levinas (1969) was taciturn on the subject of his own ordeal of surviving the Holocaust and mourning the deaths of his entire family, although his work was powerfully influenced by the atrocities of the Holocaust, leading him to formulate the notion of responsibility as "the primordial expression of 'you shall not commit murder'" (199). Levinas was also one of the first philosophers to have become disturbed by the phenomenon of National Socialism. Already in 1934, in "Some Thoughts on the Philosophy of Hitlerism," he insisted that Hitlerism was not an anomaly but a menace deeply rooted in the mentality of the West and, as such, required philosophical refutation. With lucidity and foresight, Levinas (2004) pointed out that Hitlerism was not primarily a political problem, to be solved through political stratagems, but that it corroded the very foundations of humanity: "racism . . . does not challenge this or that dogma of democracy, parliamentarism, dictatorship, or religious policy. It contests the very humanity of man" (21).

Levinas (1990) also made more direct, if undeveloped, references to the Holocaust in some of his works. For instance, in a brief section at the end of *Difficult Freedom*, titled "Signature," in which he outlined his intellectual "biography"—"a disparate inventory" of literary and philosophical influences on his thinking—he concluded unexpectedly with the statement, "It [his work] is dominated by the presentiment and the memory of the Nazi horror" (291). In Philippe Nemo's words, the Holocaust was "a hidden referent" around which Levinas's work was organized (quoted in Malka 2006, xi), even though he did not comment on it in any of his major works. As Eaglestone (2004) also remarks, "The Holocaust saturates Levinas's work," even though his responses are by no means direct (255). In "Loving the Torah More Than God," Levinas (1999) explains that his reticence on the subject was motivated by a refusal "to offer up the ultimate passion as a spectacle and to use these inhuman screams to create a halo for myself as either author or director. The cries are inextinguishable; *they echo and echo across eternity*. What we must do is listen to the thought they contain" (81; emphasis mine).[5] Reminiscent of his injunction against capturing the other in aesthetic representations, Levinas argues against appropriative thematization of the Holocaust. Yet he emphasizes that the impact of the events is enduring, and he posits that the ethical task of "listening" to the cries of the victims has become the very foundation of post-Auschwitz thought.

One of the poignant moments when the philosopher breaks his ostensive silence is the dual epigraph in *Otherwise than Being, or Beyond Essence*. The first part reads (in the English translation), "To the memory of those who were closest among the six million assassinated by National Socialists, and of millions on millions of all confessions and all nations, victims of the same hatred of the other man, the same anti-semitism." The dedication in Hebrew, placed below, commemorates Levinas's loved ones, his father, mother, two brothers, and his parents-in-law, who perished in a mass execution in Kaunas: "To the memory of my father and master, Rabbi Yehiel son of Abraham the Levite, my mother and guide, Dvorah daughter of Rabbi Moshe, my brothers Dov son of Rabbi Yehiel the Levite and Aminidav son of Yehiel the Levite, my father-in-law Rabbi Shmuel son of Rabbi Gershom the Levite and my mother-in-law Malka daughter of Rabbi Chaim. May their souls be preserved in the bond of life" (Malka 2006, 81; translation modified). In light of this epigraph, Levinas's own reflection on the constitution of the ethical subject as a witness to the existence of another can be reread as, although by no means reduced to, an act of witnessing, commemoration, and even prayer.[6] In this sense, it reminds us of Elie Wiesel's repeated recitation, in both his written works and his public appearances, of "Yitgadal v'yitkadash sh'mei rabba," the first lines of the Kaddish, the Jewish prayer for the dead in which the divine name is glorified.[7] At the same time, the doubling of the dedication can be seen as a remarkable figure of repetition in the philosopher's own work.[8]

Although Levinas's contribution to situating testimony in philosophical contexts is crucial, other contemporary thinkers have also attempted to redraw the parameters of subjectivity in terms of witnessing. In different ways and across various disciplines, authors such as philosophers Giorgio Agamben, Jean-François Lyotard, Jacques Derrida, and Kelly Oliver; intellectual historian Dominick LaCapra; and trauma theorist Cathy Caruth have all offered models in which subjectivity emerges in the process of bearing witness. Agamben (1999), for instance, describes his entire philosophical project as "a kind of perpetual commentary on testimony" (13). In *Remnants of Auschwitz*, he arrives at a general definition of subjectivity that approximates Levinas's: becoming a subject is a function of bearing witness.[9] In a more explicitly ethical formulation, feminist philosopher Kelly Oliver (2001) agrees with Levinas that we need to rethink subjectivity in light of ethics, as "response-ability, or response to address" (5). For Oliver, responsibility requires that we move beyond Hegelian recognition, because, as the paradigm that relies on the subject/object distinction, it allows the subject to subsume the other's alterity. As such, it is already a symptom of the pathology of oppression. Rather, we must reenvisage interhuman relations that are peaceful, compassionate, and respectful of difference. Although Lyotard (1988) circumvents the idiom of subjectivity, in his elaboration of the *differend* (which he defines as an irreconcilable conflict that cannot be expressed under the current rules of language), he argues that the main task and obligation of thought today, "in a literature, in a philosophy, in a politics perhaps, is to *bear witness* to differends by finding idioms for them" (3; emphasis mine).[10] Sui generis, the concept of witnessing is also central to the work of intellectual historian Dominick LaCapra, who has argued for a participatory model of researching history. Based on his consideration of the impact of testimony on historiography, LaCapra concludes that histo-riography must integrate empathy, compassion, and the work of memory into the critical analysis of historical facts. The historian bears witness not only to the events in the past but also to history's participants, often resulting in empathetic, transferential investments in the object of study. LaCapra (2004) defines empathy as nonappropriative and open to the other (in contrast to projective identification), "an affect crucial for possible ethical relation to the other and hence for one's responsibility and answerability" (77). However, the historian must remain critically aware of the transferential dynamic and a tendency to overidentify with the victims that inform his interpretive relation to the events of the past, so as to avoid the conflation of history with trauma, at the cost of analytic and normative frameworks (LaCapra 2007a, 170–74). Similarly, in Caruth's work on trauma, a psychoanalytic articulation of the subject is inseparable from bearing witness to the suffering of another person. Caruth (1996) defines trauma as a form of mental wounding that leaves no physical trace yet which is lodged at the core of the survivor's being. Since trauma is unassimilated at the time of the event and its symptoms are always delayed, the traumatic event both "defies and demands our witness" (4). Yet trauma is not merely the locus of an isolated individual's relation to the past. Rather, it is always tied to the trauma of another, and thus it may lead "to the encounter with another, through the very possibility of listening to another's wound" (8). Such ethical listening must in its turn take into account the subtle vibrations of repetition compulsion in the primary witness's speech. As Esther Faye (2001), historian and trauma theorist, insists, such listening "must be attentive thus to what repeats in a subject's speech. It must listen for the repetition of those unconscious registrations" (52). Commenting on Eric Santner's work on memory and the work of mourning in postwar Germany, Karyn Ball (2008) sums up that the critical reflection on the interrelations between history and trauma is underwritten by a commitment to "recovering the role of the individual and collective agents, who can be held accountable for their actions or offer empathetic solidarity with the traumatized and the bereaved by bearing witness to the reality of their suffering" (175).

The confines of this book do not allow for a detailed analysis of the excellent works mentioned above; let it be noted, however, that Agamben, Oliver, and LaCapra all acknowledge their debt to Dori Laub and Shoshana Felman's seminal thesis that the Shoah was "an event without witnesses."[11] All three thinkers take written Holocaust narratives or videotaped oral testimonies as their point of departure. Agamben, for example, grounds his redefinition of the subject in the necessity to speak for the *Muselmann*, that unique product of the camps about whom Levi (1993) famously wrote that they are "non-men . . . the divine spark dead within them: one hesitates to call them living: one hesitates to call their death death" (90). Although he makes no reference to Laub and Felman, in *The Differend* Lyotard also draws on Holocaust testimony in response to the plight of Holocaust survivors who were confronted with Robert Faurisson's revisionist theses about the gas chambers.

Where do these new ways of articulating subjectivity stem from? And why do they begin to manifest themselves several decades after the Holocaust? As Caruth and other proponents of trauma studies have argued, bearing witness to trauma can take place only belatedly. Caruth (1995) describes trauma as

> the breach in the mind's experience of time, of self, and the world. . . . An event that . . . is experienced too soon, too unexpectedly, to be fully known and is therefore not available to consciousness until it imposes itself again, repeatedly, in the nightmares and repetitive actions of the survivor. . . . And it is this inherent latency of the event that paradoxically explains the peculiar temporal structure of the belatedness of historical experience: since the traumatic event is not experienced as it occurs, it is fully evident only in connection with another place, and in another time. (41, 8)

Of course, thinkers and writers such as Theodor Adorno, Jean Améry, and Tadeusz Borowski noted early on that "Auschwitz" had resulted in the collapse of mainstay ethical values and epistemological concepts. The larger implications of that historical trauma could be articulated only much later, however, in the context of new cultural dominants and against the background of contemporary catastrophes. As Wieviorka has argued, such contexts did not exist prior to the Eichmann trial. Agamben (1999), for instance, suggests that the questions of contemporary relevance of survivors' testimonies can arise only after the factual "truth" of the Holocaust has been established (11).[12] Thus a meaningful context in which testimonials could be received emerged many years after the events, outside their immediate frame of reference.

If this is the case, should we consider the desire to overhaul the parameters of subjectivity in terms of witnessing—in philosophy, in literature, in art, even in historiography—to be akin to a historically situated, belated traumatic "symptom," that is, a result of thought having been blighted by a confrontation with unprecedented horror?

Is then the Holocaust narrative an example par excellence of the new notion of subjectivity, with a Holocaust survivor as the figure of a paradigmatic subject qua witness? Or, conversely, has the emergence of the amorphous genre of Holocaust *témoignage*, whether in its literary guise or in the form of videotaped accounts, made rethinking the subject in terms of witnessing both possible *and* necessary? If this is the case, Wieviorka's (2006) conclusion that the function of Holocaust testimonies was "the reconstitution of identity" (44) in the wake of shattering events would have far-reaching philosophical, ethical, and even political ramifications. In what follows, I will explore these implications by looking at two Holocaust narratives, Elie Wiesel's *The Gates of the Forest* (1966), and Imre Kertész's *Kaddish for a Child Not Born* (written in 1990), in the context of Levinas's notion of ethical substitution.

LEVINAS'S WITNESSING AS THE STRUCTURE OF SUBJECTIVITY AND THE HOLOCAUST NARRATIVE

Levinas defines ethics as the calling into question of the same—that is, of my self-identity as an autonomous subject—by the other. Since identity arises from the impossibility of escaping ethical assignation, responsibility is the primary and fundamental structure of subjectivity. As Levinas (1985) states in *Ethics and Infinity*, "The very node of the subjective is knotted in ethics understood as responsibility" (95). Prior to becoming an autonomous subject (as it has been posited by Western modernity), the ethical subject is indebted to another. In order to describe the Western subject, Levinas frequently evokes the myth of Ulysses, whose departures from home are already animated by the goal of a safe return. To Ulysses's adventure, Levinas (1986) juxtaposes the myth of Abraham, who, after his ordeal at Mount Moriah, leaves his fatherland for an unknown land and "forbids his servant to even bring back his son to the point of departure" (348). Like Abraham, the ethical self forsakes its ancestral home. It is never at rest in its identity but remains in exile, "outside the nucleus of my substantiality" (Levinas 1998b, 142), living in an affective state of vigilant disquietude. As Levinas writes in "Substitution," the seminal chapter of *Otherwise than Being*, subjectivity is constituted in recurrence, a repeated movement of going outside of oneself and withdrawing into oneself. Unlike in Hegelian recognition, where the encounter with the other culminates in the absorption of alterity, in recurrence the ethical subject ventures toward the other who cannot be appropriated into the structures of the self. As a result, the endless movement of return from the outside disallows the subject to coincide with oneself, disrupting self-presence and self-possession. As Levinas (2000) writes in *God, Death, and Time*, this repetitive misencounter with oneself is thus "an exigency coming from the other over and above the active dimension of my powers, so as to become a departure without limits in which the self spends itself without counting" (179). The self is, first and foremost, *for* the other because prior to having ventured outside of itself, it has already returned from an outside that is absolute, from the exteriority that it can never inhabit. Originating in ethical obligation, recurrence is not a matter of volition or ability (of the "I can"). Rather, in recurrence, the self remains displaced and uncomfortable, "twisted over itself in its skin, too tight in its skin, in itself already outside of itself" (Levinas 1998b, 104). The self necessarily returns to cognition, memory, and self-identity proper to will, but this sense of coherent ego always comes later, and it is possible only because recurrence, as initiated by the other whom it cannot appropriate, is prior to autonomy and self-possession. As Levinas explains, it is in the exposure to the other and in response to its needs that the subject as such is "born," although this birth will always be belated because the ethical subject never attains complete self-presence. It is important to note, moreover, that although the explicit philosophical framework of Levinas's articulation of recurrence is his polemic with Hegel, it is most likely influenced by the Judaic notion of *teshuvah*, which means "response" or "repentance." The word conveys the sense of returning to God and asking his forgiveness, in order to repair the relation with God and with those around us whom we have harmed.[13]

Since the movement of return from the nonplace of the ethical encounter is the function of my indebtedness to the other, the emergence of the subject is already testimony to the other's existence. As Levinas (1998b) writes, "The subject, in which the other is the same, insomuch as the same is for the other, bears witness to it" (146). The ethical subject is a witness before intentionality and thus before it assumes the task of witnessing. It bears witness to the source of its own obligation, the source that is radically external and that cannot be derived from consciousness.[14] This ethical testimony is not a form of knowledge or recognition: "This witness is true, but with the truth irreducible to the truth of disclosure" (Levinas 1985, 109);

that is, the truth conceived in terms of knowledge, mediated by established concepts and categories, presupposes the unmediated truth of testimony. Testimony is not anchored in memory that is a function of a conventional sense of time. The autonomous subject is indeed grounded in the temporal continuum through memory and intentionality, which are "the content" of selfhood. In its primordial capacity as a witness to another, however, the subject is the addressee of a command or a plea coming from the other, who cannot be seized in recollection. Temporality itself must therefore be reconceived starting from the time of the other, as a recurrent movement of departure and return from the nonplace of alterity, where the ethical subject is always out of step with that to which it bears witness. The subject is thus affected on a fundamental level, transcended by the diachrony of the other who signals "a past more ancient than every representable origin, a pre-original and anarchical *passed*" (Levinas 1998b, 9). The witnessing subject returns from the past that cannot be captured in memory and synthesized in the present. It lags "already in the past behind which the present delays, over and beyond the now which this exteriority disturbs and obsesses" (100).

As suggested above, Levinas considered his own work as a form of "listening to the echo" of the voices of Holocaust victims rather than as a direct commentary on the atrocities. Interestingly, the philosopher also deploys the metaphor of the echo to convey the sense of the subject's being touched by the unpresentable exteriority from which the demand to bear witness issues. The self, writes Levinas (1998b), is like a sound "that would resound in its own echo, the node of a wave which is not once again consciousness" (103), endlessly repeating after him who had called upon it in the immemorial past. The echo reverberates in the witness's speech, rippling across the surface of his or her words. It is a trope for what Levinas calls Saying, that is, the ethical essence of language as "response-ability," antecedent to communication (or the Said). Levinas (2000) frequently underscores the repetitive nature of Saying: "There is then an iteration of Saying, which is . . . a 'here I am' as the origin of language . . . bearing witness regardless of the later destiny of the Said" (198). Already transmuted into an echo, the self cannot refuse to respond, repeating after the voice whose source remains unknown. The "echoing" speech foregrounds its status as a response to the other, who is not only an interlocutor but also the source of the witness's language.

In her reflection on Ovid's representation of Echo, Gayatri Spivak offers a helpful interpretation of that mythical figure. Echo is condemned to express herself through the repetition of another's words: when Narcissus asks, for instance, "Why do you fly from me?" she answers, "Fly from me!" Since, in her verbatim repetition, Narcissus's words acquire a different meaning that expresses Echo's love, her utterances unintentionally work to foil Narcissus's desire for self-knowledge. For Spivak (1996), Echo is thus an excellent trope for "the (un)intending subject of ethics [through which] we are allowed to understand the mysterious responsibility of ethics that its subject cannot comprehend" (190). At the same time, to articulate the self figuratively as an echo is to designate it as the movement of infinite repetition, of insistent and unstoppable return of the other's voice, even against my will. In this movement, the self is simultaneously proclaimed and unsettled. Its speech is emptied of positive content and becomes echolalia, the reverberation of the infinitely distant sound "uncoupled from intention." As the echo, the self lends its voice to another, putting itself in his or her place.

Levinas's concept of "substitution," perhaps the philosopher's most dramatic expression of ethical subjectivity, captures this sense of the ethical need to put oneself in the place of the other to the point of being a hostage and expiating for the other's faults.[15] The self's relationship with itself is declared to be first and foremost "the extraordinary and everyday event of my responsibility that answers for the faults and misfortunes of others" (Levinas 1998b, 10). The self is not only called upon to answer before the other but also holds itself accountable for the other's deeds, even for the other's responsibility. Substitution entails putting oneself in the place of the other who is radically different from me. Since I can never truly assume that place and the other remains radically unknown to me, substitution is opposed to appropriative identification, even if it were to be solicitous or empathetic.[16]

What begins to emerge from Levinas's discussion of substitution via the notion of recurrence is a series of extraordinary transformations of philosophical concepts. Levinas juxtaposes "recurrence" to the Hegelian "return" of the subject founded in (self-)recognition and knowledge. Hence, the movement of return is reconfigured, paradoxically, as (Abrahamic) exile, an always singular and nonreciprocal movement toward the other. Recurrence, Levinas (1998b) proclaims, is not "self-coinciding. . . . It is a substitution for another" (146). Yet "substitution" is an ethical category that now replaces (and, according to Levinas, predates) the autonomous subject's egotistic usurpation of somebody else's right to exist. Levinas frequently alludes to Pascal's expression about the self's inalienable "place under the sun" as paradigmatic of the Western subject's egotism. In the context of Western philosophy, Heidegger's conception of "Being-in-the world" and of *Dasein*'s primordial occupation of that realm is the culmination, in ontological terms, of that process.[17]

In Holocaust narratives, the Levinasian movement of substitution is revealed in a paramount fashion, as we heard in Filip Müller's testimony, in which the survivor recounted entering the place of death and, having survived, incessantly lending his voice to the dead. Insofar as one is a witness, one is located in the victim's place, vicariously entering the unimaginable site where speech ceases, in order to bring that silence to speech. As Wiesel writes, in the second volume of his *Memoirs*, "Long ago, *over there*, far from the living, we told ourselves that . . . the one among us who would survive would testify for all of us. He would do nothing else." The witness is motivated by an obligation to lend his voice and his talent as a storyteller to those who cannot speak. As Levi famously remarked, the survivors are never true witnesses since they cannot testify to the limit experience at which only those who were permanently silenced had arrived. Rather, like Levinas's notion of ethical subject, the survivor is already a surrogate witness, speaking "in their stead, by proxy," borrowing the authority to speak from the dead (Levi 1988, 84).[18]

Agamben (1999) quotes Wiesel as having said, "I live, therefore I am guilty. . . . I am here because a friend, an acquaintance, an unknown person died in my place" (89). Toward the end of his first narrative *Night,* Wiesel recalls the events leading to his father's death. His father was by his side and sustained him throughout the ordeal of the camps, but he fell ill during the death march and, one night, suddenly disappeared from his bunk. Wiesel (1982) writes, in sorrow, "His last word was my name. A summons to which I did not respond" (106). Wiesel's recounting of that unwitnessed event also carries the trace of an even deeper wound: that of the death of his mother and his little sister, Tzipora, whom he saw for the last time on the ramp in Auschwitz-Birkenau and whom he never mentions again in *Night*. It seems that the writer is still responding to this double summons, and the impossibility to be indifferent to the call is the meaning of the witness's "speaking by proxy."

In *Fragments of Isabella,* Isabella Leitner dramatizes the substitutive displacement of the witness's voice by writing her "fragments" in the second person, as an address to her murdered loved ones. In a passage reminiscent of Wiesel's description of little children being thrown into flaming pits,[19] Leitner (1980) grieves the death of her younger sister: "I saw the flames. I heard the shrieks. Is that the way you died, Potyo? Is that the way?" (17). This heart-wrenching question is not a mere figure of speech but an intimate address to her little sister, whom "she had permission to bathe. To diaper her. To burp her. To rock her. To love her" (17). The intimacy of this address to her sister exudes a sense that Leitner is now cradling her sister in her tender words. The writer's promises to her dead mother, uttered after the birth of her second son, are just as personal: "I will tell them [her sons] to make what is good in all of us their religion, as it was yours, Mother, and then you will always be alive. . . . Mother, I will keep you alive" (103).

The sense of undeclinable duty, however, issues from more than the survivor's being a literal *port-parole* for another. As Primo Levi (1988) admits, he has also taken another's place in a more fundamental sense. He asks, "Are you ashamed because you are alive in place of another? And in particular, of a man more generous, more sensitive, more useful, wiser, worthier of living than you?" (81). In the philosophical context in which Levinas situates his work, the shame of the camp survivor is an immediate indictment of Heidegger's *Dasein*: its "being there" in the world always amounts to taking up someone else's place under the sun. In both Levi's and Levinas's terms, the survivor has almost literally lived in the other's stead.

Finally, Holocaust narratives express the testimonial exigency by mobilizing the Levinasian notion of ethical substitution and recurrence while at the same time evoking the psychoanalytic framework of traumatic repetition. To further develop this connection, I will now turn to Wiesel's and Kertész's literary testimonials. Both authors were young adults when they were deported to the camps (fourteen and fifteen years of age, respectively), and, although a quarter-century interval separates the two narratives, they resonate with each other insofar as they both represent a refashioned, allegorical return to the camp. While Levi's feat of surviving Auschwitz may have been put to doubt by his suicide in 1987, Wiesel and Kertész went on to achieve the status of emblematic survivors, and both were awarded the Nobel Prize, the 1986 Peace Prize in the case of Wiesel, and the 2002 Prize for Literature for Kertész. Both *The Gates of the Forest* and *Kaddish* can be read as revisitations of the site of trauma that the authors tried to describe before, in *Night* and in *Fateless*, respectively, as well as less directly in other works. At the same time, both narratives are also literary reflections of the ethical transformation of the subject in the process of witnessing. Admittedly, Wiesel situates his protagonist's struggle in a religious context, in continuation, or perhaps in response to, the *Night* protagonist's crisis of faith. By contrast, Kertész's main character emphasizes his lack of religious outlook, even though every page is interrupted by interjections of "good God," the calling in vain of the name of the divine, the existence of which the narrator vehemently rejects. Both novels, however, are linked by the evocation of Kaddish, the prayer for the dead, which also structures both narratives.

"AND THE SEA IS NEVER FULL": THE INSATIABLE SUFFERING FOR THE OTHER (ELIE WIESEL)

At the beginning of *The Gates of the Forest*, the main character, Gregor (an assumed name), is hiding in a cave in the forest, following the deportation of the Jews from his hometown in Transylvania and the presumed death of his entire family. At first, his father was in hiding with him, but one night he did not return after a foray to the village for food. The narrator constantly repeats that all of Gregor's relatives, indeed, all of the Jews of Romania, have been turned into clouds whose drifting presence is palpable throughout the novel: "The clouds refused to leave the patch of sky above the houses huddled together in the town below. Later Gregor understood why: they were not clouds properly speaking, but Jews driven from their homes and transformed into clouds" (Wiesel 1966, 3). One night, a stranger arrives at the hideout, claiming that his name has left him and responding with laughter to all of Gregor's queries, a laughter that makes Gregor shudder (7). Under these circumstances, Gregor, who himself has been stripped of everything, offers the nameless stranger the gift of his Jewish name, "Gavriel." This is his secret name, which, as Gregor explains, must not be pronounced in perilous times, since, like its owner, "it has gone into hiding" (13). The giving of the name is announced in the first sentence of the novel: "He had no name, so he gave him his own. As a loan, as a gift, what did it matter? In the time of war every word is as good as the next. A man possesses only what he gives away" (3). It seems that Gregor's dispossessing himself of his real name makes it possible for the narrative to begin. Gregor's gesture of giving his name away is spontaneous: he does it because he "likes to give." His subsequent journey, however, reveals the meaning of the stranger's remark, at the beginning of the narrative, that "giving is a privilege which has to be earned" (15).

As if in response to Gregor's ultimate gift—in a way, the gift of himself—the stranger begins to tell him the stories of the annihilation of Jews in nearby villages and towns. Unable to leave, Gregor has to listen to the horrifying account told by him who now bears his name. Gavriel commands Gregor, "You must learn to listen. Listening gives you the key" (44). When the story is finished, the stranger—now Gavriel—surrenders himself to the Germans, who believe they have captured Gregor. He thus literally substitutes himself for Gregor and saves his life. But before Gavriel gives himself up, he elicits a solemn oath from Gregor that he will never forget the stories of destruction that he told him. He makes Gregor promise that he will make his "the silence of the children at the hour of their death" and, in remembrance, will always follow in the footsteps of the *Tzaddik* "who sang as he walked to the ditch where the corpses of his townsmen were piled up" (21). From then on, Gregor lives a life that is beholden to the stranger, to whom he had relinquished his name and his entire world. He survives the first months after his escape from the cave by slipping into the role of a deaf-and-dumb village idiot, allegedly a nephew of his family's former servant, Maria. After he leaves the village, he joins a group of Jewish partisans, living out what would have been, as it turns out, Gavriel's life. He also keeps his promise to pass on Gavriel's legacy, and he tells the partisans the harrowing tales of destruction, "a madman's story" (129). The narrative closes years later, with Gregor's recitation of the Kaddish for his childhood friend and later the partisan leader Leib the Lion, who, in his courage and selflessness, "had incarnated what is immortal in men" (226).

Throughout the story, the narrator underscores the insubstantial nature of Gregor's meetings with Gavriel: the first encounter in the cave is described as *"apparent"* (87). It is also uncertain whether the stranger that Gregor chances upon in New York after the war is indeed Gavriel. Gavriel's actual existence is ambiguous, and the narrator repeatedly refers to his powers of an angel, lending him the aura of a mythical figure (it seems significant that, in the Hebrew Bible, archangel Gabriel is a messenger from God).[20] I suggest, however, that the character of Gavriel should be read as an allegory of the ethical obligation to suffer for the other and, in taking that suffering upon oneself, to bear witness to it. It is this ethical dimension that Gavriel's manifestation in Gregor's life has revealed; Gavriel is the ethical essence of Gregor. Thus, for Gregor, Gavriel's existence is indubitable in an ethical rather than in a factual sense. As Gregor avows, "Sometimes I doubt the existence of Gregor, but never that of Gavriel" (130).

As implied in Gavriel's name, the narrative of *The Gates* is subtended by a religious reflection on the meaning of the messianic promise. Following his spiritual apprenticeship with Gavriel, Gregor recognizes that the significance of the coming of the Messiah is that the Messiah "isn't one man, he's all men" (225). His recognition that the awaiting of messianic time is inseparable from the ethical obligation to the other, who is both most distant and most pressingly near, fulfills the stranger's earlier announcement that the underlying structure of time is related to their meeting. Wiesel writes, "Separation contains as much of a mystery as meeting. In both cases a door opens: in meeting it opens on the future, in separation on the past. It's the same door" (50).[21] In the messianic time, to borrow from Walter Benjamin, every moment is a gate through which the Messiah might enter (Benjamin 1969, 264). In Wiesel's account, in the cycle of encounters and departures, fulfilling one's obligation to the other is what ushers in the coming of the Messiah; the other is the arch of that gate.

The stranger is then the locus of the witness's identity, while the name that the witness carries and that designates him or her is always only an alias. Indeed, Wiesel's protagonist feels as if the stranger encountered in the cave had inhabited him, lending him his voice and his soul: "The voice of Gavriel vibrated within him, regulating his breathing and giving depth to his silence. He hid himself behind Gavriel's face, beneath Gavriel's star" (83). The transposition of the name in the process of witnessing indicates that the self's identity as an autonomous being is only an approximation of its ethical essence: as such, in Levinas's (1998b) words, the self "bears its name as a borrowed name, a pseudonym, a pronoun" (106). Levinas contends that subjectivity is "the possibility of being the author of what has been breathed in unbeknownst to me, of having received, one knows not from where, that of which I am an author" (148).[22] The subject therefore never truly writes the script of his or her life story, and the author of a Holocaust narrative rescinds his or her autonomous right to the authorship of that story to an unparallel degree. Insofar as the writer/

witness substitutes for another, he always lends his or her true name to the stranger.

When forced to recount, three times, the story of Leib the Lion's capture by the Germans, for which the partisans hold him accountable, Gregor realizes that "the repetition of the truth betrays it. The more I talk the more I empty myself of truth" (Wiesel 1966, 163). This leaking out of "actual truth," however, opens Gregor up to a different kind of truth—the ethical truth of testimony. Gregor increasingly suffers from feelings of guilt, a guilt that prompts him to assume responsibility for Leib's capture. Thus, even though he realizes that he is without fault, he continues to reproach himself for not being in Leib's place. It seems that, toward the end of the narrative, Gregor recognizes the ethical truth and the meaning of his suffering. As if quoting Levinas, he affirms that "the injustice perpetrated in an unknown man concerns me; I am responsible" (166), although he recognizes the nature of this responsibility only in the process of retelling the stranger's story. The gesture of putting oneself in place of the stranger thus constitutes the speaking subject as witness. As conveyed poetically in Levinas's (1998b) metaphor of the echo, the indisputable fact of the other's existence can be proclaimed only in the witness's pseudonymous voice, "through what it is capable of doing in the witness" (145). The other manifests his or her existence as an echo, reverberating in the witness's words. Ethical responsibility thus amounts to "the impossibility of being silent, the scandal of sincerity" (143), and the imperative to speak must be obeyed. This event of the other's visitation in my speech is unhinged from chronologies, from linear temporal movement. Yet it is also this repetition that enables the witness's entry into the continuum of time and space, and thus into acts of speaking and writing. I am a witness because the evanescent passage of the other through the world traces itself in my voice: "Language permits us to utter, be it by betrayal, this *outside of being*, this *ex-ception* to being" (6).

Levinas contends that the self's endless and unsettling returns to itself in recurrence, as discussed above, amount to a persecution by the other who holds me hostage and puts into question the meaning of my existence as "for-itself." Being responsible thus hollows me out, deposing over and over again the content of my ego. In *God, Time, and Death* (2000), Levinas addresses this "emptiness" at the core of my being. He writes, "It is therefore necessary that there be in the egoity of the I the risk of a nonsense, a madness" (20), and he locates the core of that "nonsense" in the scandalous fact of the other's death. It makes "no sense" because it cancels absolutely the possibility of response. This "madness" of absolute no-response, located at the very locus of meaning, refers me and consigns me to the other. In "Useless Suffering," one of the few texts in which he makes an explicit reference to Nazi atrocities, Levinas (1998b) extends this idea and argues that the "no-sense" refers not only to the other's death but also to the suffering he or she undergoes. The pain endured by another is inherently "useless" and cannot be converted into meaning, "the meaning of pain that wins merit and hopes for reward," be it religious, social, or historical (95).[23] It is also meaningless because the gulf that separates me from the suffering other is immeasurable. The only access I have to the other's suffering is through my own experience of pain. My own suffering, therefore, which in itself is equally "useless," gains ethical significance as compassion because "it alone can pry open the shell of egoity." It is "the suffering in me for the unjustifiable suffering of the other" (94), a call to the self that elicits it in its primordial and nonreciprocal responsibility. The nonsense or "madness" at the center of signification has to be affirmed as the nexus of subjectivity, affecting the self in its very identity and marking the limit of language as the vehicle of meaningfulness.[24] My concern for the other's death and suffering lies therefore at the core of the ethical relation.

Thus recurrence, the movement of return from outside of oneself, from "beyond essence," is set in motion by the nonsense of the other's suffering and death, and the exteriority from which the witnessing subject returns is the unpresentable place of that suffering. The subject's subsequent emergence into self-identity is then brought about by the awakening of the same by the other, inseparable from my fear for the other's death and suffering. Marking the other's absolute "no-response," the senseless suffering of the other commands response and designates the witness "in my culpability of a survivor," turned toward "another source of meaning than the identity of the same with itself" (Levinas 2000, 12). The meaning of the witness's speech is therefore what Levinas (1998b) calls obsession, that is, the self's being affected by the other—to the point of "madness." He writes, "Obsession . . . is inscribed in consciousness as something foreign, a disequilibrium, a delirium" (101). Since the movement of repetition, constitutive of substitution, puts the subject out of phase with itself, its speech is also dissonant, animated by significations that it cannot derive from itself. Insofar as witnessing speech is primarily Saying, that is, my aptitude to respond to the other, in which only the self's appointment by the other speaks, the words are devoid of sense and the witness's speech is obsessive. Again, the Holocaust narrative reveals this limit condition of witnessing speech, in which the "no-sense" of the other's suffering and death initiates the movement through which the I posits itself as the subject. In its primordial manifestation as witness, always accused to the point of being accountable even for the other's deeds, the subject is displaced from its sovereign position as the originator of language. Prior to being a statement, the witness's speech is already "a response to a non-thematizable provocation" (12).

In Holocaust literature, a frequent symbolic inscription of this speech, emptied of meaning by the fact of the other's suffering and death, is the figure of a "madman," usually someone who has miraculously escaped execution and has returned to warn the others. A striking example is an episode in *Bread for the Departed*, a novel by Polish-Jewish writer Bogdan Wojdowski (1997) that describes the life and disappearance of the Warsaw ghetto. In the hours preceding deportations, "a bellowing specter" is running through the streets, exclaiming words that, at the time, are incomprehensible to the inhabitants of the ghetto: "Brothers! They drive people naked into ditches and shoot them in the back. They fill in the pits and the blood flows over onto the fields. Like a watery swamp. The blood surfaces above the graves. The earth moves over those graves. . . . They have some kind of smoke. They have some kind of fire. They suffocate and they burn" (374).[25] The figure of a "madman," a *revenant* who returns from the dead, appears in almost all of Wiesel's writings. Perhaps the most memorable character in *Night* is Moshe the Beadle, a survivor of a mass execution, who returns to his village to warn the Jews of Sighet. His stories are disbelieved, and he is said to have lost his mind. As in Wojdowski's novel, the appearance of the madman marks an interruption in the narrative and the point at which the illusion of the livable, meaningful world collapses.

In *The Gates*, Gavriel is a "madman," a stranger without a name, who laughs with a "laugh, which was like no other, which did not even resemble itself" (Wiesel 1966, 3). Further, in an episode that beckons back to Wiesel's first narrative, Moshe himself returns in one of Gavriel's stories, where he is called Moshe the Mute, the nickname that becomes chillingly literal when the SS cut out his tongue; as in *Night*, he is a local beadle. In him, Gavriel recognizes the Messiah, yet a Messiah who has no powers to implore God to save mankind in the hour of terror. In a peculiar reversal, Gregor's subsequent muteness (during his stay with Maria), which encourages the villagers to deposit their innermost secrets with him and seek his succor, mirrors the character of Moshe the Mute from Gavriel's disturbing story. Just as Gavriel burdened Moshe with the responsibility for the suffering of the Jews, so does Gregor take upon himself the trespasses of the entire village, as well as the pain of their suffering, bringing to mind Levinas's (1999) description of unconditional responsibility: "He can feel all of God's responsibilities resting on his shoulders" (81). In playing the role of the "village idiot," Gregor becomes the repository of their secrets, their suffering, and their guilt.

The tension in Wiesel's narratives arises from the fact that, ever since *Night*, his testimonials have been a struggle against Moshe the Beadle's "nonsensical words" and at the same time a continuation of "the madman's" irrefutable legacy. To write about the Holocaust is to say "Here I am" to the unrelenting specter of Moshe, to be his hostage. Significantly, in *Night*, before his lapse into "madness," Moshe was young Wiesel's teacher in the kabbalah and introduced him to arcane religious knowledge. To testify to the traumatic event, to be a witness, is to repeat Moshe's fate: it means to tell stories that are insane, to utter empty words that do not deliver meaning. Yet it also means to toil against that senseless language, to compose meaningful phrases, even if they continue to abscond into "madness." The "mad" speech, the only way language can convey a Holocaust witness's message, marks the chiasmus between the possibility and impossibility of speech. In *And the Sea Is Never Full*, Wiesel (1999) writes, "The mystical madmen of Sighet, the beggars, bearers of secrets, drawn to doom, they all appear in my fictional tales. But I am afraid to follow them too far, *outside myself or deep within me*" (5; emphasis added). The madman is a stranger-within-me, whose strangeness can never be absorbed and who perseveres as the sign of absolute exteriority, the trace of which is imprinted in the witness's speech. The madman is a paradigmatic survivor and, at the same time, a trope for "a modality not of knowing, but of obsession, a shuddering of the human quite different from cognition" (Levinas 1998b, 87). He is also a symbolic messenger from the dead, who personifies the transmission of testimony between the "true" witness, whose capacity for speech was quelled by death, and the witness who substitutes for that witness and speaks "by proxy."

The identification of the traumatic kernel that refers the witness's voice to the unassumable suffering of the other can be recognized within the structure of a number of Holocaust narratives. Semprún, for instance, writes in a poised style, shaped and mediated by the author's training in philosophy and very different from Wiesel's poetic, religiously inflected idiom. However, as in Wiesel's texts, each of the numerous retellings of Semprún's (1997) stay in Buchenwald seems to swivel around a traumatic core that surfaces unexpectedly, and this sudden "memory slicing in like a scalpel" (215) corrodes the careful structure of his recollection.[26] In *The Long Voyage*, for example, the indigestible memory is a horrific episode of the death of a group of Jewish children from Poland who were torn to pieces by the SS dogs. This unnerving recollection remains unexplained within an otherwise coherent political framework of the narrative. Yet the witnessing imperative seems to stem from that senseless episode, which the narrator cannot absorb in a meaningful way. In his second fictional return to Buchenwald in *What a Beautiful Sunday!*, the narrator seems unable to cope with the memory of a group of Jews from Częstochowa, "the walking dead" who arrive after a death march from Auschwitz, walk into the room of the *Arbeitsstatistik*, where the narrator was employed with other political prisoners from France, and, in an utterly exhausted gesture, give them Hitler's salute. Semprún (1982) writes, "But you will have never forgotten, never. You will always remember, to your dying breath, the Jews from Częstochowa, standing there frozen, making a superhuman effort to stretch their right arm in the Nazi salute" (287–88). Subsequently, the narrator tries to manipulate the records so that the group would not be sent out of Buchenwald, which would mean certain death.[27] In *Literature or Life*, the "unnarratable story" is the rescue of a *Muselmann*, whom the narrator desperately tries to keep alive: "I speak softly to him. Finally, I take him in my arms" (Semprún 1997, 41). Only now does he confess to the reader that, only a week before, he was holding the dying body of his friend and teacher Maurice Halbwachs.[28] Although Semprún, a communist, never makes references to religion, both episodes, which the narrator confesses he could not have brought himself to disclose in his previous retellings, are recounted in the chapter titled "Kaddish."

"GRAVE IN THE AIR": IMRE KERTÉSZ'S
PRAYER FOR THE DEAD

Obsessive words are the insignia of the narrator's monologue in Imre
Kertész's *Kaddish For a Child Not Born*, the novel that further reveals both the complexity and the ethical straightforwardness of
ethical substitution. In a direct and unsparing manner, this account
throws into sharp relief the narratives that attempt to present the survivor's life in terms of redemptive closure (of which Leitner's retellings
are a paramount example), and it brings out hidden ruptures in those
narratives.

Kertész was nearly twelve when Hungary joined the German war
effort in 1941, under pro-Nazi regent Miklós Horthy. In March 1944,
Kertész was deported to Auschwitz, with over 400,000 Hungarian
Jews, and moved to Buchenwald and then to a smaller camp at Zeitz,
where he was liberated in 1945 (Congdon 2003, 1). He described
his ordeal many years later, in the semibiographical novel *Fateless*
(1975).[29] Already in the ending of that novel, he spoke of having lived
a borrowed existence: "I, too, had lived out a given fate. It wasn't my
fate, but I am the one who lived it to the end" (Kertész 1992, 188). In
Kaddish, first published in 1990, the narrator, who refers to himself
only as B., describes a sense of homelessness, of drifting through life
that does not seem to be his own, a survivor's endemic "rental life": "I
didn't quite live, and undeniably, this was not quite life; it was, rather,
functioning, yes, *surviving* to be more precise" (Kertész 1997, 45).[30]
Decades after the war, the narrator continues to identify his existence
with camp life, even though he feels he must constantly apologize for
his inability to leave the past behind. Again, this sensation of not being quite alive is a recurrent motif in some of the more introspective
Holocaust testimonies. The narrator of Semprún's *What a Beautiful
Sunday!*, for instance, keeps referring to his pervasive "impression
of having lived the life of someone else" (Semprún 1982, 301). He is
unable to explain this feeling to his friends or to the audiences who
come to listen to his stories of survival. When the listeners marvel at
the "thirty years since your return to life," he thinks to himself that
it is "thirty years since the last day of [my] death" (408). He perceives his existence as unreal, merely a lucid dream "of a young man
who died long ago . . . or a dream dreamed by this landscape, like a
coil of smoke hardly more substantial than the one over there" (150,
187). One of the most chilling expressions of this feeling is Charlotte

Delbo's (1995) monologue in *Auschwitz and After*, spoken in the voice of one of her Auschwitz companions, Mado. Mado confesses, "It seems to me I'm not alive. Since all are dead, it seems impossible I shouldn't be also. . . . How could those stronger and more determined than I be dead, and I remain alive? . . . No, it's not possible, I'm not alive. . . . I died in Auschwitz but nobody knows it" (257, 267).[31]

The main character of *Kaddish* relates this quasiexistence to his failure as a husband, as a writer, and as a full-fledged human being. Like Semprún, whose memory and identity are rooted in one spot in Buchanwald, Kertész (2004) is immured in the camp. As he recalls elsewhere, in a short text titled "Free Europe," his entire life after the camps was "in a way, a continuation of the camp life." Indeed, he writes, "sometimes I have a feeling that I am still standing at the foot of those hills [in Buchenwald], hopelessly looking at the scene that was unfolding in front of me" (52; translation mine). The narrator of *Kaddish* writes all the time because of the "stubborn duty" to write. Yet, unlike Wiesel, he cannot clearly articulate the meaning of this "duty": "I can't help it; if I write I remember, I have to remember even if I don't know why I have to. . . . I can't be silent about [my stories] because it is my duty, albeit I don't know why it's my duty, or more precisely why I feel it's my duty" (Kertész 1997, 21–34). The necessity to write, an "undefeatable urge to speak as if by pangs of some terrible horror" (9), propels the narrative. At the same time, it reveals the meaninglessness and illusive nature of the narrator's "survival": "If I didn't work I would have to exist, and if I existed, I don't know what I would be forced to do, and it is better that I don't know . . . ; while I work, I am; if I didn't work, who knows if I'd be?" (2–3).[32]

The underlying raison d'être of this rapid, confused monologue, however, is the narrator's compulsive need to speak to a child "not born," whom he refused to beget "after Auschwitz." Thus the text unexpectedly begins to perform the rites of mourning for the child that could have been born and whose potential existence was annihilated by Auschwitz. The narrator chooses not to "multiply the survival of himself in descendants," which painfully contrasts with Leitner's exhilaration at the birth of her two sons, whom she repeatedly calls her greatest victory over Hitler.[33] The opening sentence of the narrator's confession is the announcement of this refusal: "'No', I said immediately and forthwith, without hesitation and spontaneously" (1). The narrator exclaims this impassioned word of rejection in answer to a conventional question asked by Professor Oblach, a mediocre philosopher, with whom he has been strolling in the woods at the writers' retreat. This "screaming, howling 'No'" resounds throughout the book, a word-shibboleth that marks the boundary between the narrator's "borrowed" existence brought about by Auschwitz and the world of the living. At the same time, the pained intensity of the refusal constantly betrays B.'s longing for the presence of the unborn child: "Were you to be a dark-eyed little girl? With pale spots of scattered freckles around your little nose? Or a stubborn boy? With cheerful, hard eyes like blue-gray pebbles?" (17).

What does it mean for a witness to speak in response to a child who will not have been, whose existence was prevented by Auschwitz? The narrator views his own existence through the lens of the unfulfilled potentiality of another's life, and the refrain "my life in the context of your potentiality" is repeated on almost every page of the short novel. Thus the astonishing fact of the narrator's survival, that is, the unfulfilled possibility of his death at Auschwitz, the death that he continues to die, is inseparable from the unfulfilled potentiality of his child's birth. He qualifies his thesis as follows: "*To view your non-existence in the context of the necessary and fundamental liquidation of my existence*" (24). Kertész's existential reflection on Being-toward-death (now indelibly marked by his impossible yet actual survival) is inseparable from the child's "not-being-born" in the wake of Auschwitz. The intrinsic cause that has undercut that potentiality is revealed in the leit motif reiterated throughout the monologue: the narrator's life has been nothing but "digging the grave in the air." This rhetorical figure is astounding (albeit borrowed, as we shall see), and it brings to mind Gavriel's metaphor of Jewish inhabitants of the *shtetl* turned into clouds in Wiesel's narrative. Kertész's refrain of "the grave in the air" is just as omnipresent. The compulsion to write, to literally bury himself in his writing, is inseparable from the repetitious "digging the grave others had started for me in the clouds"; as the narrator says, "for the pen is my spade" (24).

Kaddish is also an erudite philosophical reflection, abounding with allusions to German writers and thinkers. More directly, Kertész's grappling with the enigma of his survival is clearly a philosophical but also ideological polemic with Heidegger's famed analysis of Being-toward death in *Being and Time*.[34] The only famous name the narrator conspicuously passes over in silence is that of Paul Célan, a Holocaust survivor who committed suicide in 1970, and whose verses from the poem "Death Fugue" he surreptitiously weaves into his text. Kertész writes, "There I live and occasionally I look up at the glorious air or the clouds into which I keep digging my grave with my pen, like a forced laborer, whom they order every day to dig deeper with his spade so that he play death on his violin with a darker, sweeter voice" (27). Further, "How could I have explained to my wife that my pen was my spade? That my reason for writing was that I had to, and I had to because even then they whistled to me to dig deeper, to play death's tune darker, more sweetly? How could I perform work predicated on the future using the very same spade with which I must dig my grave into the clouds, the wind, into nothing?" (66). Or, "What business do I have with literature, with your golden hair Margarete, since the pen is my spade, the gravestone of your ashen hair Julamith" (57), and, in a direct quote in German, "Der Tod ist ein Meister aus Deutschland, seine Auge ist blau" (45).[35] Like Célan's musical poem, the narrative moves in circles, with the same phrases—"I have to write," "my life in the context of your potentiality," "digging the grave in the air," "the pen is my spade"—stalking the pages like a poetic refrain.

With increasing frequency, the narrator conflates the trauma of the Nazi camps with painful childhood experiences, such as his parents' divorce and his being placed, at the age of five, in a boarding school. His understanding of "Jewishness" is also traumatic in nature, and he traces its origin to the day when he saw, with utmost horror, his orthodox aunt without a wig: "I suddenly found myself understanding who I was: *a bald woman in a red gown in front of a mirror*" (17). Since then, he has identified being Jewish with monstrosity and with a dangerous and unwanted condition that "usually carries the death penalty" (17). Being "stuck" in his Auschwitz experience causes the narrator to refract even his childhood (as well as his present existence and his future) through that traumatic lens. For instance, he refers to the students at the boarding school as "inmates" and to the weekly reports as "Appel."[36]

Toward the end of the novel, the narrator's droning voice, his "mad" speech on Being-toward-death after Auschwitz, becomes that of a "madman," as in Wojdowski's or Wiesel's tales. Kertész writes, "Occasionally, like a drab weasel left over after a process of thorough extermination, I run through the city" (94). As if mourning over his own grave and over the grave of his unborn child, which is always "the grave in the air" drifting from the chimneys in Auschwitz, the narrator ends with a prayer that evokes all the "drowned" ones of Primo Levi's

narratives: "I may drown/Lord God/let me drown/forever, Amen" (95).
Yet, by Levi's definition, the narrator is ultimately one of the "saved."
Undoubtedly, the language of *Kaddish* reinscribes the (non)experience
of trauma, and its most powerful vehicle is the displaced incantation
of Célan's refrain from "Death Fugue." With his pen turned spade, the
narrator can only "dig up" words that instantaneously turn into ash.
His inability to anchor himself in life, his "pristine homelessness," is
caused by the fact that the only home he makes for himself is the un-
locatable "grave in the air." In that sense, he occupies an empty place
structured by the contradiction that Giorgio Agamben (1999) describes
as the central paradox of subjectivity: the self's "not being able not to
be" (the irrefutable fact of the narrator's existence) and its simultaneous "being able not to be" (here, literally, his inevitable death in Auschwitz, which nevertheless did not transpire; 148). Yet this failure to
assert the givenness of his life after Auschwitz, its "facticity," to borrow
Heidegger's term, leads the narrator to the realization that his right to
be must be considered in light of another's potentiality for being. His
address is primarily a response to this exigency.

Drawing on this insight through the prism of Levinas's ethics,
perhaps we must now contest Wieviorka's (2006) assertion that
"each person has an absolute right to her memory, which is nothing other than her identity, her very being" (132). The narrator's
memories, even the most intimate ones, are indebted to those who
were and to those who would have been, with respect to whom he
feels unspecified yet irremissible guilt. In that sense, as Semprún
(1982) also discovered seventeen years after he first brought himself to write down his account of Buchenwald, "There is no such
thing as innocent memory. Not for me any more" (130), with the
feelings of guilt and shame still surging forth at the memory of being addressed with a Nazi salute. In Semprún's case, he can no longer accept the truth of his own account of the Nazi camps: he has
to rewrite it "hour by hour, with the desperate certainty of the simultaneous existence of the Russian camps, of Stalin's Gulag"
(426). Semprún's narrator now realizes that he has constructed a
redemptive political framework to make sense of what was fundamentally senseless. He must discard this memory in favor of a different kind of truth that will enable him to respond to the Jews of
Częstochowa (as well as to Ivan Denisovitch).

The narrator of *Kaddish* rushes through his monologue as if trying
to strip himself of the facts of his existence and denude his speech to

its vulnerable core. This core turns out to be an address to another, to a "you," and Kertész's (1997) narrative is unique in being written in the grammatical second-person singular. In addressing the other, he bears witness, therefore he is. His words circle impotently, "madly," around a silent core at the heart of his being, to which he refers as a primal idea that he vaguely senses and that pulsates somewhere under the simulacrum of his existence. In the course of the narration, this "idea" is revealed to be embodied in a particular individual that the narrator encountered in the camp, in circumstances that he considers most unusual. As he was lying on the stretcher (at that point, he was, as he says, one of the *Muselmänner*), another inmate, referred to as "the Professor," somehow found himself in possession of the narrator's ration of food. Convinced that the other prisoner would walk away with his meager yet life-saving portion, he was astounded when the Professor came back to him and quickly fed him, thus endangering his own life (since he was expected to remain in another section of the camp) and certainly minimizing his own chances of survival. To the narrator's astonished question, Why did he do it? the Professor answered, simply and with a measure of indignation, "Well, what did you expect?" (33). The narrator suspects that the Professor was motivated by an idea without which he "did not wish to, or what's more, probably could not live" (34), a basic idea that he must help a person in need. Amid the narrator's otherwise jaded account, this incident stands out as unaccountable within the logic of self-preservation. Moreover, the narrator comments on the Professor's behavior in a changed tone of voice, devoid of its usual sarcasm, that it is "a very important testimony to that great metabolism of fate which really constitutes life, much, much more important than any commonplaces and rational nightmares any Führer, Chancellor, or other sundry titled usurper could or would serve up" (34). The altruistic prisoner's nickname stands in accusatory contrast to the "real" professors evoked in the narrative: Hegel, Heidegger (both referred to as H.), and the fictional Oblach. In the context of Auschwitz, the narrator muses, the Professor's gesture of compassion and human solidarity was irrational and unexplainable, in direct opposition to the rationality and explainability of the Holocaust (as Kertész insists, in tandem with Agamben, among others).[37] Admittedly, the narrative ends with a gesture that invites impending death, which will be the fulfillment of, as the narrator never tires of repeating, the "digging in the air of the grave" that the others have already started digging for him. But he also states, "I dreamed again of my tasks and hopes based, I know now, on the example of the Professor" (94). This is perhaps how we can read Kertész's otherwise bewildering remark that "Auschwitz is my greatest treasure" (quoted in Adelman 2004, 1). Indeed, even the monstrosity of being Jewish symbolized by the bold aunt is responded to, however allusively, by the narrator's repeated description of his ex-wife as "a beautiful Jewess," with a full mane of red hair, who possesses a very simple yet powerful desire for life and for having children.[38]

Bearing witness—to those buried in the grave in the air, to his own inevitable yet temporarily suspended death, and to the child not born—thus constitutes the mystery of the narrator's survival, delivering him into subjectivity. The announcement of another's annulled potentiality for being in the face of his imminent and yet unfulfilled death is the proclamation of his subjective existence, of his "Here I am." The narrator's life after death, the miracle of *sur-vivre*, consists of his "being-witness." He lives for the other who was, for the other who could have been, and, finally, for himself whose existence was nearly taken away by Auschwitz, although he will never be able to find the right words to convey its meaning. The narrator repeatedly comments on the frustrating impossibility to write in another way: "I can do no differently; I am only able to depict in this manner, with my pen dipped in sarcasm . . . , as if someone continued to push back my pen constantly whenever it tried to form certain words, so that, in the end, my hand substitutes other words" (6).

In addressing himself to the child not born, the narrator transforms his "obsessive speech" into the Kaddish, the prayer for the dead that extols the divinity of the other. He writes from the guilt of having stayed alive, of "being an accomplice to my staying alive" (21), with a sense of overwhelming although indefinite responsibility—an unpayable debt of his survival that he has incurred with all the dead. Like Wiesel's protagonist, Kertész's narrator has always been accused. In Levinas's (1998b) terms, he proclaims the pronoun "I" in the accusative "declined before any declension" (142). Levinas writes that the self, the ego, is an "unavowable innocence . . . accused as unique in the supreme passivity of one that cannot slip away without fault" (121, 135). The narrator himself muses on his failure to have become a subject as defined by the philosophies of being, cognition, and transcendence: "If just for a second I could *see, know, possess* myself this way—and here of course I do not mean possessions, but simply the emergence of my identification, my sameness" (Kertész 1997, 50). This is perhaps why the narrator must remain nameless (as well as "fateless"), like the unnamed poet, Paul Célan, whose evocative metaphors nourish the narrative, and to whom, in a way, he now lends his voice and his pen. The witness's speech is initiated by the impossibility of speaking, but it is also why the subject is always a witness, why it can, and must, speak for those who cannot speak.[39] As Levinas insists, the existence of the other, "the glory of the infinite," traces itself in the witness's speech. Ultimately, the emergence of subjectivity in the movement of substitution enables the passage from the absolute impossibility of speech to the actuality of testimony. In a paramount fashion, the Holocaust narrative obliges us to pay attention to that passage and to remain vigilant concerning how this journey is accomplished.

"THE BREATHLESS SPIRIT": THE ETHICAL (RE)TURN OF A WITNESSING SUBJECT

The imperative "Remember!" issues from the time of the other, from the past that neither historiography nor individual memory can assemble. It haunts every testimony as obsessive and traumatizing exteriority, endlessly evading attempts to put it to rest. The compulsion to repeat, intrinsic to Holocaust testimonials, indicates that the subsequent retellings of the story do not assuage the need to testify or disburden the witness of that task. On the contrary, the witness, like the Ancient Mariner, suffers a "burning" demand to repeat the story; one could speak, with Levinas, of the obsessive "insatiability" of these retellings. Traumatic repetition is thus related to the ethical meaning of suffering, glimpsed by the protagonist of *The Gates* when he takes upon himself the meaning of suffering as expressed to him by the young partisan Yehuda (who dies moments later): "It is inhuman to wall yourself up in pain and memories as if in a prison. Suffering must open us to others" (Wiesel 1966, 178). Suffering—the suffering for the other—is limitless, and it grows the more one wishes to expiate for it: "the one-for-the-other is never an *enough*" (Levinas 1998b, 138). As Levinas (1986) says of Sonya Marmeladova's "inexhaustible compassion" for Raskolnikov in Fyodor Dostoyevsky's *Crime and Punishment*, the ethical desire for the other "nourish[es] me as it were with new hungers" (351). In a way, this gesture of giving, which Levinas (1998b) often expresses as "taking the bread out of my own mouth" (13), is literalized in the Professor's delivering food to another prisoner as if he had been motivated by his own hunger.

Paradoxically, the witness's responsibility is augmented the more she or he testifies. The debt is not dischargeable: it grows with each repetition of the story. The titles of the two volumes of Wiesel's *Memoirs* summarize in a succinct metaphor the demand for more witnessing: volume one is called *All Rivers Flow to the Sea,* and volume two, *And the Sea Is Never Full.* Asked whether he had not said enough about the horror that is now many years in the past, Wiesel (1995) once retorted, "Even if I wrote on nothing else, it would never be enough" (333), a formulation that underscores the urgency of the never-ending task of witnessing. Levinas (1998b) writes, "The more I return to myself, the more I divest myself, under the traumatic effect of persecution, of my freedom as a constituted, imperialist subject, the more I discover myself to be responsible; the more just I am, the more guilty I am" (112). The infinite debt incurred by the Holocaust witness cannot be discharged not only because those who cannot speak for themselves are innumerable but also because the irreducible ethical obligation, the obligation that can never be fully assumed, is the very condition of witnessing, grounding the subject that emerges from it.

How can one bear witness to the events of the Holocaust? To arrive at speech and to announce oneself as an "I" is to have already responded "Here I am" to the other. Following Levinas, we can say that one can become a witness in the sense of giving testimony to traumatic events because as a subject, one is always already a witness to the life of another. That is, it is possible to assume the concrete task of bearing witness and to remain accountable for the ways in which this task is fulfilled because to be a subject already means to be such a witness. In turn, the witness's words of testimony to particular events in the past are possible because his or her speech is grounded in the ethical essence of language, which signifies an unconditional ability to respond to the other.

Insisting on the duty to bear witness, the Holocaust narrative is written in the form of an interpellation, whereby the speaking subject emerges as the inscription of the trace of the other. The call is addressed both diachronically, to the other who has affected the witness, and proleptically, to him or her who would have been. This modality of future anterior—the "would-have-been" inscribed in witnessing—is signaled in Kertész's novel by the negative figure of

the unfulfilled possibility of the child.[40] As Levinas argues, antecedent to the time measured ontologically against the horizon of
one's own demise is the ethical time, defined by the possibility of
the other's death, for which I bear responsibility. It confers meaning on both life and death, insofar as the I lives for the other, for the
"beyond-my-death." The subject of ethics returns not only from the
immemorial past but also from the unknown future in which his or
her voice will continue to reverberate. It is in this sense that the retelling of the Holocaust story is an homage to the victims but also
a gift to future generations of rememberers. Thus in the context of
Holocaust testimonials, Levinas's shattering of the temporal ambit
of the ego tensed on itself is of special significance. It introduces the
witnessing subject who is responsible for the past before its immediate time and for the future that extends forward, beyond the horizon of its death. To be for the other means to be for those who were
before me and for those who will come after me, and to whom my
language bears witness. This entails that a work "spoken" in ethical
language is undertaken toward a horizon of the time without me, as
a passage to the time of the other. In this movement, I am always
already bereft of my work, since it is destined for the other even before it originates in me, and for the time that will continue without
me. In Levinas's (1998a) own words, "The work of memory consists
not at all of plunging into the past but of renewing the past through
new experiences, new circumstances, new wounds or horrors of everyday life. And from this point of view, it is the future that is important and not purely the past" (185).

For Levinas, the witnessing subject repeatedly turns toward the
other, although this movement of infinite approach already presupposes the re-turn from outside the periphery of the same. Recurrence
is then described as a dialectic of return and departure from the site of
trauma. We can conclude therefore that the compelling need to bear
witness after the Shoah, as it has gradually materialized itself in the
form of innumerable Holocaust testimonials, has mobilized attempts
to rethink subjectivity in terms of witnessing, the necessity that
has found its most profound philosophical expression in Levinas's
thought. I have elaborated Levinas's model of subjectivity as witnessing and related it to the repetition compulsion that underwrites the
Holocaust narrative, as well as to the witness's "obsessive" speech. It
is remarkable that Levinas (2000) frequently borrows from the language of trauma to describe the encounter with alterity: in the ethical

exposure to the other there is always "a sort of violence undergone, a trauma at the heart of my-self" (187), "a deafening trauma, cutting the thread of consciousness which should have welcomed it in the present" (Levinas 1998b, 111).[41] Drawing on Freud's work as well as on Dori Laub's study of trauma in the aftermath of the Shoah, Caruth (1996) reminds us that trauma can never be experienced directly and thus marks an interval in the temporality of the subject. This is why it returns not only in nightmares but also in the survivor's unknowing acts, "haunting" the survivor against his or her will (2). Especially important for my discussion is Caruth's conclusion that, since the experience of trauma consists in the repeated reenactment of the event that was not fully experienced at the time of its occurrence, trauma is locatable in the movement of repetition rather than in the event itself, in "the ongoing experience of having survived it" (17).

The shock of being affected by the other, which constitutes the ethical subject as a witness, cannot be comprehended or captured in memory; it is "the bursting of experience" rather than its disclosure. The encounter with alterity marks a break in the subject's experience of time; it is indeed, to borrow Caruth's (1996) term, a "missed encounter," since the self is never contemporaneous with the other or, for that matter, with itself as a fully constituted subject. Since my response to the other is an "obsession," that is, a "persecuting accusation that strips ego of its pride" (Levinas 1998, 110), I experience the being of the other on an affective level, as a suddenness that cannot be converted into cognition.

Since the accounts of traumatic events mostly convey the impact of their incomprehensibility rather than a positive content, Caruth (1996) insists that "it is in the event of this incomprehension and in our departure from sense and understanding that our own witnessing may indeed begin to take place" (56). This passage also resonates with Levinas's discovery of the kernel of "nonsense" at the heart of speech, which he locates in the suffering and death of another, and which initiates subjectivity through the necessity of response. Caruth's rethinking of trauma in terms of survival and her emphasis on the transition from compulsive "acting out" to witnessing draw attention to Levinas's positive valorization of repetition compulsion in the positing of subjectivity as recurrence and thus to his transvaluation of the concept of trauma in ethical terms.[42] Recurrence, posited by Levinas (1998b) as the trauma of persecution by the other, means to "pass from the outrage undergone to the responsibility for the persecutor, and in this sense from suffering to expiation for the other" (11). This ethical demand is especially radical in the context of the Nazi death camps, where the other often announced himself in the face of the murderer. The ethical relation designates me as responsible even for my persecutor's deeds; that is, it decrees respect for the humanity of those whose faces are hidden behind the mask of murderous hatred.[43] The "turning of the cheek," symbolic of the subject's patient passivity in the ethical relation, is a radical act that breaks the cycle of violence. The passage from the victim to the witness entails a shift from subjectivity supported by the belief in the uniqueness of my individual suffering to subjectivity that, even if it suffers itself, is unique because it is irreplaceable in its concern for the suffering of the other.

In that way, Levinas's reinscription of trauma, carried out in a strident, even violent idiom of trauma and persecution, whereby subjectivity is described as martyrdom and self-immolation, underscores the fact that the witnessing subject is not a passive victim, afflicted by the demands of the other and incapable of meaningful action. To read Levinas in these terms is to overlook the fact that his entire project is a protest against victimization and degradation, of which for him the Holocaust victim was the epitome. Admittedly, Levinas's vocabulary of "obsession, persecution, and submission" implies victimization, but these connotations themselves can arise only within the traditional understanding of subjectivity, whereby the only alternative to conquering otherness is being its victim, that is, within the very paradigm of relating to otherness which Levinas sets out to overcome. In psychoanalytic terms, therefore, Levinas's radical transformation of the notion of subjectivity—in terms of recurrence, substitution, and witness to the other—could be seen as an instance of philosophical "working through" that opens up a possibility of the future that is grounded in nonindifference, in relations with others. Hence, despite his articulation of the subject as constituted in the traumatic encounter with alterity—but perhaps exactly because he avails himself of the language of trauma on the level of what seems to be rhetorical engagement—he can give an account of the witnessing subject in positive terms, as animated by an ethical commitment rather than constituted by a play of pathological symptoms of traumatic forces. Levinas certainly never critically reflects on the way his rethinking of Hegelian recognition as "recurrence" resonates with the psychoanalytic notion of compulsive repetition. Yet, as he himself admits, in response to Philippe Nemo's questions about the genesis of his philosophical project, thinking "probably begins through *traumatisms* or gropings to which one does not even know how to give a verbal form" (Levinas 1985, 21; emphasis mine). Such a rereading of Levinas is consistent with LaCapra's (2007a) call for the "process of articulation crucial to working through [that] may counteract the symptomatic force of acting out" (170). More importantly, it reveals the underlying inseparability of the ethical and the psychoanalytic frameworks, which has crucial implications for interpretations of Holocaust testimonials.

Drawing on the idiom of witnessing, Agamben (1999) describes his own project as "listening to something absent," or finding a way to "listen to the unsaid" (14). The following passage from *Remnants of Auschwitz* is particularly striking. Commenting on a witness's account of a soccer game played in Auschwitz, Agamben avows,

> I, like the witnesses, instead view this match, this moment of normalcy, as the true horror of the camp. . . . But also hence our shame, the shame of those who did not know the camps and yet, without knowing how, are spectators of that match, which repeats itself in every match at our stadiums, in every television broadcast, in the normalcy of everyday life. (32)

For Agamben, not only does philosophy take up the task of rethinking the subject as the structure of witnessing, but also, in a way consonant with the projects of the thinkers and writers discussed in this chapter, the very task of philosophy is being redefined in terms of witnessing. Paramount in Levinas's writing and strongly resonant in the works of philosophers as different as Agamben and Kelly Oliver, a philosopher situates himself or herself in the position of a witness.

Agamben (1999) identifies the *Muselmann* as a lacuna in experience, knowledge, and speech, the point at which the very notion of subjectivity implodes. The living dead from the camps are "the *larva* [a threatening remainder] that our memory cannot succeed in burying, the unforgettable with whom we must reckon" (81). Here, the *Muselmann* is the untestifiable par excellence that gives rise to the necessity of speech. The *Muselmann* is thus the limit from which we must rethink what it means to be a subject. While Agamben's somber diagnosis that the *Muselmann* signals the catastrophe of the subject at the limit of speech is important, it is also reductive: not only does it divorce the *Muselmann* from his or her historically specific context (LaCapra 2004, 194), but it also obliterates other blind spots that lacerate Holocaust narratives. I have spoken of these breaking points in terms of the "madness" or "nonsense" that impels a witness's testimony. In Wiesel's *Night*, the threshold from which Wiesel's life of witnessing unfolded is the missed experience of his father's death, and, even more profoundly, the loss of his mother and sister. The vortex of the narrator's monologue in Kertész's text is the unpronounceable name of Paul Célan, as it coincides with another missing name: that of the child whose possibility of existence has been annihilated at Auschwitz.

The subject that emerges in the caesura between the possibility and impossibility of speech is marked by an affective mixture of grief, awe, and respect, but also shame, the shame for his or her own comfort. This singular sensation emerges as an affective trace of being beholden to the other, a sign of what Levinas (1998b) describes as "breathlessness that pronounces the extraordinary word beyond" (16). This "breathlessness" is almost audible in Paul Célan's poetry as well as in mournful passages of Wiesel's prose and in Kertész's halting monologue. Levinas's extraordinary expression connotes the mortal danger of the deprivation of air and thus of the sheer physical impossibility of speech: in reading these writers' words, we are literally breathless.[44] But it is the limit condition from which speech bursts forth, "pronouncing" the beyond, the rhythm of respiration that is inspiration for the witness's speech. As Levinas says in a conversation with artist Bracha Ettinger, "Time, our time, is already the breath of the human being with respect to another human being. Our time is the breath of the spirit" (Ettinger and Levinas 1997, 32). In another striking metaphor, Levinas (1998b) describes this speech as "the breathless spirit [that] retains a fading echo" (42). The fading echo of the voices of his murdered relatives in Levinas's own texts is perhaps the reason I always lean over the epigraph/epitaph preceding *Otherwise than Being* and think of that book as a *matzevah* in the form of a philosophical treatise. After all, as Levinas insists himself, our ethical obligation to the other, the obligation that underwrites his own philosophical work, is always directed at a concrete human being, at a face rather than at an abstract entity.

CHAPTER TWO

The Tower of Babel

Holocaust Testimonials and the Ethics of Translation

What remains? The language remains.

—HANNAH ARENDT, *Essays in Understanding*

To truly bear witness to it, one must make language anxious.

—JEAN-FRANÇOIS LYOTARD, "The Survivor"

Heart:
Make yourself known even here,
Here in the midst of the market.
Cry out the shibboleth
Into your homeland strangeness.

—PAUL CÉLAN, *Shibboleth*

HOMELESS IN THE HOUSE OF LANGUAGE

In his essay "Language in Exile," Imre Kertész (2004) explains that he writes exclusively about the Holocaust "because it does not have a language." No particular language could possibly contain the experience of the Holocaust. If there were such a language, says Kertész, it would be so full of violence and grief that it would destroy those who used it (185). Holocaust testimonies cannot be written except in "an accidental language," and they will never belong to a native tongue (196). To the extent that one must express oneself in one of the national languages, the Holocaust remains homeless in the house of language. Kertész writes, "Europeans who survived the Holocaust can tell the story of the suffering in one of the European languages; but none of these languages is their own, and neither is the tongue of the nation which the author has borrowed to write his tale" (194; translation mine). Susan Rubin Suleiman (1996), in her study of Holocaust memoirs written by emigrants in English, arrives at a similar conclusion: "All Holocaust memoirs are essentially homeless" (634). In Kertész's view, however, this "homelessness" also affects the accounts written in the survivor's mother tongue. Hence the experience of the Holocaust is "unspeakable" not because it falls outside human linguistic competence conceived in universal terms. Rather, what happened cannot be properly articulated, since no national language has been able to absorb it or to coin words and expressions capable of conveying its catastrophic dimensions. As a result, the survivor does not know "in what language I should tell the story," to quote Izolda Regensberg, the protagonist of one of Hanna Krall's (2006, 18) biographical reportages. Literary critic Alan Rosen (2005) states that "*every* language is going to be unfaithful to the camp experience, taking what existed only in fragments and rendering it in a medium that is intact. What one sees (or reads) then is the Holocaust filtered through civilized discourse, the Holocaust as it were, according to the coherence of a single cultured tongue" (6).

In this chapter, I will consider Holocaust testimonials in relation to the question of translation, understood here as both exchanges between languages within a text and renditions of the text into another language. The question of translation is pervasive in Holocaust testimonials, although relatively little critical attention has been given to this striking phenomenon, and no consistent theoretical framework has emerged to address it.[1] As implied in Kertész's remarks, a Holocaust testimony is always a translation into another language. Moreover, it is often a translation without the original, even in the case of writers such as Kertész or Levi, who returned to their hometowns after the war and penned their memoirs in their mother tongue (Hungarian and Italian, respectively).

Drawing on Lyotard's concept of the *differend*, I will refer to this experience of incompatibility between languages in which the witness struggles to convey "the truth" of his or her experience as the "translation *differend*." Lyotard defines the *differend* as a conflict that cannot be resolved because no common language or set of discursive practices exists in which two or more parties could settle their disagreement. Such a conflict unavoidably results in injustice experienced by the speakers who have been deprived of effective linguistic means to prove their cause. In Lyotard's (1988) definition, the wrong suffered by one of the parties is "a damage accompanied by the loss of the means to prove the damage" (5). By analogy, "the translation *differend*" is an instance of a conflict that occurs in the process of translation between languages, resulting in a sense of wrong when an utterance has been grievously mistranslated or when it intractably resists translation. Thus translation between languages must also be considered in relation to the fear often expressed by survivors that they commit a betrayal each time they translate what they describe as "beyond words" into comprehensible expressions. The witnesses are acutely aware that the generalizing words of testimony obscure the singularity of the events and the particularity of the lives of those on whose behalf they speak. Yet, as has already been argued in chapter one, the survivors' desire to bear witness stems from this enduring affliction of language. This paradox of translation, which traverses a vast spectrum of Holocaust literary testimonials, necessitates that we consider translation within the parameters of ethics. More specifically, I will argue that translation is inseparable from bearing witness, and in some cases, it becomes its unique condition of possibility. Although the focus here is on written works, two episodes of Lanzmann's *Shoah* will also be examined. This film is unique in its attention to translatory sequences, illuminating the dilemmas of Holocaust testimony as it becomes caught up in translation.

In his study of the role of the English language in the transmission of Holocaust testimony, Rosen (2005) notes that Jews of Eastern Europe (the population most directly targeted for extermination) were distinguished by their multilingualism. On the eve of World War II, their ability to speak several languages stood in contrast with nationalist strategies of their respective countries of residence, which promoted uniform linguistic cultures (2). As the Holocaust unfolded, the mélange of languages naturally found reflection in diaries and chronicles written during the Holocaust. Rosen shows that, in the ghettos, the choice of a language for everyday communication, as well as for writing down a record of events, reflected the language user's particular circumstances. For instance, the deliberate use of Yiddish instead of Polish in the Warsaw ghetto became an expression of Jewish solidarity, and it signaled increasingly tense relations with former Polish neighbors and a growing sense of Jews' isolation within the Polish community. However, switching from Yiddish to Hebrew (as was the case of diarist Abraham Levin or poet Yitzak Katznelson, after the wave of deportations from the Warsaw ghetto in 1942) was testimony to Zionist hope and Jewish pride in leaving what the writers knew would be a posthumous record.[2] Because those choices were by no means arbitrary, Rosen argues that we also need to consider the choice of language in testimonies written *after* the war, by survivors who, for the most part, found themselves displaced from their former linguistic communities. After the Holocaust, that choice had a profound impact on the survivors' strategies of self-identification and their ability to heal, thus determining how they remembered the events and even the very content of that memory.

According to Israel Knox, the editor of the first *Anthology of Holocaust Literature*, which appeared in the 1960s, the most "crystallized" expression of Eastern European Jewry's war experiences were memoirs written in Yiddish. For Knox, these memoirs bore witness to the atrocity perpetrated on "the essence of [Eastern European Jewish] civilization" (quoted in Rosen 2005, 9). Yet what exactly did these memoirs express and to whom were they addressed? As Annette Wieviorka (2006) points out, unlike prewar chronicles of particular communities, these individual memoirs as well as collective *Yizker-bikher* (memory books) commemorating the genocide arrived into a complete void, bereft of a community of speakers that would provide a context for memorialization and meaningful interpretation of events (27). Deprived of an addressee, confronted with a wall of incomprehension, and impossible to publish, these harrowing testimonials in Yiddish bore witness to the disappearance of the very world in which they would have been read and understood. For Wieviorka, the homelessness of Yiddish after the war resulted in an effective silencing of witnesses. She mentions, for instance, that Yiddish-language poet Abraham Sutzkever from Vilna was not even allowed to give a deposition in Yiddish at the Nuremberg trials, and his account was limited to a brief testimony in Russian.

To expose the rupture in the language of testimony wrought by linguistic displacement and the disappearance of the Yiddish-speaking community, Wieviorka concentrates on Wiesel's *Night*, which was first written in Yiddish, printed in a small edition in Brazil in 1956, and then published in French in 1958. Drawing on Naomi Seidman's meticulous comparison of the Yiddish and French versions of the text, Wieviorka notes a fundamental shift in narrative focus between the two versions. The longer one, *Un di Velthot geshvign* (And the world was silent), expressed sentiments typical for survivor accounts that emerged immediately after the war, such as the desire to overcome death and exert vengeance on the perpetrator. By contrast, in the abridged version in French, which was revised under the mentorship of the Christian writer François Mauriac, the survivor's experiences acquired a universal dimension and became an existential reflection on the human condition. This act of translation enabled Wiesel to embark on a lifetime journey of speaking for those who could not testify for themselves. Wieviorka's analysis implies, however, that this translatory gesture remains ambivalent. By universalizing the survivor's ordeal, the French version obliterated the unique experiences of Eastern European Jewry and the Yiddish world of Wiesel's childhood.

Following the war, different national governments implemented the politics of assimilation and forgetting, either forcefully (in the countries under the communist rule) or covertly (in Western Europe, Israel, and the United States). Paradoxically, these policies compounded the annihilation of *Yiddishkeit* perpetrated by the Nazis. In this context, Rosen's and Wieviorka's reflections on the fate of Yiddish during the Holocaust suggest that, just as "complete witnesses" to the Holocaust were those who "drowned" and can therefore no longer testify for themselves (in Primo Levi's memorable words), complete testimony was possible only in a language few could speak after the war.

Based on her interviews with Holocaust survivors, Polish Holocaust scholar Barbara Engelking Boni concludes that it is impossible to convey "the truth" of traumatic events except in the language in which a survivor experienced them.[3] Yet, as Suleiman points out, a significant number of Holocaust memoirs were written in the language of the survivor's adopted country. For many, if not for most survivors, therefore, the decision to speak would amount to abdicating the "truth" of their experience. Further, while in oral testimonies the voices of Holocaust survivors remain heavily accented, betraying their linguistic dislocation, the printed words in their meticulously edited memoirs conceal the survivors' "foreignness." The marks of foreignness can never be entirely erased, however; as Suleiman (1996) remarks, what remains are proper names of places and people, usually unpronounceable to the reader, and they stand out as monuments of linguistic displacement. She writes, "No amount of glossing will assimilate the foreign proper name, nor is it translatable. It is the flag of the foreign—a stubborn kernel of otherness" (644).[4]

In contrast to Engelking Boni's findings that it is easier for the survivors to speak about traumatic events in the language in which they experienced them, many survivors report that a neutral language (such as English), free from the inscription of violence, has made it possible for them to "speak" in the first place. Perhaps it is exactly because the "truth" of the experience is so strongly associated with one's native tongue that a neutral, distant language can help surmount debilitating traumatic associations. As Holocaust historian and writer Yaffa Eliach observes, "For sometimes the language stands between the writer and the horrors of the Holocaust, in that it permits him to grapple with the Holocaust in a language other than that in which he experienced it. Consciously, or perhaps unconsciously, the new language has the power to attenuate slightly the fiery pain" (quoted in Rosen 2005, 11). In those cases, the distance afforded by another language is the enabling factor in telling the story. Not quite naming what the survivor is trying to articulate, foreign words act as a protective shield that allows the storyteller to master traumatic memories and translate them into a narrative.

Considering Kertész's assertion that "the Holocaust has no language," by which he means that there is no national language in which the Holocaust story can truly be told, can we then speak of a translinguistic horizon that structures Holocaust testimony? Once again, this question will be explored in the context of Levinas's ethics, drawing on the philosopher's articulation of the ethical essence of language as Saying. I will also turn to Walter Benjamin's reflection on translation, in his seminal essay "The Task of the Translator," and consider the task of the translator as an ethical task, whether the translation occurs within the body of a single text, or the text is rendered into another language, either by the author himself or herself, or by a professional translator. In each of these scenarios, the question arises: In what sense is translation also an act of bearing witness in its own right, albeit occasionally a negative one?

The lives of both Levinas and Benjamin were deeply affected by the events of the Holocaust. Benjamin, a German Jew, took his life in 1941 on the Franco-Spanish border when he was trying to flee from the Nazis. Levinas's entire family was murdered, while he himself was imprisoned in a labor camp in Struthof, near Bergen-Belsen. Both Levinas and Benjamin worked as translators at some point in their lives, although in very different circumstances. Benjamin was a well-known translator of French literature, lauded for his rendition into German of Charles Baudelaire's *Tableaux parisiens*, while Levinas was enlisted in the French army as a translator from Russian and German, a fact that possibly spared him the fate of being sent to a death camp. Necessarily, then, the problematic of translation is present in

the work of both thinkers, and in the case of Levinas is inseparable
from the testimonial impetus that animates his philosophical texts.

LANGUAGE IN EXILE

In his short poetic prose *Conversation in the Mountains*, Paul Célan
(2001) describes two Jewish wonderers, the inhabitants of the land,
who gaze from the top of a hill upon the fertile, green valley beneath
and muse about the language that belongs to that place:

> That's the kind of speech that counts here, the green with the white in
> it, a language not for you and not for me—because I am asking, who
> is it meant for then, the earth, it's not meant for you, I am saying, and
> not for me—, well, then, a language with no I and no Thou, pure He,
> pure It, d'you see, pure They and nothing but that. (398)

This conviction that the language of the country in which they live
has never truly belonged to them, common among diasporic Jews,
permeates all of Kertész's writings. After the Holocaust, the survivors' sense of being disowned by their language became much more
acute because "Auschwitz" had rendered that linguistic exile permanent and irreparable. For Kertész (2004), the language of exclusion,
which designates those perennial strangers who are never quite welcome at the hearth in the house of language, not only sentenced them
to death in the camps but also has marked them as strangers "after
Auschwitz" (177). If the Holocaust bequeathed the traumatic memory of Auschwitz upon the Jews, says Kertész, it also took away from
them the language in which to speak about it (175). For Kertész, the
survivor's "borrowed" existence after Auschwitz is then inseparable
from an essential homelessness of the language in which he tries to
speak about his experiences."[5] He comments, in one of his essays, "I
write my books in a borrowed tongue, which in its nature rejects me
or only tolerates my presence on the peripheries of its consciousness"
(204; translation mine). After the war, Kertész returned to Budapest
to live and write amid his former community of speakers. Insofar as
he remained a foreigner within his native Hungarian, however, he
had never truly "returned home." Yet he also found a strange conso-
lation in this privation. He writes, "The more I am a stranger in my
language, the more I am credible to myself, the more credible what I
write seems to be. I like writing in Hungarian, because [paraphrasing
Kafka] the better I feel the impossibility to write" (183). For Kertész,

alienation from his native tongue becomes a necessary condition for writing, since it allows him to perceive a rupture of language "after Auschwitz" and to try to articulate this traumatic split. The national language in which Kertész writes his literary testimony is both the language of his childhood and the language in which he experienced displacement, deportation, and near-death in the camps. Before he eventually wrote *Fateless*, however, Kertész made a living as a translator from German, the language he had learned in the camps.[6] It is possible then that, for years, his Auschwitz story, which waited for so long to be told, was displaced by the writer's activity as a translator from German.

In contrast to Kertész's sense of banishment from his language, political philosopher Hannah Arendt argues that the native tongue remains a foundation of one's self-identity, especially for those who have been geographically displaced. As with Kertész, Arendt's argument is grounded in her biography. In the 1930s Arendt fled Germany to France, and then, in 1941, to the United States, where she wrote her most important works in English. In an interview with journalist Günter Gaus, broadcast on West German television in 1964, she states, "I have always consciously refused to lose my mother tongue. I have always maintained a certain distance from French, which I then spoke very well, as well as from English, which I write today. . . . The German language is the essential thing that has remained and that I have always consciously preserved" (Arendt 2005, 13). To the journalist's query as to whether her experience of persecution did not color her relation to the German language, she forcefully affirms her attachment to her native tongue and defends its "innocence": "It wasn't the German language that went crazy. And, second, there is no substitute for the mother tongue" (13). Arendt then perceives her native language as being uncorrupted by "the madness" of the Nazi regime and therefore capable of offering her a place of refuge. Arendt makes a clear distinction, however, between her loyalty to the German language and her sense of national belonging: "I, myself, for example, don't believe that I ever considered myself a German—in the sense of belonging to the people as opposed to being a citizen" (8).

Rosen makes a connection between Arendt's plea for her mother tongue and her defense of German in *Eichmann in Jerusalem*. Arendt repeatedly condemned Eichmann's bungled, clichéd German, and was indignant about the politics of translation during the trial. She was offended by the incompetence of translators from German throughout the trial, and she also praised the Israeli judges who spoke fluent German, in defiance of the official language of the court, which was Hebrew. Commenting on the confusion and rage among the Jewish community in response to the publication of *Eichmann*, Rosen (2005) implies that Arendt's ironic, distanced use of English may have been one of the reasons for the misperceptions about the book and the accusations of callousness against the author. He concludes that, similarly to a number of her fellow exiles, Arendt's writing was marked by linguistic displacement: "Insistent that her spoken English would remain that of a foreigner, her [Arendt's] writing also remained thus" (111).

Arendt's unavowed predicament is perhaps best expressed in a comment by Irit Amiel, an Israeli poet writing in Polish. Referring to her own experience of exile, Amiel (quoted in Piersiak 2004) states, "One can emigrate from a country but one cannot emigrate from a language" (177; translation mine). An awareness of being rooted in one's language and estranged from it at the same time tends to be most conspicuous in testimonies written by displaced survivors who had to acquire the language of their adopted country but chose to write in their mother tongue. For writers Paul Célan and Jean Améry, or Polish Jewish writers such as Ida Fink and Henryk Grynberg, their mother tongue has become both a vehicle of recollection and a permanent wound of exile. Unsurprisingly, these writers are often preoccupied with the question of translation, its status for post-Auschwitz speech, and its dilemmas and paradoxes, and they foreground their ambivalent status as strangers within language.

Similarly, Jean Améry (Hans Meier), an Austrian Jew, continued to write in his native German, although at the time of the publication of *At the Mind's Limit* (*Jenseits von Schuld und Sühne*) he had been living in Belgium for two decades. In the chapter "How Much Home Does a Person Need?" Améry (1986) reflects on the status of "expellees" from the Third Reich (57). For Améry, those who were forced from their communities lost not only all of their possessions but also a sense of belonging to a "people." As their neighbors became "informers or bullies, at best, embarrassed opportunists," the exiles were robbed of their origin, as if their entire past had been "confiscated" (42, 58). In contrast to Arendt, Améry grieves the loss of his native language, even though he continues to write in German. For him, a local dialect from the place of one's birth and childhood determines one's sense of self and a person's location within a network of human relations. Once an individual is removed from his "immediate place of origin" (43), his identity unravels and he no longer knows who he is. Moreover, the loss forces him to realize that, as in Célan's parable about the two Jews on a hill, the place and language he loved as a child were never truly his, as if he had "appropriated [them] illegally" (51). Améry recalls that he first became aware of this dispossession when, in a chance encounter with an SS officer during his resistance activities in Belgium, he heard him speak in the dialect from his native region in Austria. The uncanny mixture of emotions caused by the contrast between the language that he associated with home and friendship, and the uniform marking the speaker as a deadly foe, "sent here from the hostile homeland to wipe me out" (50), caused Améry to conceal his origin and to answer the officer in French. As a result, he later assumed a French-sounding pen name, since he could no longer recognize himself in the "plain German name." When even his proper name, which his friends used to call him, is, as he feels, taken away from him (reminiscent of Gavriel in Wiesel's *The Gates of the Forest*), even the memories of his friends cease to exist (44). His entire past falls away, as does the history of the country he used to call his own, its landscapes now marred by a recollection of swastikas hanging out of farmers' windows on the day of the *Anschluss*. Thus, unlike those who, by virtue of possessing religion, have created for themselves "a portable home," Améry finds himself "completely uprooted" (45). While Arendt finds shelter from the precariousness of exile in her native tongue, Améry can never be "at home" in the German language. "Home is security" (47), he writes, and his "house of language" was razed to the ground. Yet he agrees with Arendt that no substitute exists for the mother tongue. Although he has commanded the language of his adopted country, he will always stumble around in it "as if he were drunk" (48). He cannot make himself comfortable in his new language either, because an émigré can only "parrot [it] poorly." A foreign language will never become "a real friend": "*La table* will never be the table: at best one can eat one's fill at it" (52). At the same time, Améry's German is gradually "crumbling away" and atrophying, devoid of the nourishing force of life experience (the only "life experience" German brought him was the threat of death). He bemoans the expropriation of his mother tongue and fears that, as a man deprived of his proper language, he will be forever estranged from his community and even from himself. Yet, however painful, what his experiences of exile and adoption of another language reveal

to him is that the essence of any language is friendship and hospitality, of which he himself has been deprived.

"DEATH IS A MASTER FROM GERMANY"

Kertész's discovery of national languages' fundamental incapacity vis-
à-vis the Holocaust stands in contrast to assertions of linguistic supremacy—particularly of the German language. In his critical commentaries
on Heidegger, Jacques Derrida (1989) exposes the linguistic privilege of
the German philosophical tradition and the nocuous effects of the philosophers' claim that their national language (German) is solely capable
of expressing certain philosophical concepts (71). As Derrida argues (in
Of Spirit), this "monolingualism" of the German philosophical tradition has largely depended on the exclusion of Judaism and the Hebrew
language. Philosophical monolingualism is an expression of totality,
which, in the political realm, manifests as ethnonationalism, that is,
the belief that membership in the national community is determined by
genealogy and cultural heritage (Michlic 2006, 21).

In his text *Shibboleth*, on Célan's poem of the same title (quoted
in the epigraph to this chapter), Derrida recounts the biblical story
of the Ephraimites who were required to pronounce the Hebrew
word "shibboleth" when trying to escape secretly across the Jordan
River, after they had been defeated in battle by Jephthah's soldiers.
Although the Ephraimites knew the secret password, they were unable to pronounce the sound transcribed as   in the Hebrew alphabet,
saying "sibboleth" instead.[7] The impotence of their tongues spelled
death, depriving them of the "visas" that would permit safe passage
across the border. As Derrida (2005) brings out, one's ability to pronounce certain words presupposes belonging to a linguistic community whose members speak with the same "lip" or *safah*, which is also
the Hebrew word for "language." In this way, the shibboleth grants
one "the right of asylum or the legitimate habitation of a language"
(26). The linguistic frontier is where the right to pass is dispensed,
"indeed, the right to live" (1). Yet the shibboleth of the native tongue
cuts with "the double edge": it grants a corporeal mark of belonging
to a community, allowing one to be recognized as "one's own," but
it is also a declaration of difference, a sentence of exclusion that can
single out an entire people for extermination. For Derrida, the biblical
story of the shibboleth is a parable of political power, which is located
at the frontier between national languages.

Here, Derrida's thesis converges with Kertész's (2004) assertion that "xenophobia, anti-Semitism are first and foremost in *language*, and to what deeds the use of that language can lead is well known, also to those who use that language" (160). Similarly, Derrida (1986) comments, in his criticism of South African apartheid, "There is no racism without a language," since acts of racism are committed through words, which "assign forced residence or close the borders" (292); these acts are a function of a given language's political and cultural dominance based on a system of exclusion. Combating racism and anti-Semitism thus involves exposing the mechanisms of power and violence inherent in the use of language. As philosopher Berel Lang (1988) argues, since assault on people is impossible without violence perpetrated *on* language and *through* the use of language, languages must be examined for their complicity in the acts of genocide, as if they were themselves morally culpable. In a similar vein, Paul Célan's struggles against his mother tongue, and his "translating interpretations of German" (Derrida 2005, 100) expose the lethal force of language when it is tethered to political power. From the depths of his own testifying speech, Célan (2001) knows that the price of the linguistic privilege claimed by the language of the "master race" is, as he writes in "Death Fugue," that "der Tod ist ein Meister aus Deutschland [Death is a master from Germany]" (32).

In contrast to Arendt's belief that the German language resisted the madness of National Socialism, Célan (2001) exposes the corruption of his native tongue and remonstrates that German must be recovered from that madness. As he famously announces in his Bremen speech, the German language must "pass through its own answerlessness, pass through frightful muting, pass through the thousand darknesses of deathbringing speech" (395). This is why, counterpoising Adorno's dictum about writing poetry after Auschwitz, Célan insists that true poetry must now be written in the very language of barbarism.[8] In poems such as "Nocturnally Pursed," Célan wonders whether the word can be nursed back to life:

A word—you know:
a corpse.

Come let us wash it,
come let us comb it,
come let us turn
its eye heavenward. (69)

Célan compares writing poetry to a funerary ritual performed on the corpse of the German language. The solicitous care extended to the dead body of language and the intoning of "come let us,"[9] as if in a prayer, indicate that these last rites are also a dramatic rescue; language has to be resuscitated and infused with breath before it can be uttered again and spoken into existence. Only then can Célan proclaim that the German language "remained, not lost, yes in spite of everything" (395).

Before immigrating to France after the war, Célan worked in Bucharest as a translator. Yet the most notorious instance of his translatory activity is the fact that, like Améry, he "translated" his proper name from Antschel (Ancel) to a French-sounding anagram "Célan." The poet's gesture is paradoxical, since, as Suleiman has noted, proper names, by virtue of naming a particular individual, are untranslatable and do not truly belong to a national language.[10] The translation of the proper name, of the word that stands on the "edge of language" (Derrida 1985, 185), is a declaration, therefore, that the boundary between the two languages—in this case, between Célan's native tongue and the language of his adopted country—is always undecidable rather than clearly demarcated, and the name itself is the site of continuous migrations between the two. Yet the untranslatable of the proper name, which Célan translated nevertheless, reveals how narrow and precarious is the strait that allows the passage between languages. Encrypted in the name "Célan" is the mourning for the abandoned German Jewish name, as if it had to be forsaken so that it could be properly mourned and remembered. Although the labor of mourning takes place in the very language of the extermination of the Jewish name, German becomes infused with that strangeness and pried open by the poet's French idiom, as well as by evocations of mourning in Hebrew. Célan (2001) writes, in "The Sluice,"

> I lost a word that sought me:
> *Kaddish.*
>
> Through
> the sluice I had to go,
> to salvage the word back into
> and out of and across the salt flood:
> *Yizkor.* (151)

Perhaps the destruction of the proper name was also necessary for Célan's post-Holocaust speech to carry the horrific burden of the

German words, even though this translation continued to accentuate his painful exile from the *Muttersprache* (mother tongue), from the linguistic community to which he nevertheless belonged by virtue of continuing to write in German.

TRADUTTORE TRADITORE, OR
THE TRANSLATION *DIFFEREND*

The languages in which Holocaust memoirs were first published after the war or into which they were translated often reflected the dominant national politics of memory.[11] Kurt I. Lewin, for instance, wrote his account of surviving the Holocaust on the Aryan side (near Lvov) immediately after the war, and he wrote it in Polish.[12] Considering the political climate and incidents of violence against the Jews in Poland at the time, he could not publish his story there, and it first appeared in 1947, in a Hebrew translation, when the author immigrated to Palestine. The original Polish text was published in Warsaw only in 2006, following almost two decades of national reckoning with the inglorious pages of Poland's World War II history. Władysław Szpilman's diary, which inspired Roman Polański's acclaimed film *The Pianist*, first appeared in 1946, heavily censored, and it remained virtually unknown in Poland until 2001, when it was reissued as *Pianista: Warszawskie wspomnienia, 1939–1945* (The pianist: The Warsaw memories, 1939–1945) on the initiative of Szpilman's son, to coincide with the release of the film in that country. The new Polish edition, however, was preceded by a 1999 translation into English. Similar tribulations befell Ida Fink's semiautobiographical novel *The Journey* and her short stories, which were written in Polish and published in London, although they first received critical recognition after their translation into English.[13] The publication of Fink's short stories and of her novel in Poland (in 2003 and 2004, respectively) was accompanied by the author's celebratory tour of the country from which she had previously been expelled.[14] After decades of exile from their community of speakers, these Holocaust testimonials returned to their mother tongue, although this homecoming was mediated by another language (usually English) into which they had been translated in the meantime and in which they had received acclaim. The language community to which Szpilman's and Fink's accounts returned many years later, however, was not the same, while the reception of the works had been influenced by their former "success" in English.

As Rosen points out, in the decades after the war, English became the dominant language in which many of the Holocaust memoirs were written or into which they were translated; only in English could they become noticed or even published at all, even if very few of their authors initially knew that language. As mentioned above, for many survivors, the relative neutrality of English with regard to the Holocaust and its marginality with respect to languages such as Yiddish, Hebrew, Polish, Ukranian, German, and others in which the events of the Holocaust were experienced, served as a buffer against the rawness of pain and thus facilitated transmission. English was an "amnesiac language," a lens through which the fragmented, uncontainable experience was refracted and homogenized.[15]

The long saga of Leitner's "Holocaust fragments" reveals the tension between the linguistic appropriation and the palliative effect of giving testimony in English. In *Isabella: From Auschwitz to Freedom*, Leitner (Leitner and Leitner 1994) returns one more time to her Holocaust experiences in order to gather together all of her previous accounts. In the "waning years of [her] life," she wants to sum up a decades-long labor of rememoration and, presumably, achieve a sense of closure. At the opening of the book, Leitner reminisces about the moment when she reached for the box containing the scraps on which she first wrote her memories in Hungarian "and began to translate them" (16).[16] From the outset, the process of narrativizing her inchoate memories is thus enabled by translation. The language of Leitner's first retelling in English, *Fragments of Isabella*, largely preserved the rawness and intensity of the author's wartime experience, even if it was already blanketed by English and by her husband's editorial assistance. Although Leitner was already a young woman when she found herself in Auschwitz, in her memoir, she uses an emotive language of childhood, expressed in fragmented syntax, as if she were speaking in the voice of her murdered youngest sister, Potyo, whose death she continues to grieve. Throughout subsequent rewritings of her story, Leitner's style reflects not only her growing maturity but also her increased linguistic competence in the language of her adopted country, while the "foreignness" of her idiom is smoothed over.[17]

Significantly, English is the native tongue of Leitner's husband, to whom the author acknowledges a debt of gratitude. Indeed, Irving Leitner is listed as the coauthor of both *Isabella* and of one of the earlier books, *Saving the Fragments*. In the following epigraph, Leitner (Leitner and Leitner 1994) dedicates *Isabella* to her husband:

> The recall was painful.
> My husband tiptoed around
> me with deep, delicate concern.
> This book belongs to him.

Leitner's last account is followed by an epilogue by Irving Leitner, in which he in turn expresses his debt to his wife for her continuous acts of love that, as he says, have allowed him, "a distanced witness to the horrors of the twentieth century," to maintain hope. In eulogizing his wife, Irving Leitner continuously emphasizes her "innocence," which remained uncorrupted by the horrific events, and which enabled her to transform the experience of horror into an affirmation of life and an expression of human goodness and compassion.

Clasped between the dedication to her English-speaking husband and the epilogue, Leitner's narrative betrays the "husbandry" of her account by the English language. Insofar as her (unpublishable) fragments, initially written in Hungarian, were expropriated into the language in which she could (and was allowed to) bear witness, Leitner's book truly "belongs" to her husband. Yet, interestingly enough, the epilogue is not the last word in the book: it is followed, somewhat inconsequentially, by a coda titled "*Lager* Language," in which Leitner, with the help this time from Ruth Zerner (a professor at Lehman College), reflects on the mongrel language that she and her fellow inmates used in the camp. The appendix is preceded by an explanation by Leitner that she first recorded these comments "in my native Hungarian tongue almost immediately after I arrived in this country in 1945. What I did—and after so many years—I am glad I did." Leitner (Leitner and Leitner 1994) writes,

> There is an English language, there is French. There is Russian, also Spanish. There is Hungarian, there is Chinese. According to the Bible, God punished humanity in Babel with a madness of languages, but there is one language even God cannot understand—only we do, those of us who were prisoners in the shadow of the crematorium. I call it *Lager* language, and each word means a different kind of suffering. (227)

Leitner provides a succinct dictionary of *Lager*, in a form reminiscent of an elementary school lesson:

Vertreterin meant kneeling; *Studendienstkapo*, beating; *Torwache*, kicking. . . . A *Plus* meant that they might take away your sister into another *Block*. *Mengele* is selecting there in the afternoon. You are looking for your sister, but she is already up in smoke in the *Krem-chy*. . . . *Pritsch* means that fourteen of us are lying on a lice-filled plank of wood. (228)

This brief reflection on camp language, followed by a two-page "*La-ger* Lexicon," seems incongruous with the previous narrative, and it stands out within Leitner's literary corpus. The painful humor of some of her earlier writings, which stemmed from the juxtaposition of a childish idiom and the horror of her circumstances, is now re-placed by the bitter irony of her "definitions." Perhaps, situated in the book after her husband's "last word," Leitner's reflection on trans-lation is a strategic escape into *Lager* from the neutralizing effects of English in which all of her published accounts were written, and in which the linguistic plurality of her experiences was obliterated. Ironically, it is only in *Lager*, the universal language of camp inmates (rather than in her native Hungarian or in her second language) that Leitner can assert her linguistic mastery and her exclusive interpretive rights to the words which neither her husband "nor God" can com-prehend. Leitner's rewritings of her Auschwitz narrative can be seen as an attempt to break out of the silence that her native Hungarian imposed on her when she first tried to write it, and her texts manifest both that struggle and her sense of having succeeded, at least par-tially, in that endeavor.

In contrast, the story of Izolda Regensberg, described by Polish writer Hanna Krall in *The King of Hearts on His Way Out Again*, is an account of linguistic defeat that leaves the survivor immured in the silence of incomprehension and intranslatability. During the war, Izolda had only one purpose: to save her husband (Szajek) at any cost. Passing as a Pole, she smuggled goods across the border to make money for the parcels to be sent to her husband (who was incarcer-ated in Auschwitz and then Mauthausen). To achieve her goal, she escaped from forced labor in Germany and then from a transport to Auschwitz; she endured repeated rape, imprisonment in the notorious Pawiak prison, and torture at the SS headquarters in Vienna. Izolda's inventiveness and her success in securing help for her husband de-pended on her knowledge of languages: she could easily pass as Ma-ria Pawlicka because of her flawless Polish; in Germany and Austria, she used her fluent German and French to gain favors or to pretend she was a *Volksdeutche*; and she secured her husband's final release because she could chat in Russian with an officer of the liberating Russian army. Izolda's story is anything but banal; as the author comments, it is a story fit for an epic Hollywood movie. Yet Krall juxtaposes this image of an adventurous, courageous young woman, who saves her husband's life largely due to her multilingual skills, with a portrait of Izolda in her old age, immobile in her armchair and unable to learn either English or Hebrew. Izolda now lives in Israel, with her two daughters, and while her greatest wish is to tell her story, the linguistic barrier keeps her isolated behind a wall of silence. In a frustrating episode, Krall (2006) shows Izolda asking her daughter to translate her story to her granddaughter, but the truncated version in Hebrew cannot carry the weight of her experiences, and both the daughter and the granddaughter soon grow impatient. With the exception of the narrator, whom Izolda has commissioned to ghostwrite her story in Polish, there is no one with whom to share it.[18] The book ends with a scene of distressing linguistic disjunction: sitting at a birthday party in her honor, Izolda reminisces to herself about the past, as if conversing with the ghosts of her long-dead relatives and friends, while the actual conversation in Hebrew floats around her. Izolda's sense that "those people do not want to listen to me" (156) and her own inability to understand the guests is underscored by the juxtaposition, on the page, of the paragraphs in Polish and in Hebrew. Izolda's story starkly exemplifies what I have referred to as the "translation *differend*," in which the survivor has been deprived of the linguistic means to tell her story, even though the people who surround her are loving relatives rather than hostile Holocaust deniers.

Striking examples of the "translation *differend*" occur during translation sequences in Lanzmann's film *Shoah*. Unlike in written testimonies, in which survivors' foreign accents disappear, during the film, the viewers are constantly forced to negotiate a variety of cultural markers, signaled by the witnesses' accents. The unique effect of this cinematographic testimony, which frequently includes the presence of translators, lies in its mêlée of languages. By staging the Babel of post-Holocaust memory in front of the camera, Lanzmann evokes Jewish victims' linguistic predicament both during and in the aftermath of the Holocaust. Since, despite the translators' good efforts, many sentences and phrases remain untranslated, the reception of the film depends largely on the viewer's proficiency in the numerous languages spoken by Lanzmann's interviewees, which makes it almost impossible for any one viewer to follow all the linguistic nuances.

First of all, nowhere is the use of English to anesthetize the pain of an intolerable memory more striking than in Lanzmann's inter-view with Abraham Bomba. In Treblinka, Bomba was a member of the bar-ber *Sonderkommando*, charged with cutting the hair of the women who were ushered into the gas chambers. While other survivors in-terviewed by Lanzmann speak either German or He-brew, Bomba chooses to communicate his experiences in English.[19] During the interview in the barbershop in Tel Aviv, Bomba describes at length the process of selecting the barbers for the work detail and then their tasks inside the gas chambers. Bomba speaks in a dispas-sionate tone of voice and with a confident intonational pattern, which strikes the viewer as incongruous with the horrifying content of his account. His fluent performance breaks down, however, when he tries to describe the moment when women from his home town of Częstochowa walked into the gas chamber, among them the wife and the sister of Bomba's fellow barber. The women started asking Bomba questions; he recalls, "And when they saw me, they started asking me, Abe this and Abe that—'What's going to happen to us?'" (Lan-zmann 1995, 107). At this moment, the protective shield of Bomba's testimony in English crumbles, and Bomba falls silent, struggling for several minutes to regain composure. It seems that, from the start, Bomba's responses in English to Lanzmann's questions (which were asked in just as heavily accented English) serve to conceal the pain of his memory of the words he exchanged with the women whose hair he was cutting in the gas chamber and with whom, presumably, he spoke in his native Yiddish. Significantly, before Bomba resumes his account, cajoled by Lanzmann's insistent "Abe, you have to do it," he mumbles, in a low voice choked with tears, a sentence in Yiddish. In the space where Bomba's English collapses into his mother tongue, on the frontier between languages, the affective "truth" of his experience is conveyed to the viewer.[20]

By contrast, in Lanzmann's interviews with Polish "bystanders," it is French that becomes a neutralizing medium, although in an entirely different way. In the central episode with Simon (Szymon) Srebrnik, we see the former child survivor of the Chełmno death camp in front of a church in Grabów, in the middle of a group of villagers. The in-terviews are translated between Polish and French, by an interpreter who is constantly present on the screen. Lanzmann spurs the villagers

on with questions about what they knew about the mass extermina-
tions happening nearby, and their answers escalate from expressing joy
at seeing "Pan Szymek" (Mr. Simon) to an outburst of voices accusing
Jews of deicide.[21] According to Shoshana Felman, this episode stages a
reenactment of Polish Christian anti-Semitism, resulting in a revictim-
ization of Srebrnik, who remains silent throughout the scene. While
this is undeniably true, what is lost in a fluent French translation for
a viewer who does not know Polish are the background voices of the
"bystanders." While Srebrnik is silent most of the time, the translation
glosses over brief, direct, even intimate exchanges in Polish between
him and several women in the crowd. One of the women, for instance,
verifies her memories by addressing short, detailed questions to Srebrnik, to which he responds and then encourages her to speak aloud for
the camera: "Niech pani to powie!" (Please say it!). The members of the
crowd give contradictory answers to Lanzmann's questions, speaking
in chorus "Pamiętamy!" (Yes, we remember!) and "Ja nie pamiętam!"
(No, I don't remember!), and they continuously vie to correct one another ("Państwo tłumaczą źle," a man interjects [You are trying to explain it, but it is all wrong]). What disappears therefore is the complexity of this episode as a memory event, as well as Srebrnik's agency in
orchestrating it. Undoubtedly, in this scene, his testimony falls victim to
mistranslation (which is aggravated by subtitles in the English version
of the film), despite the translator's competence.

In other scenes in the film, Lanzmann interviews Polish "bystanders" at other sites of German extermination camps, such as Włodawa
near Sobibór or the town of Oświęcim. From behind the voices that
become uniformly channeled into the French translation, we hear untranslated fragments of conversations, in which the town inhabitants
argue about the details of the events, seek to confirm their recollections, and express their horror at what occurred in their neighbor-
hood. Lanzmann's interlocutors in Polish villages and small towns
are not highly articulate. Indeed, their answers to Lanzmann's questions often come out in garbled Polish, although each ungrammati-
cal phrase immediately becomes corrected in the French translation
(for instance, the grammatically incorrect "To jest taka morderstwo"
(This was such a murder) instantly becomes "Il était un meurtre" [It
was a murder]). These grammatical errors, however, are so bizarre
that one hesitates to attribute them solely to low levels of literacy
among the villagers. Perhaps the awkward manner of speaking also
indicates the speakers' inability to come to terms with the reality of

murder so close to home, and, at least for some, with their complicity in the events and their indifference to the tragedy of their former neighbors. The "bystanders'" struggle with the Polish language, which has been hardened by several decades of forgetting, during which the murdered Jewish neighbors remained unmourned, the difficulty highlighted in their speech by constant (untranslated) repetitions: "To było coś okropnego, coś okropnego" (It was something horrible, something horrible) . . . "Ja to przeżywałem, przeżywałem!" (It was really hard for me, really hard for me!).[22] Lanzmann's questions, however, in which he keeps alluding to the fact that the Poles have profited from the murder of their Jewish neighbors (with a sarcasm that, largely thanks to the translator's tact, remains undetected by his interlocutors), exude a sense of the director's moral superiority. In these sequences, the Polish language as such stands accused before Lanzmann's camera.[23] Something momentous happens during the numerous, often distressing encounters between languages in the film. Although this intense sensation resists being translated into one of the languages involved, it persists affectively, bearing witness to a profound failure of communication but also to the necessity of continuing to communicate.[24]

An occlusion of the "translation *differend*" occurs perhaps every time Holocaust narratives are rendered into other tongues by professional translators, even if the very fact of the work's being translated bears witness to the success of its testimonial intention. An example is the translation into English of Ida Fink's work. As described in her autobiographical novel *The Journey*, Fink, whose first language is Polish, also spoke German and French. In her short stories, Fink frequently interjects German expressions to convey the lethal power of the German language as the vehicle of death. When Fink's stories were translated into English, however, the translators decided to eliminate the German phrases to make the text more accessible to the English-speaking reader.[25] In translation, therefore, the fear that the sound of the German language strikes into the hearts of the inhabitants of the ghetto, its harshness when it is used as a tool of torture, and the threat of betrayal sensed when it suddenly comes from the lips of their Polish neighbors, are neutralized and disarmed. Further, the *poliglossia* of the ghetto in Zbaraż, Fink's hometown, its rich mixture of Polish, Yiddish, and Ukrainian, also largely disappears. In this case, as with the example of Wiesel's rendition of his story into French, the translation has inadvertently aided in the disappearance of the Eastern European Jewish world, although the translator's expressed intention, like the writer's, was to preserve its memory.

THE TOWER OF BABEL

Primo Levi (1988) writes, "It is an obvious assertion that where violence is inflicted on men, it is also inflicted on language" (97). The precarious condition of post-Holocaust language stems directly from the Nazi assault on language as a means of communication, as well as on particular national languages, which were annulled by the decree that those who spoke them should die. As does Leitner in her much later account, in *Survival in Auschwitz*, written in 1946, Levi (1993) conceives of the Nazi death camp as modernity's version of the Tower of Babel: "The confusion of languages is a fundamental component of the manner of living here: one is surrounded by a perpetual Babel, in which everyone shouts orders and threats in languages never heard before, and woe betide whoever fails to grasp the meaning" (38).[26] For Levi, the impossibility of communicating—of understanding the orders and obtaining life-saving information from other inmates— is the true force of extermination, more menacing than hunger or physical coercion. Survival depends on one's translating abilities and linguistic talents, which enable one to secure an extra slab of "bread- *Brot-Broid-chleb-pain-lechem-keynér*" (39). The prisoners' Babelian ordeal and their inability to communicate is why German civilians perceive them as less than human: "They hear us speak in many different languages, which they do not understand and which sound to them grotesque as animal noises" (121). In his later account *The Drowned and the Saved*, Levi (1988) writes, "The greater part of the prisoners who did not understand German—that is, almost all of the Italians—died during the first ten to fifteen days after their arrival: at first glance, from hunger, cold, fatigue, and disease; but after a more attentive examination, due to insufficient information" (93). In Levi's own perception of the camp, Babel was symbolized in the tower that the inmates erected in the middle of Buna-Monowitz: "Its bricks were called *Ziegel, bruques, tegula, cegli, kamenny, mattoni, téglak*, and they were cemented by hate; hate and discord, like the Tower of Babel" (Levi 1993, 73).

Levi (1993) conveys a sense of incomprehension and linguistic confusion by inserting foreign words into his narrative. The descriptions of the everyday goings on of the camp are punctuated by German words and phrases that are left untranslated and intrude on every page: *Tagesraum, Kräzeblock, Alles heraus* (33, 70). To every question a *Häftling* must reply *Jawohl* because in the camp there is *kein warum* (29). When occasionally Levi provides translation in parentheses, its function is to exacerbate the deadly power of the German words: "a diagnosis of *'dicke Füsse'* (swollen feet) is extremely dangerous." The German language stakes out the linguistic perimeter of the camp, and within it, the respective languages of the inmates are annihilated, reduced to meaningless and inconsequential babble. Ironically, what gave Levi the momentary comfort of feeling "human" in the camp (and what most likely enabled his survival) was passing the chemistry examination in German, as well as being addressed by the examiner in the polite plural form of address "Sie" ("Wo sind Sie geboren?" Levi 1993, 106), after which Levi was recruited for the chemical work detail. After the war, the concentration-camp German will continue to contaminate Levi's native Italian (as well as its translations into other languages), reinforcing the inscription of camp experience on the language of witnessing. In Levi's testimony, the barbs of German words continue to wound the narrative and undermine the authority of the language of the account.[27]

Levi (1988) comments that, as a result of the linguistic dispersion in the camp, the "use of the word to communicate thought, this necessary and sufficient instrument for man to be man, had fallen into disuse" (91). Those who are "drowned" perish in the deafening noise from which "the human word did not surface" and where "one finds oneself facing a human being with whom one must absolutely establish communication or die, and then is unable to do so" (93–94). Although Levi's references to Babel imply language's fallen condition marked by evil, in the camp, language slips into the grey zone "beyond good and evil," eluding even God's jurisdiction and thus the possibility of redemption.

Accordingly, Levi describes his fellow inmates in terms of their linguistic abilities and which languages they speak. Rabbi Mendi from Russia, for instance, speaks seven languages, while all of the Italian Jews, most of whom are secular and do not even know Yiddish or Hebrew, are helpless and mute. In Levi's account, fluency in camp languages, when it is employed to aid other inmates, is emblematic of a person's moral backbone and human dignity. This is how he describes Jean the Picolo, who knows both French and German and uses this knowledge to protect the members of his work detail. Levi's friend

Alberto understands all of the commands in German and Polish although he does not know these languages *per se*, but since he uses his skill to help others, he stands out in Levi's account as a symbol of dignified, uncorrupted struggle for survival. Thus translation functions in Levi's narrative as an emblem of remaining human under the circumstances in which the very meaning of humanity seems to have collapsed. True translation means "translating for the other" so that he can stay alive; the ability to translate and the uses of translation seem to have profound moral implications.

The pivotal scene in *Survival in Auschwitz* is Levi's effort to translate passages from Dante's *Divine Comedy* into French for Jean the Picolo, in order to teach him the basics of Italian. Only in the effort to translate Dante in the Nazi camp, as if his life depended on it, does Levi begin to truly comprehend the meaning of the verses that were written in his native Italian. From within Levi's broken French, Dante speaks to him "as if I also was hearing it for the first time: Like the blast of a trumpet, like the voice of God" (Levi 1993, 113). Translation provides a redemptive moment, in which Dante reminds Levi, via his own translation, "You were made men/To follow after knowledge and excellence" (113). Throughout the translation episode, Levi makes no attempt to supplement German words to aid Picolo's comprehension, although they both know that language, as if Levi guarded the moment of camaraderie between Italian and French against contamination by the language that has sought to eradicate them. The association of translation with soup, which is being carried by Levi and Picolo to feed the members of their *Kommando*, points to its quality as vital nourishment. Levi is filled with its life-giving energy, at least for a brief moment of reprieve, as he searches for the French phrases. In another telling association with nourishment, Levi recalls absorbing foreign words and expressions "like a famished stomach rapidly assimilates even indigestible food." In one episode, Levi trades a daily portion of bread for a lesson of German, commenting that "never was bread better spent." He also recalls becoming conditioned, like Pavlov's dog, to the sound of the Polish words "stergishri steri" (*czterdzieści cztery*; forty-four), the number preceding his, and he refers to the memory of those words as "the unconscious preparation for survival."[28]

The central translation sequence in Levi's narrative, which marks his effort to counter the destructive forces of Babel, is followed by the news of the Allied landing in Normandy, as if the effort of translation

and the miracle of communication amid inhumanity were causally related to the German defeat and to the author's eventual survival. The
scene also reveals the urgency of the need to translate. Levi (1993)
pleads, "Here, listen Picolo, open your ears and your mind, you have
to understand, for my sake" (113), and this compulsion to translate
Dante parallels his obsessive need to tell his story.[29] Indeed, Levi associates his effort to dredge the fragments of the poem from the depths
of memory, which has been dulled by hunger and cold, with the struggle of memory against oblivion, foreshadowing his future destiny as
a storyteller from Auschwitz. Translation thus becomes a conduit of
recollection: if memory is for Levi like a photographic film that must
be soaked in chemicals to bring the images to light, translation functions in this chemical analogy like a developer that makes recall possible by bringing words back to life. It is then a device that enables
Levi to carry the *Häftling* out of the darkness of incomprehension and
to translate him back into the human from linguistic chaos.

Like Levi's accounts, Kertész's (1992) camp narrative in *Fateless*
recreates the sounds of the mixture of languages in the camps. The
narrator, György Köves (the author's young alter ego), is surrounded
by the constant noise of incomprehensible words that float around
him, which he describes with adjectives that emphasize their strangeness ["that strange language" (93), "some sort of musical language"
(140)]. Like Levi, Kertész's protagonist arrives in Auschwitz with "a
smattering of German" that he picked up in school, which saves his
life during the selection because he is able to understand the urgent
advice from older inmates to lie about his age. In the camp, his fluency
in German continues to increase, especially after his transfer to Buchenwald. While at first Kertész phonetically transcribes the German
phrases that his narrator does not understand (*"Los ge ma rorne!* he
said, or something similar" [65]), properly spelled German words and
their translations begin to appear in the text with growing frequency
("Aber Mensch, um Gottes Willen! Wir sind doch ja hier nicht in Auschwitz" [92]). Yet despite the advantage of comprehending German
commands and of being taken care of by a fellow Hungarian inmate,
György becomes a *Muselmann* and is left for dead on the ground.
Through a series of events that, as he says, he "could never explain,"
György finds himself in a hospital and is treated by a doctor, a French
prisoner, who rewards the patients who speak his language with an
additional cube of sugar. While Levi's account implied an association
of the knowledge of foreign languages with food, György literally

tries to learn a few French words to earn the coveted sugar. He comments, "That's when I realized the truth of what they kept teaching me at home: what an important thing an education is, especially a knowledge of foreign languages!" (Kertész 1992, 143). The narrator's slow emergence from total incomprehension is signaled by his learning of words from different languages, Polish in particular, the language that he previously perceived as "strange" ("*Gyinkuge . . . gyinkuge bardzo*" ["Dziękuję . . . dziękuję bardzo" (Thank you, thank you very much)]; 150), and this process coincides with his physical recovery, followed by the liberation of the camp.

The motives of the knowledge of languages and translation as a strategy to stay alive appear in numerous Holocaust testimonials, even if the author may not reflect on them as such. Eta Wrobel, for instance, in her extraordinary account of survival in the forest as one of the leaders of a group of Jewish partisans, makes frequent references to her quick-minded use of different languages in life-threatening situations. For example, she rescues her father from jail because she can speak fluent German, in which she brazenly addresses the prison commander; or she "impulsively" exclaims a phrase in Polish (thanking Mary the mother of Jesus for rain), thus dispelling the suspicions of ax-carrying Polish peasants that she and her family were Jewish. After the war, translation continues to be Wrobel's main survival strategy, and she describes her life after the liberation in terms of survival. For instance, with the arrival of the Russian army, she interprets for the Russian officers, which enables her to secure means of subsistence for her family when they come out of hiding. On the family's first day in America, she defends her husband from a security guard in the hotel because she is the only one in the group of émigrés who already knows English.

In the introduction to her memoir, Wrobel mentions that she tried to write an account of her wartime adventures immediately after the war, but she developed shortness of breath when leaning over the pages and had to give it up. Only decades later did she resume her efforts to leave a record, for the sake of her children and grandchildren, who had been urging her to do so. It is striking that, in the story, Wrobel presents herself as an indomitable fighter, a partisan leader, whose courage shocked even an SS man into cowing to her demands. Her mental and physical endurance and her ability to withstand pain are stunning: for instance, for months she ran around with a bullet embedded in her calf and a leather boot growing into her swollen flesh. After the war, however, she shows herself unable to overcome the psychosomatic symptoms that paralyze her attempts to write. As with many memoirs penned by survivors who have told their story in a foreign language, Wrobel's account, written in a vivid yet mostly dispassionate English, is coauthored, hers with Jeanette Friedman, "a good writer and . . . a good person, a *mensch*" (as Wrobel remarks in the acknowledgments). Wrobel does not mention what the language of her first attempt to give testimony was, although we can assume it was Yiddish. Interestingly, Yiddish and Hebrew words appear occasionally in the narrative, and their choice does not seem to be random: *Tateh*, *Mammushe*, *dorfisher brot* (corn bread), *machzorim* (high holidays prayer books), *neshama* (soul), *simcha* (joy), and other expressions that refer to people, objects, or feelings that offer Wrobel sustenance. Further, the narrative is interrupted, more or less in the middle, by a poem in Yiddish that Wrobel wrote in 1943, which describes the deportations of Jews from her hometown of Lukow. The poem is followed by a translation into English by her daughter Anna Wrobel. Here translation becomes a gesture of homage by a daughter to her mother, but it also indicates that the process of intergenerational transmission of memory is necessarily a rendition into English.

Like the epigraph in Hebrew in Levinas's *Otherwise than Being*, the Yiddish poem stands as a commemorative textual *matzevah* to the murdered relatives. Although Yiddish is no longer viable as a primary means of transmitting memory, the presence of *mameloshn* (mother tongue) both holds Wrobel's story together and interrupts, irritates, and questions the logical calm and correctness of the account in English. Through her interjections, Wrobel is trying to conjure up the specter of *Yiddishkeit*, and, in that sense, the fact that her memoir is "ghostwritten" has double meaning: it is both cowritten by a professional writer and dictated to Wrobel in Yiddish by the ghostly voices of her murdered relatives. Wrobel's linguistic foreignness is also marked in a less visible way: in Polish, the author's last name (which she took after her husband) must have been spelled "Wróbel." The author makes herself at home in English, but her American "visa" will always be stamped with the elision of the diacritical mark in a foreign-sounding name.

Perhaps the most outstanding case of translation among Holocaust literary testimonials is Ruth Kluger's double memoir. In 1992 Kluger published *weiter leben: Eine Jugend*, a book she wrote in German. Nine years later, she rewrote her account in English as *Still Alive: A*

Holocaust Girlhood Remembered, refashioning the story in order to place it in the context of her American experience.[30] As in the case of Wrobel, the slight change of the author's last name, from "Klüger" in the German version to "Kluger" in *Still Alive* (both variants are cited in critical discussions and reviews of both books) is the visual mark of the author's linguistic migration. German is Kluger's (Klüger's) native tongue, although she seems to share Célan's ambivalence about that language rather than Arendt's certainty of German as an uncorrupted place of refuge. She recalls that, even as a little girl growing up in Vienna, she had an acute sense that the language she spoke was also the language of hatred directed against her, and she records her feelings of linguistic shame: "To know no language other than what those who thought us subhumans spoke!" (Kluger 2001, 87). When she visits Vienna as an adult, Kluger's feelings about her native language are just as equivocal. The German language is the only thing that still links her to the place of her childhood and that has remained unchanged, so "I speak it though I don't like it" (59). Paradoxically, only the specificity of the German language allows her to describe the atmosphere of her childhood in Vienna, whose culture was *judenkinderfeindlish* (hostile to a Jewish child). She is both "attracted and repelled" by German, and this emotional ambivalence extends to her friendships with German intellectuals.

Immediately after arriving in the United States, Kluger studied English with a passion. She writes, "New York freed me from the incompetent silence of otherness by teaching me to understand its language—English" (200).[31] *weiter leben* was written in Germany, when Kluger was hospitalized in Göttingen after an accident. At the time, she had been living in the United States for decades and referred to Irvine, California, as her "home." Paradoxically, it seems that, only having found a home in America—and, as Schaumann (2004) points out, having retold her story from the vantage point of an American citizen, the liberator of the camps—can Kluger now call herself "a German girl" (146) and recount her story in German. Conversely, she can designate Irvine as a home only because of her previous nomadism and continued exile from the mother tongue.

weiter leben met with enormous success in Germany, garnering Klüger (1992) a number of prestigious awards and earning her comparisons to Levi and Wiesel. According to the author, the German version was written for German readers, whom she challenged to confront the established paradigms of Holocaust remembrance. Although her questions were provocative and at times potentially offensive, she invited her native readers to engage in a dialogue on the discourse of remembrance and to think through the past together. The wealth of allusions to German culture in the text also served to assert her ownership of the German cultural tradition and to reclaim the heritage from which Klüger had been disowned during the war.

By contrast, the English version of the memoir is addressed to American audiences and dedicated to the memory of the author's mother. Significantly, Kluger (2001) refers to it as "neither a translation nor a new book; it's another version, a parallel book, for my children and my American students" (210).[32] Unlike the German memoir, the book received modest praise in the United States, and the critics' responses were lukewarm.[33] Although the politics of memory also informs Kluger's unique translation into English, the focus is on a personal journey of healing and repair rather than on intervening into official strategies of Holocaust remembrance. While the version in German was open-ended, as if instigating the reader to pose his or her own questions, *Still Alive* ends with a gesture of reconciliation with Kluger's mother, whom up until then she has not been able to forgive for what she perceived as years of psychological abuse, and especially for her suggestion, back in Auschwitz, that they end their lives by walking into an electric fence. The process of translation subsequently becomes inseparable from the work of mourning, during which Kluger labors to posthumously reclaim the relationship with her mother from beneath the hurtful memories of her childhood.

The story of the tower of Babel is also mentioned in Kluger's (2001) account, although it happens as if by chance, when she recalls a book of Jewish legends. She writes, "When the Tower of Babel was built, God threw colored confetti into the crowd, thus damning them to their various languages and misunderstandings: God's wrath as a painted carnival of chance" (32). Although the motif of Babel appears here in the form of a tale for children, its simplicity highlights the undercurrent of the Babelian theme in the novel. In the English text, this problematic is signaled (as in Levi and Kertész) by German words that remain untranslated. Unlike Wrobel's nourishing words in Yiddish, the words in Kluger's mother tongue are hurtful—such as *ausgehoben* (lifted out), which Kluger remembers as referring to the disappearance of her Jewish classmates during the early years of the German occupation of Vienna; *Judenschule*, the derogatory term for Jewish places of learning; and *Judenstern*, which Kluger experienced

as a humiliating sign signaling to others her inferior status (22–23)—
and appear like scars disfiguring the body of her English language.
The fact that Kluger so emphatically refuses to translate these hated
words, as if barring them from entry into her adopted tongue and
striking them out of dictionaries, betrays their perseverance in her
memory as somatic traces of alienation and linguistic shame.[34]

Preceding the last chapter (or "station") of her English book,
Kluger quotes Adrienne Rich, from the poem "Prospective Immi-
grants Please Note":

> Either you will
> go through this door
> or you will not go through.
>
> The door itself
> makes no promises.
> It is only a door.

Rich's poem speaks to immigrant experiences, yet it also alludes to
the threshold between languages, where the newcomer is both a wan-
derer halted before the door as well as her own gatekeeper. As in the
parable "Before the Law" (to which the poem seems to allude), the
nomad knows that, in Kafka's words, "No one else could ever be
admitted here, since this gate was made only for you" (Kafka 1971,
4). It is always up to the traveler to decide whether she will close that
door or continue her journeys. The struggle to come into her own as
a witness takes place at this linguistic threshold, in the caesura of her
divided speech.

Kluger's unique translatory achievement draws attention to the
centrality of translation in Holocaust testimonials. Indeed, one might
now wonder, considering that thousands of Holocaust memoirs have
been published in the last few decades by authors who are often bilingual, why Kluger's was the only such attempt (at least the only well
known and successful one). What layers does Kluger's uncommon
translation mobilize in the two languages that she has set in motion?
Undoubtedly, her unique form of double address opens up the two
languages to each other. Yet Kluger's twinned text broaches the question, which I will explore shortly, of what her testimony must necessarily disavow in the movement of translatory exchanges.

THE TASK OF THE TRANSLATOR:
TRANSLATION AS TESTIMONY

Contributing to the debate about the limits of Holocaust representation, Berel Lang (1988) argues that these limits depend on cultural and sociopolitical contexts, as well as on a particular community's value systems. This also means that traumatic events are both experienced and remembered against the backdrop of these cultural expectations. A national language is a medium in which these contexts and values are shaped, and through which a particular community judges the moral weight of what is represented as fact and determines the criteria of inclusion in the official historical narrative (343).[35] Since the translator moves between different linguistic communities, he or she must take into account the moral consequences of the use of a particular language and consider the linguistic mechanisms of exclusion and repression practiced by a given community.

In his essay "On Language as Such and the Language of Man," Walter Benjamin (1986) argues that the allegory of the Tower of Babel symbolizes the inferiority of the words with which man names things with respect to God's creative word that speaks things into existence (318).[36] In another text, "The Task of the Translator" (1969),[37] Benjamin writes that the task of translation is to redeem language's "fallen condition" and to bring dispersed languages closer to what he calls "pure language." Pure language is the "inaccessible realm of reconciliation and fulfillment between languages" (75), which means that languages are a priori interrelated, and translation can bring out their higher kinship. Every language then possesses an inherent quality of translatability, regardless of whether a person capable of translating it may ever exist. The actual work of translation thus reveals the unattainable horizon of linguistic possibility toward which every text is destined. The text always "calls" for a translation, and this call is a promise of future communication. From within one language, translation addresses itself to a wholly other tongue, although its mission is to solicitously watch over both languages. For Benjamin, the life of literary works thus receives "highest testimony" in translation: renditions into other languages bear witness to the work's life but also to its afterlife, its posthumous survival (76). Like memory, translations are always belated, and they mourn the passing of the original text; translating (*übersetzen*) is always a form of surviving (*überleben*), the work's "stage of continued life" (71). For that reason, they convey the work's demand that it remain unforgotten, even if this claim were never to be fulfilled by men. But, more importantly, the task of the translator is not only to ensure the mere survival of the text but also to transform it into something more and better, beyond the means of the author.

Ironically, the English translation of Benjamin's essay obscures that the German word for "task," *Aufgabe*, also connotes "giving up" or "failing" (de Man 1986, 80). Although translation engages both the language of the original and the target language, it also necessarily fails to attain the goal of perfect communication. Yet this defeat, this betrayal intrinsic to every act of translation, stems from the lack in the very language of the original, from *its* failure to express what it has always already disarticulated and sent into exile. Translation then reveals "the suffering of the original language": the fact that exactly in the place where we feel most at home and familiar—in our original language—"this alienation is the strongest" (84). And this is why, ever since Babel, languages are destined for translation; why the translator's task is a mission—"the commitment, the duty, the debt" (Derrida 1985, 177)—to reveal a language's originary indebtedness to that which it has always excluded. We do not know to whom the translator is obligated, but it is from the place of this inarticulable alterity inherent in every national language that a work calls for translation. The task of the translator, Benjamin (1969) continues, "is to release in his own language that pure language which is under the spell of another, to liberate the language imprisoned in a work in his re-creation of the work" (80). Translation renders the familiar sounds of the native tongue foreign, uprooted from their native soil, *unheimlich*. It exposes the traces of what the language has excluded, yet to which it remains indebted.[38] Instead of striving to preserve the status quo of the target language, the translator must allow a domestic language to be "powerfully affected" (81) by the foreign tongue in order to release the traces of that inscription. Simultaneously, the translator is also the guardian of the frontier between languages, the one who regulates the migrations of meanings: he ensures their safe passage or halts their uncontrolled proliferation. Translation is thus an injunction to a national language to be deeply self-reflective about what it has excluded, and to confront its investments and assumptions.

In the postulate that translation bears witness to the original text, Benjamin's articulation of the translator's task resonates with Levinas's idiom of responsibility, as developed in chapter one. For Levinas, the primacy of the subject is put into question by its ethical relation with the other. The self's existence is primarily testimony to the life of another, while its speech is an echo whose source remains unknown. The metaphor of the echo in Levinas's description of ethical subjectivity is reminiscent of Benjamin's (1969) own formulation of the task of the translator: "The task of the translator consists in finding that intended effect [*Intention*] upon the language into which he is translating which produces in it *the echo of the original*" (76; emphasis mine). Perched on the periphery of language, translation calls into the "language forest. . . . It calls into it without entering, aiming at that single spot where the echo is able to give, in its own language, the reverberation of the work in the alien one" (76). Translation is a response to the summons from another language, the language of the other. In the context of Levinasian ethics, my obligation to the other is unconditional because I am responsible whether I will it or not. Benjamin's postulate of "pure language" reveals that the translatory imperative is similarly undeclinable and irreducible, and it obtains even if no translator for the work will ever be found. In the border crossings between languages, translation reveals that I come into being as a speaking subject—a member of a linguistic community—because I am indebted to what my language has excluded, to what remains outside its borders, "on the periphery." The translator's mission is to keep a vigil over the target language and to bring out what that language remembers, what it has disowned, and what it will continue to forget. After all, the translator is the one who knows how to pronounce these foreign-sounding, unpronounceable proper names, and she is aware, perhaps painfully so, of their status as the mark of alienation.

In arguing that language is primarily constituted by the self's aptitude to respond to the call of the other, Levinas distinguishes between the ethical essence of language (Saying) and language in its communicative function (the Said). The translator is always turned toward the ethical horizon, yet in his everyday practice, he attends with solicitude to the plastic and contextually molded surface of language. What Levinas calls the Said always appears in its concrete manifestation as a national language. Levinas then seems to conceive of Saying as a moment that escapes the totalizing intention of a particular language. In so far as Saying originates in the other's call for help that I cannot decline, it resonates with Benjamin's conception of "pure language"—the horizon of communicability between languages, toward which the text is solicited by a call from another language.

It is interesting that, throughout his profoundly innovative reflection on the ethical essence of language, Levinas—a Lithuanian Jew, raised in a Yiddish- and Russian-speaking household—never comments on his own displacement within the French language. According to his biographer, Salomon Malka, Levinas's heavily accented French and his struggle with the French syntax bore the mark of "the suffering of language," signaling his estrangement from the language in which he wrote all of his work.[39] Not unlike the authors of the Holocaust testimonies described above, Levinas remains estranged from his linguistic community. Perhaps the only intentional inscription of this foreignness in his work is the double epigraph in *Otherwise than Being*, which consists of a general dedication to the six million victims, written in French, and a personal tribute in Hebrew to his murdered relatives.[40] The cipher of linguistic and also of philosophical alterity (the Hebrew script would have been illegible to a majority of Levinas's philosophical readers) is impressed on the body of Levinas's main work. Even if this alterity remains unthematized (in the work dedicated to the discussion of alterity), the epigraph is a sign of the translation *differend* that opens up in Levinas's silence on the question of translation. It can be argued that the philosopher's activity as a translator, which likely ensured his survival during the Holocaust, as well as his translatory struggles throughout a lifetime of writing, have profoundly informed Levinas's thinking about language as primarily listening to the other. In a way, for Levinas, "translatability" belongs to language on a fundamental level; in Benjamin's understanding of the term, as indebtedness to the language of the other and its aptitude to reach out and respond to the other's call.

Finally, looking ahead to the discussion of "silence" in chapter three, let us note that, although he is silent on the topic of translation, Levinas himself insists that silence is a part of speech rather than its limit. In the context of the multiplicity of languages that Levinas himself passes over in silence, there arises the question of the translatability of silence. Just as Kertész and others ask to what language Holocaust speech belongs, it is important to inquire whether "Holocaust silence" is a part of a given language. If it is, how to translate that silence? We have seen that Bomba's silence in *Shoah* destroys his carefully wrought protective shelter of the English language. What language did Bomba's silence belong to? As I have suggested, it may have "belonged" to the language that was not even mentioned during the interview with Lanzmann, the language in which Bomba addressed the women from his hometown in the gas chamber and which erupted during his traumatic collapse. Is silence more perceptible in one's native tongue or in the language of translation? Through interminable translation sequences in Lanzmann's film, silences become almost audible as they become increasingly unbearable to the viewer. The silences in Holocaust testimonials also signal translation *differends* between the linguistic communities in which the discourse about the Holocaust is formulated and in which its narratives are embedded. A translation of the testifying word is always a translation of the word that has been "ensilenced" (Célan's [2001] *das erschwiegne Wort* [78]) by the uniqueness of that which the generality of words has erased. As Derrida (2005) remarks in his text on Célan's poetic witnessing, bearing witness is sometimes silent, yet the poem addresses even in silence (96). Graphed in the caesuras that fracture the words in Célan's poems, this silence calls for translation, while also marking the limit of the poem's translatability. Yet, as we have glimpsed in the translations of Fink's short stories, impatient translation can also smother that silence. Babel, the threat of the untranslatability of testimony, its being halted on the border and forbidden passage, pervades these migrations. As Benjamin (1969) has already cautioned, there always exists a danger inherent in translation that "the gates of a language . . . may slam shut and enclose the translator with silence" (81).

Benjamin's thesis that translation points to an inaccessible region of reconciliation between languages is informed by the cabalistic concept of *tikkun*, that is, messianic mending and restoration.[41] The process of translation is like putting together the fragments of a broken vessel (78); it gathers and rejoins words that have been scattered and abandoned across different languages, or, as in the case of the languages of Holocaust testimony, of words and phrases that have been rendered meaningless by violence. For Benjamin, the sense of translation's "fidelity" to the original is not that it reproduces the original but that it produces an effect of harmony, that it reflects "the great longing for linguistic complementation" (79), even if, as Benjamin writes in "Theses on the Philosophy of History," this is only "a weak messianic promise"(264).[42] In the post-Auschwitz context, Benjamin's understanding of translation as a promise of communicability can thus be related to what Canadian philosopher Emil Fackenheim has articulated as *tikkun olam*—a whole and unconditional act of mending that bears upon every aspect of post-Holocaust existence. Fackenheim (1994) writes, "It is precisely if the rupture, or the threat of it, is total, that all powers must be summoned for a mending" (253), although he adds that, from the start, we must accept that the post-Auschwitz *tikkun* can only be fragmentary.[43] Orienting itself toward that future, translation announces a pure event of communicability, even if the actual words are always marked and interrupted by strangeness.

In the examples of translatory exchanges in Holocaust testimonials, we have repeatedly seen gestures, not always successful, of trying to mend the broken bonds with the past, perhaps most profoundly experienced in Kluger's retranslation of her memoir. If the motif of Babel in Holocaust testimonies is emblematic of a radical rupture of language "after Auschwitz" and of the shattering of human ability to communicate, translation, in its various manifestations, is animated by the promise of the *tikkun* of language, however fragmentary. Because Holocaust translations expose the consequences of violence *on* language as well as violence perpetrated *by* language, they also posit a new imperative, which French writer Maurice Blanchot (1995) formulates as "May words cease to be arms" (11). The question of translation is then central to Holocaust testimony because, oriented toward "pure language," it is primarily an articulation of this hope. Its function is to initiate and sustain communication and to transmit the possibility of addressing the other. Tellingly, Benjamin (1969), like Levi, when giving an apparently arbitrary example of language's intention to communicate, chooses the word for "bread," the symbol of nourishment and preservation of life: "The word *Brot* means something different to a German that the word *pain* to a Frenchman. . . . As to the intended object, however, the two words mean the very same thing" (74). Holocaust testimonials, as they are infused with the translatory imperative, foreground a similar need—not a cognitive desire to impart facts on the reader but an insistent plea: "Are you listening?" In this sense, as Thomas Trezise (2001) has written, "A survivor speaks otherwise" (62), in defiance of the "total linguistic barrier" that Levi says he faced in the camps. In the context of bearing witness to traumatic events, translation also becomes a vehicle of healing, rescuing the words of those who were almost destroyed by the violence of language.

As mentioned in chapter one, Levi recalls the presence in the camp of a three-year-old boy, paralyzed from the waist down, whom the inmates named Hurbinek. The child kept repeating words that resembled sounds in different languages but which no one in the multilingual crowd of Auschwitz inmates was able to recognize. As Levi

(1979) notes, because Hurbinek tried so desperately to communicate, "everybody listened to him in silence, anxious to understand, and among us were the speakers of all the languages of Europe" (198). According to Agamben (1999), Hurbinek's attempt to escape from the abyss of nonspeech is the true site of testimony, where the witnessing subject comes into being (38). Agamben refers to Hurbinek's nonsensical words as incomprehensible "sounds." What truly matters for the inmates that listen to him, however, and what Agamben overlooks, is that these sounds arise in the gaps between languages. Each of the inmates hopes that perhaps they belong to his mother tongue, so that he, in his turn, will be able to respond to the child. Hurbinek, a child without a mother tongue, embodies the orphaned condition of post-Holocaust language, as announced by Kertész. An abandoned, motherless child, Hurbinek is also a symbol of the vulnerability of that language. Yet the testimonial imperative stems from the need to make Hurbinek's nonwords comprehensible in the particular languages of those who witnessed his anguished efforts to communicate. This seems to be Kertész's mission: if he writes about the Holocaust because it has no language, he does so to give it a language. The space of translation is where the dispersed languages meet, and where the voices whose "paths" would otherwise never cross begin to call to one another and to address one another. There is no "common language" to speak about the Holocaust, and what Holocaust testimonials bear witness to first and foremost is this abyssal, Babelian condition of post-Holocaust speech. Yet, what survivors, their descendants, and those who listen to their stories *do* share is this resounding absence of the common idiom, a radical disjunction of speech (which has been referred to as the "translation *differend*"), and they are committed to forging passages across this divide.

What transpires in the occurrence of the translation *differend* is the feeling that there are differences in what individual languages can express, and translators bear witness to these differences. Their efforts to find the "right" word imply this ethical inflection: their responsibility is to initiate communication, and they do so by lending an ear to the other, by exposing themselves to the harshness of the alien sounds that they make reverberate in their native tongue. The ethical injunction of Holocaust translations is, to quote Adorno (1967), that "we think with our ears" (19). As Benjamin implored us, "Do we not, ourselves, feel a faint breath of the air in which people of yesterday lived? Do not the voices to which we lend our ears carry an echo of voices now extinguished?" ("On the Concept of History," quoted in Didi-Huberman 2008, 170).

Kertész (2004) asks, apropos post-Auschwitz speech, "For whom is this language destined?" (181). According to Célan (2001), the poem can be "a message in a bottle, sent out in the—not always greatly hopeful—belief that somewhere and sometime it could wash up on land, on heartland perhaps" (396). It is a gift destined to an unknown future, and its hope "has always been to speak . . . *in the cause of an Other*—who knows, perhaps in the cause of a *wholly Other*" (408). Like Célan's poetic speech, the translating word drifts toward the unknown for the sake of an encounter, opening the door to the other who arrives from the future, and it is marked by the accents of those to whom it is addressed. That is why the task of the translator is to interrupt a national language's complacency by disseminating the echoes of foreign word-visas without which linguistic borders would remain impassable. In the process, native words are transformed from an inscription of belonging into the mark of strangeness. They are evicted from what is most properly "mine" and dispatched toward an experience of the multiplicity of languages. Because it brings out the mark of difference on the body of language, translation can potentially stand guard against linguistic ethnonationalism, remaining vigilant against the sedimentation of words into tools of oppression, exclusion, and discrimination. Translatory exchanges between languages in Holocaust testimonials also bring out the fact that the violence of the Holocaust, which penetrated the German language during the war, did not leave other European languages intact, as we have seen in the case of Lanzmann's indictment of the Polish language in *Shoah* (the director's objectionable manner of conducting interviews with Polish "bystanders" notwithstanding).

Regardless of her own linguistic tribulations, Arendt's attention to the importance of translation during the Eichmann trial, as it was sharpened by her experience as an exile, shows that the issue of translation pervaded and structured the event that inaugurated "the era of the witness." As Wieviorka (2006) remarks, the question of the choice of language is at the heart of testimony, since it posits the question, where does one testify from and what does one testify to (32)? In his essay "Poetics and Politics of Witnessing," Derrida (2005) draws an analogy between testimony and translation. The truth of testimony is vested in the singularity of the event to which one bears witness and thus is a matter of belief. Yet a witness is always held to the standard

of objectivity and historical truth. Derrida brings out a parallel between translation's crossing of linguistic frontiers and testimony's
crossing the borders between "an act of faith," a subjective "space of
believing" (78), and the order of knowledge where the proof of events
has to be procured. In a way, testimony is always both an act of translation and it resists translation. "But," asks Derrida, "what would an
untranslatable testimony be worth? Would it be non-testimony? And
what would a testimony that was absolutely transparent to translation be? Would it still be testimony?" (69). Derrida concludes that the
relation between translation and testimony is a necessary one, and it
is maintained by this aporetic conundrum of testifying speech.

Ultimately, Kertész's comment that the Holocaust has no language
points to a unique Babelian predicament inherent in virtually all Holocaust memoirs, even if its manifestations vary significantly. If the
Holocaust exceeds the means of verbal representation at our disposal
(it is "unspeakable"), it signifies, first and foremost, that it cannot
be expressed in the idiom of particular languages. This "unspeakability," however, is signaled and born witness to in the space of the
translation *differend*. Translation is then the means par excellence of
searching for new idioms in which to bear witness, and many of the
authors of Holocaust testimonies, of which I have discussed only a
few, take up the challenge of this "task of the translator."

If, as I argued in chapter one, the witness is born in the self's recurrent journey toward the other, translation, by its nature, is already a
repetition. It is a return to the same in a different tongue, whereby the
original comes back as a gift of (another) tongue. The accounts of Holocaust experiences, from the death camps, from the ghetto, from the
hiding places on the Aryan side, describe states of being for which no
words exist in national languages, the lacuna which the writers (and
often also their translators) have endlessly tried to convey. The Holocaust is extraterritorial with respect to national languages, or, at least
in the speech of survivors, it constitutes each language's inassimilable
remainder, although those who bear witness in these languages always hope that, in the process of transmission, they will finally "say
it right." Witnesses always translate the untranslatable into one of
the comprehensible languages and familiar expressions, aware that
their speech is a mistranslation, an instance of *traduttore traditore*.
Paradoxically, to an extent, translation effaces the very thing it seeks
to preserve, and in consequence, it fails to deliver what it has been
consigned to bring forth. But what witnesses-translators succeed in

conveying, perhaps often against their expressed intention, is both the experience of that failure to translate and the desire for further translation. Here translation is the cipher for witnessing.

The weakness of Holocaust testimony—its lack of a specific discourse or narrative, and, first and foremost, the absence of a national tongue in which it can be properly conveyed—makes it vulnerable to appropriation. Within the scope of Levinas's ethics, which I have expanded upon to address the issue of translation, however, this weakness is also its greatest strength in at least two respects. First, the vulnerability and "homelessness" of this language, the intrinsic otherness that is revealed in translatory misencounters, offers a possibility of undoing the linguistic privilege or supremacy of one language over the other. This constitutes a credible effort to lend ethical and political content to the clichéd promises of "Never again!" Secondly, Holocaust testimonials foreground the communicative imperative and are structured as an address to another, demanding a response. Since, as I have argued, testimonials always involve some forms of translation, through this summons, they have a potential to create communities of speakers along different, multiple, and intersecting axes of belonging, communities of rememberers yet-to-come.

CHAPTER THREE

Lending an Ear
to the Silence Phrase

Holocaust Writing of the Differend

It takes a poet to describe it, I don't have the words.

> —ABA BEER, Holocaust survivor

La réalité a souvent besoin d'invention, pour devenir vrai. C'est-t-à
dire vraisemblable.

> —JORGE SEMPRÚN, *L'écriture ou la vie*

The disaster, unexperienced. It is what escapes the very possibility of
experience—it is the limit of writing. . . . Which does not mean that
the disaster, as the force of writing, is beyond the pale of writing or
extratextual.

> —MAURICE BLANCHOT, *The Writing of the Disaster*

WRITING THE *DIFFEREND*: THE MEMORY PHRASE
"REMEMBER!"[1]

At least since the broadcast of the contentious TV miniseries *Holocaust* in 1978, a number of Holocaust testimonials were labeled "con-
troversial" because of the challenge they posed to the established
boundaries between creditable responses to the atrocities and "mere"
aesthetic productions. Contentious representations of the Holocaust
included Art Spiegelman's comic book *Maus*, Binjamin Wilkomirski
alias Bruno Doesseker's fake Holocaust memoir *Fragments: Memories of a Wartime Childhood*, Norman Finkelstein's polemical study
The Holocaust Industry, Roberto Benigni's Oscar-winning film *Life
Is Beautiful*, Peter Eisenmann's *Memorial to the Murdered Jews of
Europe* in Berlin, and the art exhibit *Mirroring Evil: Nazi Imagery/
Recent Art* at the Jewish Museum in New York, among others.[2] The

controversies surrounding these works gave rise to lengthy debates, in both academia and the popular media, signaling a crisis in the realm of Holocaust memorialization. What these debates also revealed, however, was a problematic relation between ethics and aesthetics in a diverse body of works subsumed under the category of Holocaust representations. As such, they laid bare a need for a new idiom in which to express these works' intertwined yet contradictory claims: of commemorating the dead and working through the traumatic past, on the one hand, and providing aesthetic pleasure on the other.

Despite the pronouncements about the "unspeakability" of the Holocaust experience, the testimonial imperative that has inspired Holocaust literature over the last few decades has been animated by a hope that the survivor's tale can be shared, indeed, translated and retranslated into a common idiom that carries the message "Remember!" Yet the disputes over the different modes of remembering the Holocaust have been acrimonious. Indeed, one "has a feeling" that these conflicts cannot be resolved in the common language of the injunction to remember. French philosopher Jean-François Lyotard bids us to heed such feelings because they often signal that something cannot be phrased in the language that is currently available; an intractable remainder resists the efforts to share the Holocaust story. Lyotard, let us recall, insists that the task of "thought" today is to bear witness to the *differend*, whether it is expressed in the form of a philosophical inquiry, a literary work, or a work of art. Lyotard defines the *differend* as a conflict that cannot be equitably resolved because no rule exists to which both claimants could appeal when seeking a just solution. As a result, either one or both parties in the conflict suffer injustice, without hope for restitution; they feel victimized because they are deprived of a language in which they could express their grievance. Under the current rules of language, their case has become literally "unspeakable."

Lyotard was prompted to write *The Differend* in response to Robert Faurisson's spurious claims about the nonexistence of gas chambers, which the Holocaust denier supported with scientific data and archival research. According to Lyotard, Holocaust survivors were victimized by the demand from Faurisson and his cohorts that they provide a scientific proof for the mass extermination of the Jews. Hence, in a lecture "Discussions or Phrasing 'After Auschwitz,'" Lyotard (1992) proposed that the task for philosophy in the post-Holocaust era was to "link" to the name "Auschwitz" in novel ways, that is, to search for idioms other than those that are governed by the rules of scientific knowledge (364). These innovative genres of discourse would allow the injustice to be articulated and the memory of "Auschwitz" as "the most real of events" to be preserved.[3]

The conflicts between different ways of representing the Holocaust indicate that a multitude of *"differends"* arise within what can be called the Holocaust genre of discourse. Lyotard (1988) defines genres of discourse as ways to "link together heterogeneous phrases, rules that are proper for attaining certain goals: to know, to teach, to be just, to seduce, to justify, to evaluate, to rouse emotion, to oversee" (xii). The Holocaust genre of discourse is animated by the obligation to remember the atrocities of the Shoah for the sake of the future, as expressed in the imperative "Remember!" Using Lyotard's language, I will refer to this crucial phrase, repeatedly evoked in Holocaust testimonials, as the "memory phrase." For Lyotard, each phrase is constituted in conformity with certain rules or regimens, depending on whether its purpose is to describe, to question, to show, to order, and so forth. Under this definition, the memory phrase, grammatically a mood expressing a command, is unique in its peremptory demand to remember.

According to Lyotard, in order to constitute itself as a unified genre that can fulfill its specific purpose, a genre of discourse must suppress unresolvable conflicts that inhere in its structures. Analogously, the unity of the Holocaust genre of discourse can be maintained only by concealing the gaps that open up within it. Specifically, this chapter focuses on the *differend* between the contradictory claims of ethics and aesthetics in Holocaust literary, artistic, and philosophical testimonials, that is, a conflict between the piety of memory and the iconoclastic impetus of art called upon to convey that memory. The works that belong to the Holocaust genre of discourse, guided by the memory phrase "Remember!" are determined by the tension between these two imperatives. Subsequently, a Holocaust scholar today, as well as anyone wishing to remember the Holocaust for the sake of the future, is confronted with the task of bearing witness to that *differend.*

Lyotard's forays into philosophy involve continuous negotiations in the border zone between ethics and aesthetics, where he continuously redraws their respective territories. Yet Lyotard's critics accuse him of collapsing distinctions between ethics and aesthetics, and between politics and art. Allen Dunn, for instance, objects to what he sees as a contradiction inherent in Lyotard's articulation of the *differend*: it stands for both an ethical call for justice and an aesthetic celebration of heterogeneity.[4] Such criticisms, however, ignore Levinasian inflections of Lyotard's take on aesthetics, that is, his efforts to give voice to what cannot be heard under the current rules of language. In the context of debates about the limits of representation and the politics of Holocaust memory, Lyotard's central concept of the sublime, the term derived from traditional aesthetics, remains relevant exactly in so far as it has informed his formulation of the *differend*, arguably an ethical and political concept.

The thought of the sublime informs many of Lyotard's texts.[5] Starting with Kant's definition in *Critique of Judgment*, where the sublime already serves as a bridge between aesthetics and ethics, Lyotard reads the sublime over and against Kant, as the moment which upsets the architectonics of the human mind and fractures the unity of the transcendental subject instead of grounding it, as was the German philosopher's claim. The sublime arises when the subject attempts to represent either infinitely great objects, such as a raging ocean or a mountain range (mathematical sublime), or ideas of reason, such as humanity, unity, or freedom (dynamical sublime). The experience of the sublime then results from imagination's failure to provide a representation corresponding to the idea. Stretched to its limits, imagination "plunges into the abyss," and it can do no more than signal its failure to present what exceeds its capacity as the faculty of presentation. This signal comes as a shock, "the feeling of a momentary checking of vital powers" (Kant 1951, 82) and erupts in the sensation of simultaneous pleasure and pain: the distress of imagination's sacrifice and the satisfaction of having gestured, even if only in a negative fashion, toward the higher realm of the suprasensible. This sensation of imagination striking against its limit never becomes present to a perceiving mind. As such, the sublime cannot be experienced as a moment in the temporal continuum, to be retained in memory or anticipated in the future. Impossible to recover in representation, the sublime "cracks open . . . a framework placed over the manifold [of sense impressions]," eluding imagination's effort to conceptualize this experience (Lyotard 1990a, 32).

What Lyotard emphasises in his postmodern rereading of Kant, however, is not the paradox of negative presentation, that is, the presentation of the unpresentable as such, but the experience of bearing witness to the intensity of feeling when the *event* of presentation, of

mind putting into shape, is taking place. For Lyotard, Kant's evocation of the sublime betrays the nostalgia for the ineffable presence
(an organizing or unifying principle, such as God). By contrast, Lyotard's sublime departs from Kant's negative aesthetics, and it refers
to the presentation that the unpresentable *is*, that it is occurring. It
signals, through an indeterminate feeling, the minimal occurrence of
the question, Is it happening? (*Arrive-t-il?*), which stands for the very
event or rather "eventing" of presentation. Abandoning the fixity of
the beautiful form, the formlessness of the sublime yields an aesthetics of movement, in which the figure that stands for this experience
continuously eludes being captured in a determinate shape. Always
awaiting the future of possible presentation, however, it signals the
infinite possibility of figuring and imagining.

Drawing on English philosopher Edmund Burke's description of
the sublime as the sensation of overcoming the threat that nothing
will happen anymore, of which the fear of death is the uttermost expression, Lyotard argues that the sublime, as an affective testimony
to "Is it happening?" is an experience of warding off such terror. This
momentary feeling of astonishment and delight at being alive, however, is unpresentable and eludes consciousness. The occurrence of
"Is it happening?" is infinitely simple: that it happens, says Lyotard
(1992), precedes the cognitive question pertaining to what happens:
"Or rather, the question precedes itself. . . . The event happens as a
question mark 'before' the happening as a question" (197). Here, Lyotard argues for the primacy of affective certainty that something is
happening, over cognitive knowledge of the content of that event. In
Lyotard's reformulation, the sublime does not mark a transcendent
moment of unattainable elsewhere, but the *here and now* of the event,
signalled by the intensity of feeling.

In a later text, "L'inarticulé ou le différend même," Lyotard
(1990b) refers to the singular sensation of the sublime as an "affect
phrase." The affect phrase is inarticulate because it does not present
anything in terms of positive content, and its time is always the time
of the "now": "a feeling appears and disappears entirely at every instant . . . it is completely new each time" (202). This is why this feeling, which Jewish American painter Barnett Newman once called
"a sensation of time," poses a conundrum for memory: how *will* the
mind remember it? Lyotard (1990a) writes, "When the sublime is
'there' (where?), the mind is not there. As long as the mind is, there
is no sublime. This is a feeling that is incompatible with time, as is

'death'" (32). Yet it signals that something that exceeds consciousness has touched the mind and that, as such, it can be remembered. Thus what the memory phrase "Remember!" strives to present is a sensation that one is engaging with the past, and this feeling precedes the knowledge of what happened. This is not to dismiss the relevance of factual knowledge and thoughtful understanding but rather to underscore that it is this paradoxical affect that animates the desire to continue to understand and know in the first place. Thus already in Lyotard's writings on art it becomes apparent that the stakes he articulates in the concept of the postmodern sublime exceed the realm of aesthetics in order for the philosopher to explore thought's underlying imbrication in *aistheton*, that is, in sense perception and the materiality of the *here* and *now*.

A detailed examination of the passage from the sublime as the placeholder for the unpresentable (in Lyotard's essays on art) to the politicoethical concept of the *differend* (in *The Differend*) lies beyond the scope of this chapter. Let us note, however, that Lyotard elaborates the transition as well as the continuous intertwining between the two sets of concepts already in *Just Gaming* (*Au juste*, 1979). In that book, while engaging with Kant's theories of imagination, Lyotard responds to Jean-Loup Thébaud's questions about social justice. He argues that Kant's definition of aesthetic judgment, as that which allows for a free play of the faculties of the mind, opens up the possibility of "thinking outside of the concept and outside of the habit" (Lyotard 1985, 82) and thus resisting totalitarian conceptions of society. When, shortly after, Lyotard publishes *The Differend* in the politically laden context of emergent Holocaust denial in France, the idiom of the sublime comes to inform the notion of the *differend*, coined by Lyotard to communicate the ethical and political stakes of the paradoxes of unpresentability. The shift entails a change of focus from issues of representation in visual arts to representability as it bears upon acts of linguistic expression and their complicity in perpetrating social and political injustice, with the focus on the *differend*'s resistance to representation in language. Lyotard's examples of injustice range from Holocaust denial, the atrocities committed by the Stalinist regime, the demands for autonomy by the Martiniquans, to copyrights issues. Surprisingly, Lyotard himself does not reflect on the nature or underlying stakes of this transition from the sublime—an ostensibly aesthetic concept— to the *differend*; articulating it, however, allows us to foreground the philosopher's attempt to radically rethink the dynamic between aesthetics, ethics, and politics.

Importantly, in addition to his definition of the *differend* as an expression of the irresolvable conflict between incompatible claims, Lyotard (1988) argues that the term denotes "the unstable state and instant of language wherein something which must be able to be put into phrases cannot yet be" (13). This moment of language exerting itself to express what currently eludes it, which often signals a conflict between competing genres of discourse, becomes repressed when one genre of discourse, such as the cognitive genre (focused on statements of knowledge about the true and the false), prevails over the others that also struggle to make a claim. As a result, the fact that the utterance *is* taking place, the event of its arriving into speech, is obliterated. Thus genres of discourse are modes of forgetting that "it" happens as an event of language *here and now*, in the singularity and simplicity of its occurrence. The *differend* remains nevertheless, demanding that it be articulated, although the only link between the various incommensurables is "the silent feeling that signals that the *differend* remains to be listened to" (141). The proleptic "yet to be phrased" of the *differend*, currently signalled by silence, is what calls upon possible future utterances. The unpresentable of the *differend* signals the event of phrasing, that is, the astonishment that new phrases are taking place, even though there could have been "nothing." For Lyotard, then, it is the eventing of the phrases coming into speech that is unpresentable, and *not* (as, for instance, in Giorgio Agamben's reading of Lyotard) the referent of the phrases, such as "Auschwitz." In so far as "Auschwitz" is a paramount name that demands that we continue to phrase what is not presentable under the regimen of knowledge, "Auschwitz," for Lyotard, "is the most real of realities" (58).[6]

Lyotard pays special attention to the phrase that he calls "obligation," that is, to the utterance expressed in the form of a command or order. A command places emphasis on the addressee (who is obligated) while leaving unmarked the instance of the speaker (from whom the obligation issues), as in the sentence "Open the door!" In the "phrase of obligation," the speaking subject is situated in the position of a hostage to the voice that commands, and it is displaced from the privileged position of the originator of phrases. Obligation, according to Lyotard, is therefore a preeminently Jewish phrase, as witnessed in the injunction "Hear, Israel!" The Jews, as Lyotard (1990a) explains, after Levinas, are the community bound by the "law of listening, which cannot spare it the despair of never hearing what the voice says" (22). They are the people who bear witness to the commanding voice. To convey the sense of the absolute nature of this obligation, Lyotard (1988) quotes Levinas, from *Quatre lectures talmudiques*: "They act before they harken!" (111).[7] The imperative "Hear, Israel!" is empty of content, but the necessity of responding or a demand for further phrasing is already inscribed in it.

In light of this reading, it is no coincidence that the post-Holocaust attempts to express the wrong perpetrated on the Jewish victim have surfaced in the form of the obligation "Remember!" (*Zakhor!*), which has been referred to as the memory phrase. In the context of Lyotard's theory of phrases, we might ask, "What happens to 'Remember!' when it comes along?" Further, does the command "Remember!" make sense? Is it "meaningful?" (17) Within the Holocaust genre of discourse, the *differends* proliferate on the edges of the memory phrase, where we cannot formulate what it is exactly that we must remember or how we are to remember "it." What distinguishes the memory phrase from the "Jewish" phrase of obligation is that, while the command "Hear, Israel!" conceals the name of the divine addressor but designates the addressee as the people of Israel, the imperative "Remember!" leaves both instances unmarked.[8] Who is its addressee? Is the addressee singular or plural? Namely, is the event of memory always an individual and unshareable experience or, conversely, can it only truly take place if its content can be communicated to other members of a community of speakers? Although responding to a command is necessary because the phrasing of the command immediately presupposes a response or reaction, even if it were to be a negative or silent one, the addressee's choice of *how* to respond is unpredictable. Lyotard gives an example of a situation in which a command, which was intended as an obligation, misfires when it is interpreted within a different linguistic regimen: during a battle, the officer in command shouts "Avanti!" and jumps out of the trench, to which the soldiers reply "Bravo!" and do not move. Analogously, the addressee of "Remember!" can respond with "Well said!" a phrase that indicates approval yet does not result in an action, or with a dismissive "Why should I care?" which expresses indifference. Both of these utterances signal that the addressees do not consider the command to be incumbent on their subsequent utterances or actions: they have not listened, although they may have heard. A phrase is obligatory, Lyotard explains, only "if the addressee feels obligated" (108). Secondly, if the addressor instance of the obligation is unmarked and the speaker unknown, where is the phrase "Remember!" arriving from? Who bids me to never forget?

One can imagine the command to remember, for instance, to be a voice coming from a gas chamber. This is the voice that Polish poet Jerzy Ficowski, the author of a moving volume titled *A Reading of the Ashes*, imagined hearing when he read the testimony of Rudolf Reder, the survivor of the death camp in Bełżec. Reder overheard a child, who was being pushed into the gas chamber, cry out seven words: "Mommy! But I was good! Dark, dark!" For Ficowski (1981), those heart-wrenching, plaintive words impose an imperative to repeat them, and to let them resonate in his own poetic lamentation, "Seven Words":

> And one empty place is calling, calling
>
> You who aren't afraid of me
> Because I am little and I'm not even there
> Do not deny that I was
> Give me back the memory of me
> These post-Jewish words
> These post-human words
> Only those seven words.[9]

The seven words arrive from a site to which the poet is barred entrance: from the place of the child's unwitnessed death. In the poet's imagination, this place is absolutely "empty" because no physical traces exist of those who died in the gas chambers, and even their memory, like the record of the little boy's name, has been lost. This memory, Ficowski continues, "paled/not because of the horror/it has been paling for thirty years."[10] The poet cannot reconstitute this place in imagination, even if, by the impact it has on him and the power of the obligation commanded by the voice, he knows it to be the most real of places. This failure of imagination, however, is what animates his repeated attempts to speak about it and thus to continue to remember.

In Ficowski's example of the memory phrase "Remember!" the addressor has withdrawn, commanding the poet to speak precisely by this absence. If the abyss between the speaker and the addressee of the command is unbridgeable, the phrase "Remember!" signals the radical otherness of the voice that demands remembrance. Yet this

absence, this "emptiness," places a demand on the listener, the demand that is unconditional in the sense elaborated by Levinas, as developed in chapter one. Perhaps the most powerful expression of this
sense of undeclinable duty has been expressed in Primo Levi's (1993)
poem "Sh'ma" (written on January 10, 1946). The poem merits full
citation:

> You who live safe
> In your warm houses,
> You who find, returning in the evening,
> Hot food and friendly faces:
> > Consider if this is a man
> > Who works in the mud
> > Who does not know peace
> > Who fights for a scrap of bread
> > Who dies because of a yes or no.
> > Consider if this is a woman,
> > Without hair and without a name
> > With no more strength to remember,
> > Her eyes empty and her womb cold
> > Like a frog in winter.
> Meditate that this came about:
> I *commend* these words to you.
> Carve them in your hearts
> At home, in the street,
> Going to bed, rising;
> Repeat them to your children,
> > Or may your house fall apart,
> > May illness impede you,
> > May your children turn their faces from you. (11; italics mine)[11]

Primo Levi was a self-professed atheist, for whom reciting Dante or,
on the practical level, chemical formulas rather than the Hebrew Bible
brought a measure of solace during his ordeal in Auschwitz. Yet his
account is prefaced with a paraphrase of the Jewish prayer Sh'ma, in
which Jews are commanded absolute obedience to Lord their God lest
he "will close the heavens" and the people shall perish. Levi's version
of Sh'ma contains none of the promises of prosperity and renewal that
animate the original prayer. Unlike in the text of Deuteronomy 6:4–9,
which directly calls upon the wrath and the promise of the Lord, the
name of God is missing in Levi's rendition, while "a man who works
in the mud" and a woman "without hair and without a name" are
the disastrous remnants of God's once glorious creation. The command to never forget and to repeat the story to the children seems to

issue from those who have been deprived of voice and denied memory. This substitution of the divine voice is blasphemous, at once impossible and necessary. The phrase "I commend," which in the original prayer is pronounced by God, strikes terror in the reader's heart and underscores the absolute nature of the demand. As Lyotard points out, what we designate as "the absolute" means that it cannot be presented as such. Yet, as both Lyotard and Levi insist in very different contexts, it can be presented, that is, spoken about or responded to, in the utterances that follow the command. This response manifests itself in the repetition of "hundreds of thousand of stories" from the Holocaust, which Levi calls "the new Bible" (1993, 65–66). For him, the retelling of the story offers a measure of hope that humanity will continue, even if the essence of what it means to be a human being has been put into question. However, the addressee's failure to heed this new command threatens absolute rupture and the forbiddance of the future. When "your children turn their faces from you," worse than the wrath of God is the ultimate cessation of the events of language. Humanity is damned when there is no one who will link onto the survivor's phrase.

Although "Remember!" obligates us unconditionally and demands a response, determining the nature of that response is fraught with difficulties. The injunction is marked by indeterminacy, bidding "us" to engage in memory events without the criteria to determine what constitutes the adequate content of that memory or who is a competent rememberer, adequate to the task of witnessing. In the opening chapter of his much later reflection *The Drowned and the Saved*, Primo Levi (1988) makes an attempt to establish who has such authority to remember properly. He assures the reader that his own recollection is complete and "unaffected by drifting" (35), unlike the memories of the perpetrators and their descendents, who are prone to distort the past. Yet even Levi fails to convince us of the survivor's superior ability to remember and convey his memories to us truthfully. Earlier, in *Survival in Auschwitz* (written in 1946), Levi (1993) remarks, for instance, that "many things were then said and done among us: but of these it is better that there remain no memory" (16). In *The Drowned and the Saved*, he confesses that those who do have that authority, the "complete witnesses," have all "drowned," and his own testimony is thus only writing "by proxy" (84). Overall, Levi's formulations suggest that to bear witness to "Remember!" we must respect the indeterminacy and alterity of the voice that bids us to

remember, a voice that issues from the place that cannot ʟ
in familiar categories. If this is the case, no one, not even a sᴜ
vested with the absolute authority to prescribe it or to judge ᴜ
stance of someone else's memory. Of course, many of us makᴇ
claims, especially those who teach and write in the area of Holocᴀ
studies, because we often consider ourselves to be the appointed guardians of Holocaust memory. Lyotard, however, speaking of Lanzmann's
Shoah, cautions against "granting oneself the authority to speak"
because it often means the silencing of those "who are claimed not to
have the authority to speak about it" (Carroll 1990, x).

Lyotard explains, in *The Differend*, that each utterance discloses
its own "phrase universe," which, apart from the addressor and the
addressee, also contains the sense of the sentence (its meaning) and
the referent (that which the utterance is about). Yet what exactly is the
referent of "Remember!"? The reality that this phrase designates is
not signified in the phrase, but this radical obliteration of the referent
demands that the command be followed by descriptions, by endless
recitations of "I will never forget this or that . . . ," as in Elie Wiesel's
(1982) famous passage from *Night*:

> Never shall I forget that night, the first night in camp, which has
> turned my life into one long night, seven times cursed and seven
> times sealed. Never shall I forget that smoke. Never shall I forget the
> little faces of the children, whose bodies I saw turned into wreaths of
> smoke beneath a silent blue sky.
>   Never shall I forget those flames which consumed my faith forever.
>   Never shall I forget that nocturnal silence which deprived me, for
> all eternity, of the desire to live. Never shall I forget those moments
> that murdered my God and my soul and turned my dreams to dust.
> Never shall I forget these things, even if I am condemned to live as
> God Himself. Never. (32)

By conjuring this terrifying image, Wiesel pledges remembrance to the
children whose murder he witnessed upon his arrival in Auschwitz.
To convey the impossibility of adequately describing this experience,
however, he evokes the biblical significance of the number seven and
expresses his homage to the burning children in terms of his relation
with God.[12] Just as the children were being burnt, these images are
now scorched into the writer's memory, and his own description is
like a seal that will "sear" them, to recall Levi's version of Sh'ma, in
the reader's mind. But grafting images onto the empty site of the children's death also betrays that memory; they can only be an imperfect

and iconoclastic semblance. Lyotard (1988) writes, "Impertinence is to link onto the command by a commentary on a command, and not by its execution" (85). A poetic image is a form of commentary, and in that sense, Wiesel himself is "impertinent," albeit his "betrayal" is a necessary one since "one must, in any case, speak (*dire*)" (Lyotard 1992, 364).

The incommensurability between "Remember!" and "factual" knowl-edge about the Holocaust is inevitable, since we can only ap-proximate many of these facts in "fearful imagination," to use Hannah Arendt's (1958, 441) apt expression. Still, the possibilities of respond-ing to the imperative "Remember!" are innumerable. In the context of Holo-caust memory, therefore, the predominance of the cognitive genre conceals the conflict between factual knowledge and the ethi-cal imperative to remember, perpetrating the erasure of the *differend*, especially when a survivor cannot procure an empirical proof of his ordeal or when she remembers it inaccurately. We can argue there-fore that when knowledge claims decide what constitutes acceptable Holocaust testimony, the phrase "Remember!" will be factually legiti-mated, but it will vanish as a phrase of obligation.[13] History, under-stood as the genre of cognitives, the depository of things remembered, forgets the very happening of the memory event and the moment of its transmission. In a way, this process of forgetting is necessary, so that a historian can continue narrating. As shown in various post-Holocaust contexts, however, factual historical accounts enter into a conflict with the ethical imperative to remember, and Lyotard cites the case of the French historian Pierre Vidal-Naquet, who wants to refute Faurisson's false claims by using the traditional tools of his discipline.

Although Lyotard's reference to Vidal-Naquet is only cursory, his comment merits further inquiry into the French historian's dilemma. In *Assassins of Memory*, Vidal-Naquet (1992) juxtaposes his own irrefutable knowledge of Holocaust facts with the denier's dubious justifications, which he says can only be compared to the claim that "the moon is made of Roquefort cheese" (xxiv), thus reducing the op-ponent's argument *ad absurdum*. Yet in the course of the book, just as Levi's claim to "absolute memory" was undermined by his own observations on the nature of memory, the French historian is forced to question his ability to provide the necessary proof. Vidal-Naquet vacillates in his response to the denier because, on his own confes-sion, as a Jew, he is also motivated by a desire for vengeance, the ob-jective that contravenes basic principles of the cognitive genre. Here he quotes Chateaubriand's famous pronouncement that the historian is "charged with avenging the people." Although in the preface Vidal-Naquet states confidently that "what is at stake here is not feeling but truth" (xxiv), he later confesses that he has been guided by the feeling of vengeance and an ethical obligation to the dead rather than the task to establish historical facts. As a result of this contradiction, the historian ends up with a sense of failure in carrying out his duty. In the last essay of the book, whose tenor differs considerably from the confident statements in the opening chapters, Vidal-Naquet refers to his own work as "a melancholic essay" and, in lieu of a factual conclusion, cites in full the text of a tango by an Argentine poet, whose verses are chilling to a reader who has trusted Vidal-Naquet's former assurances about the infallibility of knowledge:

> This world was and always will be a sty
> A jackass the same as
> A great professor
> There is neither punishment nor reward . . .
> It is all the same . . .
> The one who kills, the one who cures. (142)

The historian sets out to rescue the memory of the victims from the infamy of the Holocaust denier's "war against memory" (Primo Levi's phrase; 1988, 31). He ends up, however, in the position of a victim, that is, in Lyotard's (1988) terms, as someone who seeks to express a grievance but "is divested of the means to argue" (9). Vidal-Naquet's initial allegiance to the regime of historical truth gives way to what can only be described as relativism, tinged with melancholy. However, the historian's predicament corroborates Lyotard's thesis that the feeling, "the silent phrase," must be heeded. As if in an effort to come to Vidal-Naquet's aid, Lyotard (1988) argues that "a historian pleading for the trial's revision will be able to object at great length that the crime has not been established in its quantity. But the silence imposed on knowledge [the silence into which the historian collapses in the end of his book] does not impose the silence of forgetting, it imposes a feeling" (56). This silence is a sign that something is happening that cannot be articulated within the discourse of history. Silence, for Lyotard, is also a phrase that demands further linkages: "There is no non-phrase. Silence is a phrase. There is no last phrase" (xii). In order for a historian to become attentive to the silence coming from the place where the victims' suffering went unwitnessed, he or she must "break with the monopoly over history granted to the cognitive regimen of phrases, and he or she must venture forth by lending his or her ear to what is not presentable under the rules of knowledge" (57).

Holocaust literature frequently illustrates preponderate silence imposed on the survivor's phrase. For example, in Ida Fink's (1996) dramatic piece "The Table," a prosecutor is trying to establish the truth about an *Aktion* in a small-town ghetto during which twelve hundred Jews were murdered. He solicits corroborative evidence, required to bring the murderers to justice before the law. The eyewitnesses' accounts during the interrogation, however, are inconsistent, even contradictory, and it becomes frustratingly obvious that no positive proof of the crime will ever be established. Instead of proof, the witnesses offer descriptive judgments:

Witness:	"The square was black with people"
Prosecutor:	"'The square was black with people' is not completely accurate."
Witness:	"It was a sunny, cold day. There was snow in the streets. The snow was red."
Another witness:	"Oh, you want proof, don't you? The snow on the town's streets was red. Red! Does that satisfy you?"
Prosecutor:	"Unfortunately, Mr. Zachwacki, snow does not constitute proof for judges, especially snow that melted twenty-five years ago." (141, 149, 156)[14]What really matters—the nightmare of the selection process and the enormity of the crimes, as the result of which the entire Jewish population of the town perished—cannot be ascertained. The traumatic experience is signalled, however, by the silences that cloak the prosecutor's frustration and the witnesses' anguish as they desire to procure the evidence of the crime. This feeling or "an affect phrase," which is inadmissible under the rules that constitute the genre of history, resists the hegemony of knowledge phrases and calls for another way to express the wrong.

THE SILENCE PHRASE

As mentioned above, Lyotard's book was largely a response to the silence of Holocaust survivors and their inability to prove the wrong they had suffered vis-à-vis the Holocaust denier. Lyotard writes that the *differend* is surrounded by silence, although silence is also a phrase in which one or more instances—addressor, addressee, sense, or referent—have been muted. Silence in place of a sentence could mean the addressors' inability to speak, due to their lack of authority to do so or an external constraint that prevents them from speaking, or it could signal language's failure to communicate the meaning of the event. It could also indicate the nonexistence of the referent, that is, of the object to which the phrase is referring, and this is how a Holocaust denier chooses to interpret a survivor's silence. Finally, it may suggest the addressee's lack of authority or, as in the case of German philosopher Martin Heidegger's inexcusable silence about the Holocaust, his incapacity to listen. Here, Lyotard (1990a) condemns Heidegger's "mute, leaden silence that lets nothing be heard" (52), which stifles the imperative to render historical justice to the victims. In each case, however, silence is not a cessation of speech but a relation of speech, a sign that further phrasing is necessary.

The theme of silence in the wake of the Shoah, the strife between speech and silence in testimonies, and the challenge of rendering traumatic events in language, have long been central to discussions about Holocaust representation. Lyotard insists that, to find an idiom to express the wrong suffered by the victims—an injustice that has deprived the survivors of the means to express their suffering—the negations bearing upon their stunted phrases have to be withdrawn, in the utterances issuing from "us." The survivors' speech arrives from the abyss of silence, where language was threatened with absolute cessation, yet it delivers these silences to us, the commentators, historians, teachers, members of the public at commemorative ceremonies, who speak about them. Our commitment to listen to that silence stems from the ethical imperative to remember. We often overlook, however, that silence is also a powerful *rhetorical* figure, the figure of the sublime, as ancient rhetorician Longinus already knew when he was writing *Peri Hypsous*,[15] and this aesthetic dimension often lends force to that compelling silence.

An example we may recall from the previous chapter is the barber shop episode in Lanzmann's interview with Abraham Bomba in *Shoah*.[16] To reiterate, Bomba gives a lengthy account of his gruesome task of cutting women's hair before they were gassed. The description continues in a dispassionate tone of voice, until he recalls the day when the women from his home town of Częstochowa entered the gas chamber. At that moment, Bomba breaks down, and the viewer is subjected to several minutes of agonizing silence. As LaCapra (2007b) points out, this "Beckettian" sequence, while being perhaps the most distressing to watch, is also the most carefully staged one in the film (220). It is shot in a barbershop in Tel Aviv, in which Bomba continued to work as a barber after the war (although he retired years before the interview). Bomba is then asked to "play himself," to reenact his gestures from "back then." The theatrical effect of the episode is enhanced by the presence of mirrors, which, reminiscent of the famous mirror episode in Orson Wells' *Citizen Kane*, cast multiple reflections of the participants. For LaCapra, this elaborate staging, dissimulated before the camera, poses a major difficulty in discussing *Shoah* as a "fiction of the real" because "in it survivors both *play* and are themselves. Any boundary between art and life collapses at the point trauma is relived, for when the survivor-actor breaks down, the frame distinguishing art from life also breaks down and reality erupts on stage or film" (220).[17] In the text of the screenplay Bomba's protracted silence is transcribed by ellipses: "A friend of mine worked as a barber—he was a good barber in my hometown—when his wife and sister came into the gas chamber . . ." (Lanzmann 1995, 107). Within the film's aesthetics, the hiatus in the interview with Bomba can be read as the culmination of Lanzmann's antimimetic strategy. Yet as LaCapra notes, this radical disruption in the film's already fragmented narrative also marks the collapse of the distinction between "art" and "life," between the aesthetic exigencies of this staged drama and the moral imperative to bear witness. The viewer is forced to voyeuristically participate in the breakdown of Bomba's theatrical mask, reflected in the crumbling of his carefully composed and inexpressive facial features, and the shattering of his crafted, accented English.

A very different example from the history of Holocaust cinema is a scene in Polish director Andrzej Wajda's *Korczak* (1990). The film tells the story of the renowned Polish Jewish teacher, children's right advocate, and paediatrician Janusz Korczak (born Henryk Goldszmit), who perished in Treblinka together with his wards from the Jewish orphanage in Warsaw. According to the legend, conveyed in the film, Korczak chose to accompany the children to the gas chambers of Treblinka, although he had had numerous offers of assistance to escape to the Aryan side. Toward the end of the film, following a sequence when the children from the Warsaw ghetto orphanage board a cattle train at the *Umschlagplatz*, an empty frame runs for several seconds—nothing but the grainy surface of the screen. During this unconventional cinematic pause, the film seems to hesitate as to how to continue the narrative. Eventually, instead of arriving in Treblinka, the children are shown jumping off the train in slow motion and running across a meadow behind the banner with the logo of the orphanage, a four-leaf clover on one side and the Star of David on the other. Wajda's allegorical rendition of the finale of the Korczak story provoked controversies, with Lanzmann striking a particularly condemnatory note.[18] As film critic Terri Ginsberg argues, the vociferous debates about *Korczak* reflected conflicted ideological positions that dominated the political climate at the time of the film's release (at the cusp of the collapse of the Soviet empire), and they were shaped by quarrels about the function of Holocaust memory in those political contexts. Ginsberg, however, finds the critics, on all sides of the discussion, equally guilty of inattention to the film's "phenomenological aesthetics," that is, its techniques of staging the events of memory. In support of Ginsberg's interpretation, it can be argued that the "silence" of the film's empty frames foregrounds the disjunction between its lyrical poetics and the moral imperative to remember the deaths of Korczak's children. Yet the disconcerting feeling caused by the empty cadres, an unusual filmic device, which signals a threat of nothing to see and nothing to hear, summons in the viewers of the film the memory phrase "Remember!"

In print, such silences are usually marked with ellipses, and many Holocaust memoirs are punctuated with this unique stylistic device, repeatedly suggesting a momentary termination of speech. In diaries written in the midst of horror, which were published after the war but whose authors perished, sometimes without a trace, the ellipses indicate the missing pages or the sentences broken off in the middle, and many Holocaust diaries end haltingly that way. Dawid Rubinowicz, for instance, was twelve when, on March 21, 1940, he began recording the events in his Nazi occupied village of Krajno. His diary stops in midsentence, in the entry on June 1, 1942, and we can surmise that the author was suddenly interrupted and then prevented from returning to complete the sentence. Rubinowicz (1981) writes,

> When the two women caught sight of the Germans they began to flee, but were overtaken and arrested. They intended shooting them on the spot in the village, but the mayor wouldn't allow it. They then went into the woods and shot them there. The Jewish police immediately went there to bury them in the cemetery. When the cart returned it was full of blood. Who . . . (87)

In another example, Petr Ginz, who, at fourteen years of age had already demonstrated his talents as a writer, poet, newspaper editor, and painter, kept a diary until two months before he was deported to Theresienstadt (Terezin). Following a terse report, dated July 1, 1942, that Ginz's grandmother received "the summons to the transport" (Pressburger 2007, 154), the diary ends with two "empty" entries: "28.VII. 1942–1. VIII. 1942: *no entries* [editor's note]; 5. VIII. 1942—7. VIII. 42: *nothing written* [editor's note]." The handwritten dates signal the author's intention to fill the empty pages in the future and his hesitation over the blank pages, although he never committed the intended words to the page. We know now, however, that in Theresienstadt, Petr continued to write poems and to paint, and he edited the weekly magazine *Veden*, written by a group of boys who lived with him in the same house in the camp, the documents that were recovered and later deposited at Yad Vashem.[19] In 1944 Ginz was trans-ported to Auschwitz, where he perished.

On the other hand, unlike in edited diaries, in memoirs written after the war, the silences in the form of ellipses are inscribed purposefully by the author. Leitner (1978), for instance, in *Fragments of Isabella*, suspends her narrative with ellipses numerous times. In one of the opening chapters, she writes: "Yesterday . . . yesterday, May 29, 1944, we were deported" (13). Through the simple use of ellipses, she conveys both the unbridgeable gulf that separates the "yesterday" of Auschwitz from the "yesterdays" of her postwar chronology *and* the crushing proximity of that memory, which continues to cleave all of her seemingly normal, present "yesterdays." Further in the book, she recalls how she and her sisters were hiding in a barn after their escape from the death transport, and they were nearly discovered by a Nazi soldier. She wonders, "What happened? Was the wind blowing our scent away from the dog? We are not dead. There is no bullet in our chests. . . . We are alive. . . . He [the SS officer] is gone" (80). Here, the dots qualify the sensation expressed in the simple statement "We are not dead," and they mark the temporal abyss that separated, in the space of a few minutes, the certainty of imminent death and the moment of yet another reprieve. Similarly, although Vidal-Naquet's (1992) "Holocaust genre of discourse" is very different from Leitner's, the historian also uses ellipses in the perplexing last chapter of his book. He writes, for instance, "No need to name them [those who maintain the quasimonopolistic hold on memory], the reference will be understood. As for the rest . . ." (140). In stark contrast to his pronouncements in the preface, Vidal-Naquet's refutation of Faurisson trails off into uncertainty in the concluding sentence of the book: "Will truth have the last word? How one would like to be sure of it . . ." (142).

Another deliberate stylistic inscription of silence is the use of parataxis, the rhetorical device of placing related clauses and phrases in a sentence without the use of connecting words, and when the clauses are linked, a comma or a coordinate conjunction (such as "and") is used, instead of a more complex syntactical construction. The use of parataxis, especially in the literary descriptions of the Nazi camps, serves to communicate a sense of disjunction and chaos, as if all the causal links, which normally give us a sense of order and coherence, had become inadequate or failed. For example, in his semibiographical short story "This Way for the Gas, Ladies and Gentlemen," Polish writer Tadeusz Borowski (1976) opens with a paragraph that grammatically conveys this sense of dispersion:

> All of us walk around naked. The delousing is finally over, and our striped suits are back from the tanks of Cyclone B solution, an efficient killer of lice in clothing and men in gas chambers. Only the inmates in the blocks cut off from ours by the "Spanish goats" still have nothing to wear. But all the same, all of us walk around naked: the heat is unbearable. The camp has been sealed off tight. (29)

The story proceeds in these short, fragmented segments for twenty-one pages, without a single subordinate conjunction that would bring a semblance of cohesion to the narrative. Similarly, Charlotte Delbo (1995) begins her harrowing account in *Auschwitz and After* with a series of disjointed sentences, as in the following excerpt:

> People arrive. They look through the crowd of those who are waiting, those who await them. They kiss them and say the trip exhausted them.
> People leave. They say good-bye to those who are not leaving and hug the children.

> There is a street for people who arrive and a street for people
> who leave.
> There is a café called "Arrivals" and a café called
> "Departures."
> There are people who arrive and people who leave. (3)

As if strewn around on the page in panicked disarray, the con-
fusing (and confused) sentences exude the sense of chaos and incomprehension experienced by the inmates who have just disem-
barked from a transport.

As Lyotard (1988) remarks, referring to Erich Auerbach's
famous comparison between the Greek and the Hebrew styles of
writing,[20] parataxis connotes the abyss of "not-being" that opens
between phrases. Parataxis is "the conjunction that most allows
the constitutive discontinuity (or oblivion)" (67). In the context
of Holocaust literature, it is often those simple, usually unnoticed
rhetorical devices that bring us to the brink of that abyss. In the
course of the reading, we are shocked, surprised, but also re-
lieved that *it* is being said, even if there could have been nothing: no story, no words, no traces left. Ellipses and parataxis in
Holocaust testimonials are then the simplest rhetorical figures
of silence. They convey what Lyotard refers to as "the sublime,"
that is, the minimal occurrence of "Is it happening?" the event
of memory as it is taking shape in each instance of reading and
writing.

IN DEFENCE OF THE SUBLIME: BETWEEN ETHICS
AND AESTHETICS

Lyotard diagnoses, as did others before and after him, the impossibility of aesthetics "after Auschwitz." Importantly, however, he
urges us to acknowledge that art persists nevertheless. While it
is dead as a mere expression of beauty and the source of aesthetic pleasure, it continues in its capacity to deliver the "nothing" of the event. The task of the artist is to bear witness to this
gesture of art, to the event that signals its own unpresentability
but also its endless desire to imagine. For decades, the events of
the Holocaust were evoked as the paradigmatic unpresentable.
Unsurprisingly then, their representations have yielded themselves to analyses in terms of the sublime, defined by Kant as

negative presentation.[21] As Geoffrey Hartman, for instance, has argued, Holocaust representations are not only infinitely inadequate to the horror and the extent of suffering, they also underscore our inability to conceptualize what happened, even if we must concede that, since what happened was perpetrated by rational human beings, it must be conceivable. Hartman credits Lyotard for having the courage to "save" aesthetics "after Auschwitz," especially considering the Nazi effort to aestheticize politics, which ultimately led to the degradation of aesthetics. Hartman emphasizes the ethical and political significance of Lyotard's aesthetics, since it offers a challenge to the destructive impact of the fascist conception of *Kunstwerk* on post-Holocaust culture. In Hartman's view, Lyotard's recourse to the sublime was intended to demonstrate the price "humanity" has paid for its desire for stability and unity, achieved at the cost of eliminating difference and dissent.

In recent years, however, critics have targeted the evocations of the sublime in reference to the Holocaust, focusing on the dangers of negative presentation, that is, the failure of imagination to "present the unpresentable." LaCapra (2004), for instance, views Lyotard as the proponent of the "transcendent sublime," which, by displacing a theological frame of reference, can only emphasize lack, loss, and unknowability. LaCapra cautions that, in Holocaust contexts in particular, such fixation on a displaced, unattainable absolute prohibits constructive processes of working through trauma. In his more recent work on the relation between the discourse of history and the transmission of trauma, LaCapra (2007a) returns to the sublime to caution against converting historical trauma into a celebration of ecstatic excess that offers a given social group "a quasi-transcendental entry into the extraordinary" at the cost of the historical anchoring of the event (167).[22] In *Remnants of Auschwitz*, Agamben (1999) argues, specifically targeting Lyotard's use of the sublime, that insisting on the unrepresentability and unspeakability of the Holocaust "contributes to its glory" (33). To cast Auschwitz beyond the pale of language is to make it wondrous, and thus to unwittingly sanctify the destruction. As a result, the evocations of the inexpressibility of Holocaust suffering have become mere ritualistic clichés, often recited during commemorative ceremonies. Such repetitions, warns Agamben, release us from the duty to strive to understand what happened. Complacent representations of the Holocaust, however, are also what troubles Lyotard, although his concern is not merely that they prompt us to abdicate the duty to know but that they do not move us anymore, while feelings, intense feelings, which he associates with the sublime, compel us to search for new idioms to express them.[23] Thus, contrary to Agamben's assertions, Lyotard's objective is not to enshrine the Holocaust as an incomprehensible event but to insist on the need to search for innovative ways to express what happened.[24] In that sense, rather than being fettered to the unspeakable that stunts our desire to know, bearing witness to the unpresentable of the *differend* is an injunction to speak: to find new significations and linguistic competences, that is, new "ways of phrasing the wrong that a victim has incurred, and that inhabits the victim's overall power of doing things with words" (Gasché 2007, 296). The memory phrase, after all, is an attempt to link onto the shocked silence, onto the speech that was annihilated by horror, and it affirms that the mind has not capitulated in confrontation with the abyss. Thus, as Holocaust testimonials have repeatedly illustrated, without being moved by this "feeling," without the desire to imagine what we cannot grasp in imagination, *we may not feel the need to know and to understand in the first place.*

In "The Unspeakable," Thomas Trezise (2001) explores the polysemy of the term, and he urges Holocaust scholars to distinguish between its different senses. Firstly, "the unspeakable" can connote "unsayability" in a linguistic and cognitive sense, insofar as this traumatic historical event exceeds the verbal means at our disposal (39). The second sense is mainly ethical, conveying a claim that a given act is so morally repugnant that it falls outside existing normative frameworks. The unspeakable acquires yet another signification when it is placed within a sacralized framework, outside the sphere of the profane, whereby it cannot or ought not to be spoken about. What traverses these three most common uses of the unspeakable, however, is that they all conflate a cognitive (factual) claim about the impossibility of presenting the object and a normative claim that invokes a prescription against presentation. This failure to distinguish between the two discursive regimens prevents us from recognizing to what extent the linguistic medium, that is, a prevailing representational consensus, as well as dominant cognitive categories and normative frameworks have "been disrupted and altered by the Holocaust as an event" (41). As Trezise also suggests, the rejection of the unspeakable disregards the question of "who speaks": namely, it is a form of censoring and silencing the survivor for whom this evocation is a complex rhetorical device, perhaps serving as a protective shield in a psychoanalytic sense. This leads Trezise to conclude that, while the dogma of unspeakability in a cognitive sense must be rejected because it amounts to an abdication of the duty to learn and understand (as is also Agamben's point), what remains and what emanates from the survivors' evocations is exactly the ethical claim that we listen, or, in Lyotard's idiom, that we "lend an ear" to what still remains to be phrased.

Guided by Lyotard, I would argue that Holocaust art and literature, as well as the debates that surround them, must acknowledge and pursue both "the pain of silence and the pleasure of invention," the affective paradox of the sublime. It is this ambivalent sensation that announces what is unpresentable, that is, the advent of the memory event. In bearing witness to the *differends* surrounding "Remember!" this event ungrounds both ethics and aesthetics, and it radically displaces their respective domains. For instance, Wiesel's graphic description of little children being murdered does not merely move us as a horrific fact. It compels us to remember because it is an incantation, a dirge whose rhythm, complemented by the rhythm of our reading, probes the immeasurable depths of grief. Admittedly, Wiesel himself draws a line between "truthful" accounts (such as autobiographical *Night*) and fictional representations, shuddering at the thought that the Holocaust experience might become aestheticized through literary means and he himself might become "a peddler of agony."[25] In his essay "First Royalties," for instance, Wiesel describes a storytelling contest organized in Auschwitz by a kapo, the winning prize of which was two bowls of soup. Young Wiesel won the contest with a story describing a sumptuous Shabbat meal he supposedly had just eaten. As he confesses to the readers, he was unable to enjoy his hard-won meal: "And nausea welled inside me, uncontrollable, overwhelming. I had the oppressive feeling that it was my story itself I was swallowing" (Wiesel 1971,

85). Wiesel's tale is a compelling allegory of ethical dilemmas involved in aestheticizing suffering. And yet perhaps this "nausea" is also a signal that the *differend* between the aesthetic and the ethical is occurring, and that it demands to be accounted for. This also means that heeding the duty to pass on the tale always involves negotiations between the ethical injunction to remember and aesthetic demands that are indispensable in order to convey that injunction.[26]

Rhetorical and aesthetic considerations continue to be downplayed in the debates on post-Holocaust memory, echoing Emmanuel Levinas's (1969) pronouncements that "the games of art" are injurious to ethics (347). The suppression of aesthetics in commentaries on Holocaust literature and art occurs in the name of the ethical injunction to remember. This ethical imperative is often insisted on, moreover, by survivors who rightfully demand that their difficult stories be heard by secondary witnesses, and that they reverberate, as Levinas wrote, "into eternity," as a warning for future generations. During a public interview with second-generation artist Lily Markiewicz (2002), for instance, Holocaust survivor Helena Jockel intervenes as follows: "What I demand from the artists: to engage in it. . . . What I think is, these people who survived, who have some guilt, should promise to work, to preach, to acknowledge their guilt in some way" (34–35). For Jockel, heeding the ethical imperative is the ultimate guarantee of Holocaust memory, rather than Markiewicz's use of innovative artistic techniques.[27] And yet, in a private conversation on a different occasion, in response to my expression of ambivalence regarding Benigni's "comic" treatment of the Holocaust in his film *Life Is Beautiful*, she commented, "Finally something beautiful has come out of that horror!" Here Jockel's endorsement of Benigni's unortho-dox Holocaust aesthetics echoes Aharon Appelfeld's dictum "Only art has the power of redeeming suffering from the abyss" (quoted in Kaplan 2007, 1). Bearing witness to the conflict between ethical and aesthetic phrases, between the demand for responsible witnessing and the need for "something beautiful," allows us to discuss, teach, read, and experience Holocaust literature and art as *memory events* rather than as mere illustrations of the command to remember or, on the contrary, as aesthetic manifestations of the paradox of negative presentation, devoid of the ethical force.

Lyotard's negotiations between ethics and aesthetics bid us to acknowledge the sensation of "Is it happening?" as both an ethical expression of injustice and an aesthetic gesture, and it is in the space of the *differend* between them that we experience the opening that allows for memory events. The principle that governs the presentation of "Is it happening?" the occurrence of memory taking place, does not rely on any set of criteria or rules for what constitutes an adequate representation because it is indeterminate and new each time. Lyotard (1989) refers to the constitutive power which takes up that law and strives to "present" it as "imagination": "Imagination is not only the power to judge; it is a power to invent criteria" (17). Imagination is that which searches for a means of expression without a rule, which reaches for an untried possibility, for the next possible phrase. Its task is not, as Kant may have desired, to wrestle the unity of the subject out of conflicting forces. Rather, imagination brings the faculties of the mind into movement, into agitation that presents that "it" is happening indeed, and this is the minimal law that "Remember!" calls forth. In the occurrence of "Is it happening?" we glimpse the persistence of the memory phrase and the affirmation of its ability to continue. This does not mean that we are awaiting a Gertrude Stein of Holocaust literature or a Marcel Duchamp of Holocaust art for this to happen; it has happened already, in many of the works that the readers of Holocaust literature are familiar with.[28] In each instance of remembering, however, we have to allow it to happen again. In advocating nonrepresentational modes of speaking about the Holocaust, Lyotard cites Lanzmann's *Shoah* as an example of perhaps the only work that heeds this imperative.[29] This generous assessment of the film, albeit well-deserved, seems unfair to a host of other works inspired by the Holocaust. From Célan's hermetic poetry to Mindy Weisel's abstract paintings, these testimonials defy the demand for realistic depiction, always in search of a new means of imagining and expressing what seems to elude representation. In this minimal ethical sense, imagination labors against the totalitarian impetus of the Nazi regime to eradicate the victim's capacity to imagine. As witnessed by Charlotte Delbo (1995),

You may say that one can take away everything from a human
being except the faculty of thinking and imagining. You have no
idea. One can turn a human being into a skeleton gurgling with
diarrhea, without time or energy to think. Imagination is the first
luxury of a body receiving sufficient nourishment, enjoying a mar-
gin of free time, possessing the rudiments from which dreams are
fashioned. (168)

To draw on the idiom of the sublime as reinterpreted by Lyotard,
Holocaust memory today is seized with the terror of its own imminent disappearance, of its not happening any more. We hasten to
absorb that terror into all-too-familiar representations and man-
tras of "so it never happens again," recited at commemorative ceremonies and repeated in student papers. Lyotard (1990a) reflects,
"One will say, 'It was a great massacre, how horrible!' . . . One
cries out 'never again' and that's it! It is taken care of" (26). By
contrast, the acts of reading and writing, the memory events that
respond to "Remember!" in an instance of the *here and now*, have
the potential to keep it alive. The memory phrase resists being
dominated by any single genre of discourse, be it historical knowledge (the genre of cognitives), the ethical imperative to remember
the victims (expressed in phrases of obligation), or "mere" representation for the sake of aesthetic pleasure. In continuously challenging the rules of what constitutes proper ways of representing
the horror, it defies the impersonality and anonymity of Holocaust
memory, the features that would otherwise allow its "referent" to
sink into oblivion.

For those who care, it is terrifying to think that one day no
one may want to respond to "Remember!" the posthumous phrase
issuing from the dead who insist on becoming phrased. The scandal surrounding Binjamin Wilkomirski's book (as well as other
fake memoirs that have emerged since then) can be read as a symptom of the terror that the memory of the event will vanish and
be replaced by vacuous simulacra.[30] We despair of our inability
to remember accurately if we can no longer distinguish between
the authentic voice of a legitimate victim and the chaff of constructed memory. Many examples of Holocaust literature, however, both autobiographical and fictional, have proven capable of
producing "the shock, the sublime intensity producing ontological
dislocation" (Lyotard 1992, 206). Warding off the fear that nothing will ever be said anymore, these testimonials signal the interval

in which bearing witness occurs, in the *here and now* of the memory event. They offer us assurance that not only is speaking necessary but also, as Edmund Burke already knew, "it is in our power to effect with words combinations that would be impossible by any other means" (Lyotard 1992, 205).

Lyotard (1990a) writes, "Philosophy as architecture is ruined, but a writing of the ruins, micrologies, graffiti can still be done" (43). For Lyotard, philosophy is a genre of discourse whose rules remain to be sought; in that sense, the sublime, the experience of indeterminacy, is the critical essence of philosophy. Yet is not the Holocaust genre of discourse also such writing of the ruins whose task, like that of the philosophical genre, is to proceed without a rule? Lyotard (1988) asks, "But what if the stakes of thought concerned *differend* rather than consensus?" (84). Arguably, the same question pertains to Holocaust literature and art, which have been summoned into existence "after Auschwitz" by the memory phrase "Remember!" The links from one sentence to another, or one image to another, are not determined by the rules of how to remember the victims of the Holocaust but by "a quest for a rule" (97). Ultimately, Holocaust literature is not only about knowing but also about feeling, always anew, posing a challenge of how we can share an affect that seems unshareable. Reaching beyond what can be recovered in knowledge, it is "indebted to the memory of fundamental non-memory and . . . obliged to recognize this debt" (Carroll 2000, x).

Lyotard (1990a) proposes that the unforgotten, which endures in the forgetting of the origin of the voice, cannot be represented without being missed again:

> Whenever one represents, one inscribes in memory, and this might seem a good defence against forgetting. It is, I believe, just the opposite. Only that which has been inscribed, can in the current sense of the term, be forgotten because it could be effaced. . . . One must, certainly, inscribe in words, in images. One cannot escape the necessity of representing. But it is one thing to do it in view of saving the memory, and quite another to try to preserve the remainder, the unforgettable forgotten, in writing. (26)

Ultimately, the withdrawn referent of "Remember!" cannot be remembered for what it was because something that never ceases to be forgotten persists at its core,, where remembering and amnesia occur at the same time. A happening of the memory phrase is withdrawn from representation, "but this concealment lets something else show, this contradictory feeling of a 'presence' that is certainly not present, but which precisely needs to be forgotten to be represented" (Lyotard 1990a, 4).[31] Ordinary memory merely accomplishes forgetting, in order to construct coherent narratives of events. Lyotard admonishes, however, "It must even be sufficient that one remembers that one must remember, that one should" (38). Here, Lyotard takes his cue from one of Eli Wiesel's Hasidic tales. In the epigraph to *The Gates of the Forest*, Wiesel (1966) tells the story of a rabbi who intercedes with God to save his people, although he has forgotten the words of the prayer: "Then it fell to Rabbi Israel of Rizhyn to overcome misfortune. Sitting in his armchair, his head in his hands, he spoke to God: 'I am unable to light the fire and I do not know the prayer; I cannot even find the place in the forest. All I can do is to tell the story, and this must be sufficient.' And it was sufficient."[32]

Holocaust testimonials are the writing of the *differend*, which searches for the ways to express the impossibility of either truly remembering or forgetting what cannot be remembered, although, yes, we know now, and we fear, that it will fall into oblivion. In the chap-ter "The Referent, the Name," Lyotard (1988) compares the aftermath of the disaster experienced by survivors to the consequences of an earthquake in which all instruments for the measurement of the cataclysm have been destroyed and therefore it cannot be scientifically proven (56). Similarly, Polish Jewish Holocaust writer Julian Stryjkowski, in his semiautobiographical novel *Wielki strach* (Great fear, 1980), tells the story of an elder of a Jewish community who pleads for assistance after their village has been razed to the ground by a fire. When asked for a report on the fire, he answers that the report has been burned with the village: when the record of the disaster cannot be procured, the conflagration is absolute. But Stryjkowski insists that this does not mean that the sufferers can be cast into oblivion, and that is why he wants to give them a voice in his own writing. The task of Holocaust literature, art, and criticism today must be seen as bearing witness to "Is it happening?" of the memory phrase "Remember!" so that the question mark is not snuffed out. Therefore, as Lyotard

argues against Faurisson, one must find discursive means to vali-
date survivors' traumatic experiences when the language of factual knowledge proves inadequate to this task. To evoke Lyotard's
seismic metaphor, we must allow ourselves to feel the tremors
along the fault lines of memory, even if all the instruments for the
measurement of their impact have been destroyed. The duty of artists, critics, and teachers who consider themselves to be guardians
of Holocaust memory is to listen to the rumblings of the *differend*.

Today, we are left with the important task of, yet again, "lending an ear" to "Remember!" Lyotard (1988) enjoins us to continue phrasing, to go on speaking about the endlessly indeterminate "it" to which the memory phrase refers. He writes, "The
presentation entailed by a phrase-case is not presented in the universe that this phrase presents. . . . But another phrase-case can
present it in another universe and thereby situate it" (71). A diary
recovered from the ruins of the Warsaw ghetto (from Emanuel
Ringelblum's Oneg Shabad archive), Zvi Kolitz's fictional story
"Yosl Rakover Speaks to God" (about the last Warsaw ghetto
fighter trapped in the ruins and awaiting death), and Jerzy Ficowski's poem "Two Mothers" (which commemorates the rescue of
his future wife Elżbieta from the Warsaw ghetto)[33] belong to very
different genres, although they all allude to events from the same
period of history, and that took place in the same location. They
now resonate with one another in the phrases that issue from us,
who read and speak about them. Only in the utterances that follow these accounts can we create the conditions for the stories to
meet and speak to one another. This memory work also includes
creating a discursive terrain in which the stories of victims and
those of perpetrators can be considered together and instigate
reflection. Philosopher Avital Ronell mentions *Shoah* as an example of a cinematic work that creates conditions for such meetings to occur because it brings together accounts that are worlds
apart even if they happened in the same place and at the same
time, such as, for instance, the report of SS-*Unterscharführer*
Franz Suchomel, in charge of the gassings in the death camp of
Treblinka, and the testimony by Abraham Bomba, the prisoner
in Treblinka. In the camp, there was no communication between
the SS and the inmates, since the only objective was to make the
prisoners die. Thus their "phrases" were so radically disparate

that, as Lyotard argues, not even a *differend* existed between them. The *differend* therefore emerges as the most minimal condition of bearing witness, and when the utterances are disjointed to the extent that the *differend* no longer arises between them, the threat of the dissolution of language is at its highest. That is why it is crucial that the most incommensurate of voices, even those belonging to perpetrators, are invited to cohabitate in the viewer, and they obligate him or her to remember and reflect. To read, for instance, the Auschwitz diary of *SS-Obersturmführer* Johann Paul Kremer, who performed selections and oversaw gassings in the camp in 1942,[34] alongside *Night*, in which Wiesel deliberately refrains from talking about the Nazi perpetrators, is revealing of what the writer chooses to leave unsaid. Contrasting clandestine images of the members of the *Sonderkommando*, the infamous inhabitants of the grey zone, to whom Primo Levi refers as National Socialism's greatest crime, with the photographs of laughing Nazi functionaries resting in a nearby resort after a day's work in the death camp, invites reflection on the question of moral responsibility, complementing historian Christopher Browning's description of the Nazi killers as "ordinary men" or political philosopher Hannah Arendt's statements on the "banality of evil."[35]

In his Holocaust comic book *Maus*, Art Spiegelman offers a compelling image, which can serve as a concluding illustration of Lyotard's injunction to continue "phrasing after Auschwitz." In one of the panels of volume two, we see the cartoonist during a psychotherapy session, in treatment for depression following the success of *Maus I*. He draws himself shrunk to the size of a diminutive child mouse. The therapist, himself a Holocaust survivor, says, "Anyway, the victims who died can never tell their side of the story, so maybe it's better not to have any more stories." The Spiegelman character replies, "Uh-huh. Samuel Beckett once said: 'Every word is like an unnecessary stain on silence and nothingness.'" The next panel *is* "silent," with wisps of smoke from two cigarettes winding around the little mouse figures instead of speech bubbles; indeed, this is the only entirely silent panel in the book. Yet, in the next picture, Art "links on," over the abyss of the wordless frame: "On the other hand, he said it" (Spiegelman 1991, 45). Here, as in the case of other works I discuss in this book, to Allen Dunn's (1993) warning that

"it is dangerous to conflate the artist's need for discontinuous origi-
nality with a death camp victim's plea for justice" (220), one must
answer, Yes, I am running that risk each time I link my own phrase
onto the memory phrase "Remember!"; nevertheless, to paraphrase
Kant's categorical impera-tive, "I ought to."

CHAPTER FOUR

Poethics of Disappearing Traces

Levinas, Literary Testimony, and Holocaust Art

A face is a trace of itself, given over to my responsibility, but to which I am wanting and faulty. It is as though I were responsible for his mortality, and guilty for surviving.

—EMMANUEL LEVINAS (1998b, 91)

Pas de trace, pas de nom.
Pas de trace de pas.
Pas de trace, de trace de pas.

[No trace, no name.
No trace of the (no) step.
No trace, the trace of the (no) step]

—RÉGINE ROBIN (2002, 146)

ERASURES

In one of the interviews about his film *Shoah*, Claude Lanzmann commented that he had to work with "the disappearance of traces. . . , with traces of traces of traces" (quoted in Robbins 1987, 252). The motif of traces structures one of the film's opening episodes, in which Simon Srebrnik, a survivor of Chełmno extermination camp, returns to the site of murder many years later. We see him walking through a serene, rural landscape flanked by a forest, his eyes trained on a sight that remains invisible to the viewer. Suddenly, Srebrnik nods his head in a gesture of recognition, points to a large field covered with grass, and says, "Ja, das ist das Platz" (Yes, this is the place). This unremarkable scenery is now unscathed by the signs of the violence to which it was witness. For Srebrnik, however, it bears the imprint of the crime, the traces of which only his description in front of Lanzmann's camera can etch in the viewer's imagination. "The place" is an image of absence: it withholds the signs, draws them into itself. Indeed, even Srebrnik's voice seems to retreat from *das Platz*: as he says, he cannot describe what happened there. In an attempt to bring forth an image, the survivor walks away from the camera, stepping along a concrete ledge overgrown with grass, outlining what must remain invisible. With his footsteps, Srebrnik traces a figure of what he previously described as the ovens in which many people were had been burned. Walking around the perimeter of the death camp, Srebrnik traverses as well the immense distance that separates his present account from the time of his past experience. While ostensibly the landscape does not change in front of the camera, Srebrnik's footsteps transform the place and return it to the viewer re-marked with the absolute difference of that past. Even the tranquil chirruping of birds suddenly sounds jarring against the survivor's recollection that, in that place, two thousand bodies were burned every day. To recall a phrase coined by Israeli poet Irit Amiel, this is indeed "a double landscape."[1] Srebrnik offers little more than a silhouette of a forgotten outline. But his footsteps have initiated a journey of memory, releasing the traces of the past from under the landscape covered with thick grass.

In one of his essays, Levinas (1986) reminds us, "We must not conceive of a work as an apparent agitation of a ground which afterwards remains identical with itself" (348). The survivor's work of recollection does not perceptibly transform the landscape, yet "the agitation of the ground" wrought by traumatic memory radically distorts the site, rendering it unfamiliar, *unheimlich*. While Srebrnik's footsteps stake out the circumference of what neither his words nor his gestures can conjure, the entire scene seems to suddenly shift into a different dimension, collapsing into the invisible horror that his words have summoned. By registering this imperceptible shock, the tectonic shift between the two worlds that Srebrnik's footsteps are straddling, the viewer becomes implicated in the ethical task of bearing witness. In this way, as Robbins (1987) argues, the film's way of "'letting us know' is to render us responsible" (256).

The motif of the trace functions in Levinas's work on many levels. Levinas's biographer Salomon Malka points out that the trace is a privileged trope in the philosopher's work, and the title of his own account of the philosopher's life is *Emmanuel Levinas: La Vie et la trace* (translated into English as *Emmanuel Levinas: His Life and Legacy*; 2006). According to Malka, the trace stands both for the invisible presence of the other, which is the cornerstone of Levinas's ethics, *and* for the impact of the Holocaust on his work and life.[2] In response to Malka, the translator of the book, Michael Kigel, cautions against reducing the philosopher's work to a form of "bondage [to the Shoah] that lords over [Levinas's] entire intellectual development" (Malka 2006, xvii). Yet he himself alludes to the disaster's reverbera- tions in Levinas's work as a *pure trace*, a complex, nonphenomenal figure of a traumatic wound that cannot be retained in memory and confronted in a direct way.

The force of Levinas's ethical project hinges on the question of *how* to bear witness to alterity without reducing difference to a legible form. He asks, "Does there exist the signifyingness of signification which would not be equivalent to the transmutation of the other into the same?" (Levinas 1986, 348). Can there be a relation "with an absence so radically withdrawn from disclosure and from dissimulation?" (354). The opening to the suffering of the other in ethical speech does not oc- cur in disclosure, and it cannot be represented. Instead, the other arises as if behind the image in which he or she is presented. Thus, within the purview of ethics, the notion of the "trace" offers Levinas a way to con- ceive of nonappropriative manifestations of alterity, beyond the totaliz- ing grip of representation, as expressed most fully in his seminal essay "The Trace of the Other." The trace signals the ultimately undisclos- able face of the other, which both accompanies its own appearance in the sign and disengages itself from thematization. The other "as it were breaks through his own plastic essence, like someone who opens the window on which his figure is outlined" (351). In the trace, the other overflows the knowable and emerges only as "a surplus over the inevi- table paralysis of manifestation" (351–52), signifying a presence that has never appeared within the coordinates of my world: "It disturbs immanence without settling into the horizons of the world" (352). Since the trace has interrupted the continuity of my representations, it cannot be mastered in consciousness and memory; it is always slipping into the past more preoriginal than the past that can be captured in thought and recollection. It does not simply lead to the past, as memory would, but rather it signals a relation with the past that does not appear in the pres- ent, that is outside presence and outside presentation. The trace, which betokens the time of the other, is "incommensurable with the present, always already in the past, over and beyond 'now', which this exterior- ity disturbs and obsesses" (Levinas 1998b, 86). "An insertion of space in time" (Levinas 1986, 358), the trace is the origin of temporality, as it has been already opened up by the other.

Levinas's (1986) thinking of the trace is anchored in the biblical meaning of the invisible presence of the divine. "He shows himself only in his trace, as is said in Exodus 33," he writes (359).[3] God manifests himself through the prohibition of seeing his face, allowing only the glimpse of his back. Levinas hastens to add, however, that to be human in the image of God does not mean to merely abide in the divine trace but to "go toward the others who stand in the trace of illeity" (359). "The Divine can only be manifested in my neighbor" (Levinas 1996, 159), in the flesh-and-blood human existents: the invisible face of God is revealed as a nonphenomenal inscription in the other, especially the other who interpellates me in his vulnerability and need. The commandment to respect the divinity of another human is God's commandment, and Levinas cites Jeremiah 22:16: "He judged the cause of the poor and the needy: then it was well. Is this not to know me? says the Lord" (Levinas 1996, 159).[4] In that sense, Levinas's elevation of the other in the notion of the trace remains rooted in Judaism, in the belief that, in David Patterson's (2006a) words, the assault on the human during the Shoah is the "assault on the Holy One Himself . . . , a desecration of the Invisible One who invisibly imparts the Divine spark to the human being" (145).[5] Yet, as James Hatley (2000) stipulates, "The nudity of the face [the ethical primacy of human suffering] institutes a necessary atheism, in which G-d steps aside, is emptied out or contracts so that the one can come before the other as this particular other" (118).

The centrality of the motif of the trace for Levinas (1969) cannot be separated from his critique of modernity's paradigm of representation, as it coincides with philosophy's arrogation of the other. In his view, representation is ultimately "a determination of the Other by the same, without the same being determined by the Other" (168). The collusion of representation with power is epitomized in dominant aesthetic practices, and it is no coincidence that Levinas refers to war making as an "art." As he exhorts in *Totality and Infinity*, "The state of war suspends morality. The *art* of foreseeing war and winning it by every means— politics . . . is opposed to morality" (21; emphasis mine). Consequently, Levinas saw National Socialism as the culmination of Western philosophy's aversion to alterity, its being "struck with the horror of the other that remains other—with an unsurmountable allergy" (346), and he would agree with Walter Benjamin's warning, in his 1936 essay "The Work of Art in the Era of Mechanical Reproduction," that "all efforts to render politics aesthetic culminate in one thing: war" (Benjamin 1969, 241).

Thus, if Western philosophy, according to Levinas (1986), was founded upon the conquest of the other, the "games of art" (347), as he says disparagingly, epitomize this subjection. Starting with his early essay "Reality and Its Shadow" (1948), he repeatedly cautions against the egotistic and appropriative tendencies of aesthetics, complicit with totality and destructive of radical otherness: "There is something wicked and egoist and cowardly in aesthetic enjoyment" (Levinas 1987a, 142). By relating to its object through resemblance, the image neutralizes ("murders") the living relationship of the face-to-face. The ethical relation, on the other hand, is nonrepresentational, since it leaves no room for mimetic distancing in ethical proximity with the other, the experience which is both disruptive and intimate. Levinas later reiterates this view in *Otherwise than Being*, although by then his criticism of literature and art is less unforgiving. He writes, "Art is the pre-eminent exhibition in which the said is reduced to a pure theme, to absolute exposition, even to shamelessness, capable of holding all looks for which it is exclusively destined. The said is *reduced to the beautiful*, which supports the Western ontology" (1998b, 40; emphasis mine).

What strikes us in these formulations is that, when Levinas denigrates aesthetics, he situates it solely within the realm of the beautiful, which he denounces as complicit with totality and thus injurious to the other. He writes in the preface to *Totality and Infinity*, "Morality . . . will have gone beyond the *canons of the beautiful* to proclaim itself as unconditional and universal when the eschatology of messianic peace will have come to superpose itself upon the ontology of war" (Levinas 1969, 22; emphasis mine). Thus, despite Levinas's insistence that ethics, or justice, requires the overcoming of aesthetics, it is possible to argue that his indictment of aesthetics, his distrust of the image in which the other is seized, does not foreclose a possibility of post-Holocaust aesthetics; on the contrary, it opens up the way of thinking aesthetics "otherwise," outside of what Levinas condemns as egotistic "canons of the beautiful." This alternative, nonappropriative aesthetics refers to literary and artistic practice that is already ethically informed (even if unbeknown to its author). It is "art for the other," in which the desire to produce an image in which the other is captured already presupposes ethical responsibility and which is, in Levinas's reference to the Holocaust poet Paul Célan, "*the interruption of the playful order of the beautiful* . . . , a seeking for the Other" (Levinas 1996, 46; emphasis mine).

A reevaluation of Levinas's views on art in light of the preponderance of ethics reveals an unexpected rapprochement between Levinas's conceptualization of the ethical as an unconditional giving of my world to the other and French philosopher Jean-Luc Nancy's reflection on the relation between ethics and aesthetics, which he articulates in the notion of "the sublime offering" (*l'offrande sublime*). Nancy's insistence on the primacy of the ontological cannot be reconciled with Levinas's ethical premise that radical alterity falls "beyond Being" and that therefore the opposition between immanence and transcendence is unconditional. For Nancy, openness to the other does not presuppose severance from being: it remains within the ontological horizon. In "Unsacrificeable," for instance, Nancy (1991a) stipulates, "There is no 'outside. . . . ' What we used to call 'transcendence' would signify rather that appropriation is *immanent*" (37). Yet, in the vicinity of aesthetics, the writings of both philosophers reveal a remarkable similarity of idioms. In "Of Divine Places," for example, Nancy (1991b) writes, "It is always in extreme destitution, in abandonment without shelter or protection, that man appears, waxes or wanes before the face of God. Whenever he presents himself, God brings about destitution or denuding" (147). Moving away from traditional aesthetics, Nancy speaks of the sublime as an absolute gift of imagination that opens up the possibility of both aesthetics and ethics. In a gesture analogous to Levinas's critique of traditional aesthetics, Nancy unmasks a correlation between aesthetics and epistemology: the canons of the beautiful always secretly serve the unifying tendency of reason. Since the pleasure of the beautiful lies in the discovery of the unity of the heterogeneous, its enjoyment is always appropriative.

Although Levinas never discusses the sublime as such, except to refer to the text of the Talmud as "sublime," its idiom often inflects the philosopher's description of the ethical relation. For example, he accentuates a dimension of verticality, which is opened up by the metaphysical desire for the other. The other, the Most High, hovers over the same; the self is humbled by the magnitude of what it cannot master, by its "superiority of the superlative, this height, this constant elevation . . . and let us say this word, this divinity" (Levinas 1986, 357). The trope of immense altitude is central to the various articulations of the sublime; it is reflected, for instance, in Kant's word for the sublime, *Erhabene* (from *erheben*: to rise, raise, lift, or transport upward). The sublime is conceived in terms of ascending movement, in which the subject is both humbled and elevated. For Levinas (1987a), the self's infinite approach toward the other is "a fundamental movement, pure transport" (94). Interestingly, then, Levinas's condemnation of the beautiful is expressed through the reverberations of the idiom of the sublime in his own use of poetic figures.[6]

In his essay on French surrealist writer Michel Leiris, "The Transcendence of Words" (1949), Levinas (1989) refers to ethics as a disturbance amid aesthetic quietude. "The real rent" in the fabric of the ego derives from "the need to enter into a relation with someone, in spite or over the harmony derived from the successful creation of beauty" (147). Although Levinas is critical of Leiris's bypassing of ethics for the sake of ideas as the font of language, he interprets the writer's notion of *biffures* (which gave title to Leiris's book) as a promise of opening onto the ethical, likely relating it already to his own notion of the trace. For Leiris, the neologism *biffures* equivocates between the meanings of "erasure" (from *biffer*) and "bifurcation" (from *bifer*). The ambiguity of Levinas's reflection on aesthetics is therefore most poignantly brought out by what now must be seen as the *figure of the trace*, the trace of the other. For Levinas, the trace is both that which signifies through its own erasure and, when invested with ethical signification, which "bifurcates" from the path (of the same) toward an unknown destination (in the immemorial time of the other). I propose the term "poethics of disappearing traces" to convey Levinas's complex articulations of the figure of the trace. The neologism "poethics" (*poéthique*), coined by the French poet Michel Deguy, describes the movement of *poiesis*, of imaginative fashioning of the world, which is always already an ethical gesture. The term "poethics of traces" also conveys Levinas's conception of language as divided into its ethical essence, Saying, and its phenomenal manifestation in the Said. Language, for Levinas (1998b), is initiated by an interpellation that issues from the other, through which the self has already been summoned to respond, "before language scatters into words, into themes equal to words and dissimulating in the said the openness of the saying exposed like a bleeding wound" (151). Saying is then the trace of the other's passage through language, the dimension that cannot be captured in representation. It is literally an unconditional readiness to respond, prior to any act of speech. As such, Saying will have already opened language to the other and revealed it in its primordial function as always "for" the other. Ethical speech supports alterity, to which it is always already addressed, rather than absorbing it in the Said, and it signifies that, through my words, I offer the world to the other: "The glory . . . glorifies itself in my saying, commanding me through my mouth. . . . [It] circumscribes me and orders me by my own voice" (Levinas 1985, 110). Speaking the world to the other and for the other is an unconditional gift, for which I do not seek repayment or gratification. In turning toward the other, I am already bereft of words, since I do not truly own the "house of language" that I inhabit. For Levinas (1986), this "radical generosity" always underlies my work. It then requires the ingratitude of the other, since "gratitude would in fact be the return of the movement to its origin" (349). For Levinas, only the work that does not anticipate "the triumph of its cause," a reward to be reaped in one's lifetime, can escape being walled up in immanence, and open itself toward the future. Such absolute giving of oneself to the other falls outside the present in which the self would temporally coincide with the other. It interrupts the subject's journey "home to itself," like Ulysses, "who through all of his peregrinations is only on the way to his native land" (346).[7]

A Levinasian poethics of disappearing traces will allow us to probe further the intersecting borders of ethics and aesthetics in literary and artistic Holocaust testimonials. It is remarkable that Levinas's most powerful, unqualified endorsement of a work of fiction—a product of aesthetic imagination—is his review of Zvi Kolitz's "Yosl Rakover Talks to God," a moving novella about the last fighter in the Warsaw Ghetto. In his dying hour, the protagonist proclaims his faith in God, although he also defies his authority for having abandoned his people. The essay was first delivered on the radio in 1955, and then published as "Loving the Torah More than God" in 1963 and included in the volume *Difficult Freedom*. Levinas (1999) marvels, "I have just read a text that is both beautiful and true, true as only fiction can be" (80), and he recommends this text as a "bearer of Jewish learning" and as a spiritual resource. "Yosl Rakover" also rings authentic for Levinas (1990) because it is "fiction in which all of us who survive recognize ourselves with a sense of vertigo" (80). Despite his distrust of aesthetics, Levinas singles out a work of imagination as a site in which spiritual truth can be rekindled, and in which deeply buried traumatic memory can be reengaged. Considering that, to the best of my knowledge, "Loving the Torah" is Levinas's sole engagement with Holocaust literature, this unique affirmation of a work of fiction is momentous,[8] signaling, perhaps, that Holocaust literature is indeed the site where Levinas's view of aesthetics can be fruitfully reexamined. It also indicates that, just as ethics, in the novel sense that he has given it, has informed Levinas's efforts to "think aesthetics otherwise," the need for alternative representational strategies and aesthetic categories in the wake of the Holocaust has deeply informed his innovative conceptualization of ethics, even if the philosopher himself would have never directly expressed such a view.

FOOTPRINTS: THIS IS (NOT) A PLACE

The motif of "footsteps" in the Srebnik episode of Lanzmann's film that opened this chapter leads us once again to the work of Ida Fink (1996), the Israeli writer of Polish Jewish descent. Fink fled from a small-town ghetto in Poland in 1942, survived the Holocaust on the Aryan side, and moved to Israel in 1957, following repressions by the Polish communist government.[9] In a short story titled "Traces," from the volume *A Scrap of Time*, the main character, like Srebrnik, returns to a place from the past, which in her case is the town that formerly contained a ghetto of which she was the sole survivor. During a meeting with the town's present inhabitants, someone passes her a faded copy of an amateur photograph of the ghetto in its last stages and asks her to describe it. She comments, "There is a lot of white in it; that's snow. The picture was taken in February. The snow is high, piled up in deep drifts. In the foreground are traces of footprints; along the edges, two rows of wooden stalls. That is all. Yes. This is where they lived" (135). The woman speaks reluctantly and pushes the photograph away: "I prefer not to be reminded" (136). She then suddenly changes her mind and asks the interviewer to write down her recollections because she wants to leave a record of the fate of the children who were murdered in the ghetto. The interviewer interrupts her, "What children? What trace?" "A trace of those children," she replies (137). The speaker identifies the footprints in the photograph as most likely left by the members of the local *Judenrat* when they were being marched to death following the discovery of a group of children in the attic of the *Judenrat* building. These footprints are in turn an index that leads her to recall a group of children, who, when the SS officers brought them out of the attic, shouting at them to identify their parents, remained absolutely silent. Although the traces of the children themselves disappeared—it is only their parents' footsteps that are visible in the photograph—the narrator's reminiscence will now provide testimony to the children's courage. Since the speaker alone survived the liquidation of the ghetto, she is the only one who can testify to the vanished presence of its former inhabitants; this is why, after the break, she would tell her audience "how they were all shot." Without the speaker's commentary, no one would even notice the footprints in the picture, or at best they would remain inconsequential. They are mute signs, whose meaning escapes the eye, while the witness's speech is a conduit through which the precarious passage of the condemned ones into remembrance can be effected. Her testimony now becomes a fragile shelter, protecting its inhabitants from oblivion, although, like the footprints in the snow, barely visible in a faded photograph, these words are also threatened with erasure. In a gesture analogous to Lanzmann's decrypting of the traces, the unnamed narrator in Fink's story is trying to capture in words the phantom materiality of the footprints left by the people just about to suffer a horrifying death. The woman's brief narration is also haunted by the absence of another witness: the photographer who captured the scene. She wonders who he was and where exactly he must have been positioned to take the picture. The readers never learn how the photograph survived the war, but they are suddenly summoned before that invisible eyewitness who must have been standing just outside the frame of the picture. In both the Srebrnik episode and in Fink's story, the viewer/reader in turn becomes a witness to an unseen spectacle of annihilation. In a way, the readers of Fink's story must step into the place of the invisible photographer, as if substituting for a specter, so that they can relive that scene in their imagination. If, as Jill Robbins (1987) remarks, the annihilation was aimed not only at the individuals but also at "survivor testimonies, which are the *language trace* of the event" (252; emphasis mine), the reader is called upon to take up the labor of memory in imaginative substitution and partake in an act of rescue in which she herself becomes a repository of disappearing traces.

In Fink's short stories, the witness's speech is constantly threatened, and the narrative voice is painfully frayed between the time of the storytelling and the time of the events, at once unbearably close to and infinitely removed from the horror. Often the first-person narrator (and presumably the author's *port-parole*) reenacts a double role as one of the victims and as the sole surviving witness. In several stories the narrator describes the life of her own condemned community, as if posthumously bearing witness to herself. In the title story in the volume *A Scrap of Time*, for instance, the narrator gives an account of what it was like to be watching the roundups from the hiding place: "Hidden in the dark interiors of our apartments, with our faces pressed against the window panes damp from rain and our rapid breath, we, reprieved until the next time, looked out at the condemned" (Fink 1998, 23). The narrator marvels at her compulsion to use the pronoun "we" when describing the *Aktion* in the ghetto: "I should not have written 'we,' for I was not standing in the ranks, obeying the order that was posted the previous evening. . . . I wasn't thinking about why I avoided the gate that led to the street" (Fink 1996, 4–5). The startling coincidence of the moment of storytelling and the time she was watching her neighbors and relatives being marched to death gives the reader a sense that the witness's position is precarious, as if she were still living in peril. Because her voice is so fragile and appears to be threatened with imminent extinction, the reader is compelled to listen intently.

Fink makes it clear that the events the narrator witnessed cannot be reconciled with her life in the present. During the events, the experience of the condemned inhabitants of the ghetto did not comply with familiar norms, and it shifted into a new zone that could not be captured in everyday language. Their time was "not measured in months and years" (Fink 1996, 3) but in the escalating horror of new words such as "roundup," "*Aktion*," and "deportation." Yet the task of the storyteller is to allow that other time to creep into the crevices of the present and to continuously disrupt its tranquility. Only a memory that lets itself become distressed in this way will be able to convey the disintegration of the fundamental categories of time and space in the lives of the condemned. In the opening paragraph, the narrator describes the witness's struggle to break through the constraints of chronological time, although her efforts to palpate the horror with words seem crippled:

> I want to talk about a certain time not measured in months and years. . . . For so long I have wanted to talk about this time. . . . I wanted to, but I couldn't, I didn't know how. I was afraid, too, that this second time, which is measured in months and years, had buried the other time under a layer of years, that this second time had crushed the first one and destroyed it within me. But no. Today, digging around in the ruins of memory, I found it fresh and untouched by forgetfulness. (Fink 1998, 3)

Often the narrator is a collector of pieces of conversation from which she will reconstruct what happened. In the story "A Spring Morning," she picks up a comment that was in turn overheard by a curious on-looker who watched a procession of people being marched to their deaths. As they were crossing a bridge, one of the condemned men suddenly remarked, "The water is the color of beer" (Fink 1996, 45). The onlooker, about whom Fink remarks ambiguously that he was a lucky "possessor of an Aryan great-grandmother," overheard the comment and shared it with several friends over dinner later in the day, dismayed with the incongruity between its trivial content and the speaker's awareness of his imminent death. The narrator picks it up from one of those inadvertent witnesses and uses it to weave a lon-ger narrative about the final hours of a family of three. Marched out of their house, the father (who made the unusual comment when the condemned were crossing the bridge) instructed his daughter to run and hide among the crowd waiting in front of the church. The little girl obeyed, but she was spotted and shot to death. The negative wit-ness, whose appetite for dinner was not ruined by what he had seen, accidentally salvaged the overheard sentence, the sole testimony to an extinguished life. By unfolding the accidental comment into a story, the narrator thus released the trace of that life into an unpredictable trajectory in language. Without her effort, the memory of the victims would have disappeared, buried in the nearby forest.

Similarly, in the story "Sabina under the Sacks," the narrator hears about the last moments of Sabina and her daughter Dora, just before they were discovered in their hiding place under a pile of empty sacks in the corridor of the *Judenrat* building. Lives such as Sabina's, she confesses, are unremarkable and "float past the edges of our mem-ory" (Fink 1998, 101). Shortly before her death, Sabina and her baby were sent back to her parents by an abusive husband who spurned his wife for her refusal to "fulfill conjugal duties." Yet the narrator ad-mits that Sabina's last moments "have etched a permanent picture in [her] mind" (101), even if she heard about them only secondhand and "by chance." The storyteller has to make an effort to capture these fleeting, inconsequential bits of recollection, and to drag them from *their* hiding places. Fink does it quietly, as if in a whisper,[10] but her gentle, subdued words free the stories of those who perished from the parentheses of history.

Since Fink's narrators are constructed as recipients of the stories of others, their temporal continuum is shot through and thus preempted by the time of the other, by that other time. Like the guest speaker in "Traces," they have become a precious repository of memory, and they regard sifting through the ruins of memory to be their duty. This duty also designates them as witnesses. Although the story "The Pig" is written in the third person, its main character, similarly to the narrator in "A Scrap of Time," observes the scenes outside from his hiding place in a peasant's barn. For days, the man looks through the crack, which is his only connection to the world and allows him to keep his sanity. Yet when he sees a truck convoy carrying the remaining Jews from his town to the place of execution, he pulls himself away in horror and covers his eyes. Although now he yearns to see no more, he quickly shakes off his weakness and resumes his task: "'I can't,' he said and slumped into a corner, but he stood up again and watched without blinking" (Fink 1996, 81). In inviting and recording this account, the narrator, in turn, must withstand its traumatizing impact and initiate a chain in the transmission of memory, prompted by the knowledge of another's impending death. In some of the stories, the account is passed from speaker to speaker, and the narrator must guard that tenuous passage. At any time, the transmission could be interrupted, and the trace of the victim's extinguished life would disappear irretrievably. For instance, in "Behind a Hedge," the narrator relays the account of a housekeeper, Agafia, who in turn describes to her employer the execution of a group of Jews in the nearby woods, which she watched secretly. She reports, "When they started shooting again, I jumped up and wanted to run into the woods, so I wouldn't have to see. But I didn't run. Something kept me there and said to me: 'Watch. Don't shut your eyes.' So I watched" (19). Since the older woman does not want to listen to the gruesome report, Agafia retorts, "We have to know about it. And look at it. And remember" (17). To look at the ghastly spectacle is excruciating, yet not averting one's gaze from the scene of murder is the witness's burdensome duty.

The pain of witnessing is often exacerbated by a sense of shame or even crushing guilt. It manifests, for instance, in the feeling of shame experienced by the narrator of "A Scrap of Time," who chose to run and hide in the bushes near the river instead of joining her friends and loved ones as they were being marched off to their deaths. Similarly, a young man in the story "Splinter," who was thirteen when his mother was taken away, recalls that, when the Germans arrived, his mother pushed him into the corner behind the door, where he stayed until the end of the *Aktion*. He confesses, "Because you know, when my mother pressed me against the wall with the door, I grabbed the handle and held on to it. . . . I would give a great deal to let go of that handle . . ." (Fink 1996, 126). The elderly woman in "Behind the Hedge," following Agafia's gruesome report, recalls chasing out a young Jewish couple who were making love in her garden. As she later realizes, she stole the last moment of happiness from the girl before she was caught in the roundup and executed. The memory is difficult to bear, and her housekeeper Agafia verbalizes her vague sense of culpability when she asks, "Am I saying you're guilty of her death?" (19).

The decision to listen and respond to an account of horrors, to assume its onus of pain and dread, is a difficult one. Several stories in both volumes tell of survivors' cautious attempts to disburden themselves to a close friend or lover after the liberation, and their frustration when the interlocutors turn a deaf ear. In "Night of Surrender," a young Jewish woman who survived in the German countryside on false papers yearns to say the three words "I am Jewish" that she did not dare to utter throughout the war. She also wants to discard the lies about the parents who died in the uprising, and tell the true story about the murder of her mother and father, which she witnessed from her hiding place in a wardrobe. Yet she cannot bring herself to say all this to her boyfriend, an American soldier, despite his assurances that all he wants is to soothe her pain, to "bring [her] up all over again, teach [her] to live again" (Fink 1996, 98). When, on the last day of the war, she finally tells her boyfriend the truth, he advises her to continue with her life under an assumed Aryan identity, not because of anti-Semitism, he contends, but because "it'll be easier that way" (101). He denies Klara, alias Ann, her wish to unburden herself of the past and of the fake persona she has constructed for herself. Ironically, he chooses to collaborate in the erasure of memory, in what he believes to be the survivor's best interest. By forbidding her to talk about her parents' death, he colludes with the murderers in eradicating the traces of their existence. Further, by remaining content with the girl's invented story of her Aryan life, he refuses to acknowledge the rent in the fabric of his own world produced by her Jewish difference. Similarly, in "Splinter," a young girl begs her boyfriend to "not talk about that day any more . . . , you can't talk about it all the time, without stopping" (123) and then falls asleep when the boy finally brings himself to tell her about what happened to his mother. It literally hurts to receive the sharp splinter of another person's memory, so the girl is protecting herself from that pain.

Several stories in both of Fink's collections portray survivors who are looking for their loved ones. The writer's task, which is in turn to

be carried on by the reader, is an analogous quest, invested with the
same passion, devotion, love, despair, and often false hope. A short,
dramatic piece, also titled "Traces," records a young woman's search
for information about her sister. She conducts a series of interviews in
the village where her sister was hiding during the war and examines
what she believes was her hideout. She comes across a few clues: initials are etched on the windowsill, and a few scraps of a love letter remain in a drawer—one of which alludes to the hidden woman's own
attempt to efface the signs of her existence: "Have to wipe out every
trace. I shall always . . ." (Fink 1998, 165). Unfortunately, none of the
pieces of information can be corroborated, and the only eyewitness is
a mentally challenged boy who claims to have seen the young woman's sister during the war. He also saw her after the Germans left,
which would have meant that she did survive; at that time, she had a
baby with her. Considering that the girl was only fourteen and that
the only doctor in the village did not deliver the baby, the accuracy of
this testimony is tenuous at best. Indeed, the elder of the village keeps
repeating, "I never saw her, never even heard of her. . . . Nobody here
ever heard of her" (155, 160). The woman's quest for certainty about
her sister's fate is clearly futile—she despairs that "now that I have
found a trace, I have the feeling that I'll never find her" (179). Yet her
stubborn desire to discover the clues allows that disappeared life to
emerge in her speech. The memory of her sister becomes a lasting although indiscernible mark, touching those around her, even if this effect cannot be articulated. After the woman leaves, the villagers begin
to recall certain details, as if only then the girl about whom no one
knew or wished to know suddenly became a presence among them.
The man living in the house, for instance, now remembers finding a
cradle when he first moved in. Undoubtedly, the woman's search has
yielded no concrete proof of her sister's presence in the village, but,
unbeknownst even to her, she ruptures the villagers' unintentional
conspiracy of silence and releases her sister's memory from the crypt
of oblivion. In a way, perhaps because it is so intangible, the sister's
memory can no longer be erased. Fink's play leaves the reader with a
feeling that the woman must have lived in the village and most likely
survived, but also with certitude that she will never be found. In either case, we know that her now (re)marked absence will continue to
disturb even those who never directly acknowledged her existence.

Fink's narratives foreground the erasure of traces: from the start,
the witness's task is impossible, not only because the murderer has

destroyed the evidence of the crime but also because people in hiding during the Holocaust stayed alive by obliterating the traces of their former lives. For instance, in "The Tenth Man," a handful of Jews who return to their native village after the liberation are still wearing the disguises that saved their lives, and their neighbors can barely recognize them. Ironically, only those who "lost their faces" have managed to survive, and Fink pays special attention to their faces. Chaim, the carpenter, the first man to arrive, is utterly transformed into a withered, shrunken man, but "most important, he had no face. It was completely overgrown with a matted black thicket of hair" (Fink 1998, 103). The second man, a farmer, "has a face white as a communion wafer," which was unusual for someone who used to spend so much time outside. The appearance of two grain dealers is distorted by their "swollen faces" (104), while the teacher's wife shows the "drawn face of a peasant woman" from beneath the plaid kerchief (Fink 1996, 103). A dry goods merchant's features are hidden behind a perpetual smile, which "astonished everyone, because no one from this man's family had survived" (Fink 1998, 105). These masks cannot be easily discarded. As in Klara's case (from "the Night of Surrender"), they bring comfort because they conceal the horror of what their owners went through; with the disguise, no questions need to be asked. By the end of the story, a handful of survivors are still unable to form a *minyan* to commemorate their dead ones with a prayer. The awaited tenth man never arrives, symbolic of the absence of all those who will never return (Farmulska 2006). With the villagers indifferent to their fate and no one to come to their aid, even those remnants of the once-thriving Jewish community fade away: the white face of the farmer "shone less often in the window," and the dry goods merchant, who has been haunting the railway station, awaiting his wife, is no longer noticed. Without the witness willing to acknowledge the face beneath the mask, the traces are threatened with disappearance. It is now up to the witness to continue waiting for the arrival of the tenth man from the past she herself cannot possibly remember. Bearing witness thus becomes a quest for the disappeared faces that memory cannot conjure.

In the story "Henryk's Sister," a woman searches for a glimpse of her husband's features in the face of his twin sister. Henryk was murdered during a failed escape attempt when the house where the couple was hiding in the countryside was surrounded by the gestapo. Henryk's family, who left the country before the war, blames his death on his widow: "You know, the one who did not want to go with us" (Fink 1998, 139). As the woman is looking at the face of Henryk's sister through the window in the café where they are supposed to meet, she recalls the circumstances of her husband's death, trying to remember what his face looked like. The image that returns to her, however, is blank, and she repeats, several times, "He had no face. . . . He had no face" (140–41). Instead, she recognizes Henryk in the face of his twin sister: "It's Henryk reincarnated in his beautiful sister" (137). The woman does not enter the café, and the sister walks away, unaware that her own visage now substitutes for the murdered face of her brother. In a way, the evocation of the person's face literally confers life on the murdered person who is being remembered, although the unsubstitutable face is already deferred in the "mask" of another, in a chain of substitutions. Here the face signifies as the ethical force that breaks through the death mask and defies death itself.

In all of Fink's stories, the frequent motif of the masks that cover "true faces" and threaten them with oblivion is also symbolic of the layers of words with which the storyteller necessarily covers the persons and events she is describing. Fink's narrators often falter in midsentence as they realize that their words can only circumvent the events and never truly touch the horror. In the process of testifying, words acquire an uncanny quality; the instability of everyday expressions and the resulting equivocations and tensions in the narrative point to language itself as a suspect in the crime. As the chasm between words and what is happening in the story is widening, language seems increasingly treacherous even in the simplest of phrases. Fink conveys this deceit in the titles of her stories—"A Spring Morning," "Description of a Morning," "An Afternoon on the Grass," "Birds"—as if the reader were to expect cameos of rural tranquility rather than an account of brutal murder. The most innocent of words become grotesquely distorted by their context. In a short, untitled vignette in the volume *A Scrap of Time*, a young pregnant woman runs after a convoy of old Jewish men being escorted by the SS to the nearby ravine, shouting "Zei gezint, Tate!" (Be well, Papa!). The narrator witnesses this scene from her hiding place, and, to her, those well-wishing words of farewell are ominous. Although language is the bearer of the trace of the other, it is always ethically equivocal. One can also use words to shield oneself from horrifying truths. In the story "Description of a Morning," for instance, the husband protects himself with torrents of words against his wife's reticence and her memory of their daughter who died during the couple's escape from the ghetto. But this verbal buffer carries a price: although words can subdue the horror and thus facilitate physical survival, they often drown the voices of those who need a different kind of speaking, a speaking that, as Fink's narrators know, is first of all listening.

The deceitfulness of words also emerges in the tension between speech and silence. The inflections of silence in Fink's stories are many—the breathless silence of the hidden, the speechlessness of the crowds being led to the site of an execution, the stillness of the earth just before the thundering arrival of the cattle train. The story "Jean-Christophe," for instance, describes a group of young women, members of the work detail at a nearby camp, sitting on the grass in a forest clearing, near the railway tracks. As the women wait for "the thundering of the train," the forest is silent: "There were no birds, but the smell of the trees and flowers was magnificent. We couldn't hear anything. There was nothing to hear. The silence was horrifying because we knew there was shooting going on" (Fink 1996, 32). In "A Spring Morning," silence blankets the scene of a massacre: although the forest floor appears to be somewhat "trampled," "all around was quiet. Not even a bird called out" (40). Terror and imminent death are always announced by silence. The crowds awaiting deportation or marching to the places of execution are mute, as if their speech had already been quelled.[11] One of the tasks the witness/narrator sets for herself is to pry these different silences from the informers' words and let them "speak." She must use language without engulfing the places where words break off because it is also in the silences that penetrate, interrupt, and question speech that the other leaves a trace. While silence can be an impenetrable veil that obliterates traces, it can also allow them to emerge from the deluge of everyday speech.

Within the parameters of Levinasian ethics, the self is primordially a witness to the existence and suffering of another human being, and it is incumbent on it to respond. As we have heard from Fink's narrators, many do not act on that obligation and they choose a negative response, turning away for fear of being wounded by the memory of another or by another's memory. By exposing themselves to being wounded, however, Fink's storytellers are messengers who enable the recurrence of traces in language. The engagement with Fink's literary testimonials, which foreground the movement of traces in becoming witness, allows us to glimpse the opening onto a different thinking of the aesthetic from within Levinas's ethical thought. According to Levinas (1969), memory anchors the I in the temporal continuum "after the event" (56), in chronological time that is a function of consciousness and intentionality. Retention in memory, however, presupposes an ethical time of the witness that cannot be measured by clocks, the time that opens up as an interval in which I am for the other. The modality of that time is the not-yet, which approaches from across the divide that separates me from the other. It is not a swarm of possibilities that the self can apprehend and realize. For Levinas (1998b), representation corresponds to chronological time, and it amounts to "the assembling of being in the present, its synchronization by retention, memory and history, reminiscence" (140). The time of the other, by contrast, is the past that no memory can follow, an immemorial, "utterly bygone past" (Levinas 1986, 335) that cannot be folded into temporality.

The movement of approach toward the invisible other is for Levinas the essence of the ethical relation, and it is that relation that institutes language. If speech presupposes an interlocutor and an eagerness to listen, the first-person narrator in Fink's stories is a trope for the ethical nucleus of language: she is an astute listener who has relinquished her right to tell her own story for the sake of the other. Prior to reconstituting the others' lives in her language, she listens with patience and openness, allowing the stories to reach her from that distant shore. The act of listening is a bridge across the interval between the two times, between the past events and the time of the witness's later account, even if the distance will remain impassable.

The ethical necessity to listen stems from the witnesses' concern for the other's death: in Levinas's (2000) words, "My being affected by the death of the other is precisely that, my relation with his death. It is, in my relation, my deference to someone who no longer responds, already a culpability—the culpability of the survivor" (12). This pre-original culpability destabilizes the self to the deepest core of her being, "to the point of fission" (16). The other's death, the wound of the other's non-being (rather than the fear of my own mortality) is what truly affects me: "We encounter death in the face of the other" (105). This is why, in Levinas's (1998b) evocative metaphor, for the witness, the suffering of the other is like "a thorn burning flesh" (50). The witness experiences it on a somatic level, as a painful shock. Hence the ethical essence of language—the self's aptitude to listen and respond—is intertwined with the sensibility and vulnerability of the body, with the physical exposure to the other's pain. This openness means that I respond to the other with absolute patience and vulnerability. Such absolute passivity, prior to the "I can" and my ability to distinguish between active and passive modes of response, designates an unconditional willingness to receive the other, an attitude of unprejudiced welcome that allows the trace of the other to inscribe itself in my speech. Because I am passive in this sense, because the other needs me, I must act on his or her behalf; as a storyteller, I must search for words that would allow me to do so. Importantly, Levinas (1986) emphasizes that a trace is not a cipher that the other leaves behind to be decoded: "He who left a trace in wiping out his traces did not mean to say or do anything by the traces he left" (357). In the trace the other signifies outside intentionality, in the very movement of effacement.

As we have seen, one of the recurrent motifs in Fink's stories is the obliteration of the victims' faces. In light of Levinas's notion of the face as the expression of my ethical beholdenness to the other, Fink's evocation of faces must also be read as a figurative expression of an ethical injunction. For Levinas, murder is always aimed at the face of the other; yet because only the other's sensible appearance can be annihilated but not his or her alterity as such, the face escapes violence: it is always alive. Expressing the interdiction "Thou shall not murder," the face speaks with the force of ethics that obligates me unconditionally. Although the blurring of its contours threatens to cast the memory of a person into oblivion, the narrator takes up the task of reasserting the primacy of the face, of recovering it as a haunting, everlasting presence, beyond the specificity of the image. In fact, the trope of the face functions as an index of the moments in which the other as absolutely other is evoked and upheld. The other becomes indirectly manifested in the face and thus, paradoxically, casts off the dead shell of the image. As Levinas (1986) puts it, the face is "like a being who opens the window on which his own visage is taking form" (351), attesting to its own appearance precisely by vanishing from the visible sign. The face, which signifies an upsurge of responsibility behind its visual manifestation, attends representation but is never absorbed in it. For Levinas, I bear witness to the other in addressing myself to him or her, although the other never appears to me except as a mask. Yet "the mask presupposes a face" (355): "The face of the other in proximity, which is more than representation, is an unrepresentable trace" (Levinas 1998b, 116). In passing on the trace, the narrator's words are thus the site of unconditional hospitality where the face is welcomed.

She opens up the possibility of an encounter with the face, even if that entails enduring the pain that afflicts her—and subsequently her readers—from behind the mask. What this aesthetic equivocation of Levinas's notion of the face reveals is that it must now be thought of in terms of trace-structure, as the infinite spacing and temporalizing of the face-to-face encounter, which mark the untraversible distance that separates me from the time and space of the other.[12]

HANDPRINTS: TOWARD THE OUTSIDE (OF THE FRAME)

Can the face speak in a work of art? In "The Sublime Offering," Nancy (1993) argues that, in representation, the object is always "in retreat" and withdrawing from the image of itself. The sublime then refers to a movement of continuous erasure of what imagination is striving to represent, whereby imagination presents nothing except its failed effort to outline a finite figure. Instead of setting up a figure, the contour can point only to its own vanishing, signaling an incessant effacement of form. This failed effort and the simultaneous necessity to represent are announced through "this tiny, infinite pulsation. This tiny, infinite rhythmic burst that produces itself infinitely in the *trace* of its own contour" (42; emphasis mine). The essence of the sublime in art, Nancy concludes, is that "art should be exposed and offered" (50). That is, rather than being for itself in gratuitous aesthetic enjoyment, art is a preoriginal gesture of giving of itself in the opening of the figure to the outside. In contrast to the beautiful, which relies on the precise limit of the figure, the sublime refers to the unlimited (and the endlessly unlimiting). Thus, like Lyotard, Nancy moves away from a traditional understanding of the sublime in terms of the negative presentation of the unpresentable to focus on its indeterminate, interruptive, and "unlimiting" nature. He concludes that, ultimately, the sublime is not about presentation; rather, its essence lies in the un-bordering and dissipation of the fixed form.

In the context of the sublime, it is possible therefore to conceive of Levinas's notion of the trace as a sublime *figure* or the figure of the sublime, although the philosopher himself would likely protest that it is not a figure or a concept. Perhaps its force lies in the fact that it is so minimal—truly the figure of absence that is nevertheless indelibly present—especially since it lacks the visual connotations that permeate Levinas's earlier trope of the face. Inversely to Kant's aesthetic theory, however, where the sublime extends from the aesthetic toward the suprasensible and therefore toward the ethical, the sublime figure of the trace, conceived as the (never fulfilled) possibility of bringing forth the image of the other, is a bridge from the ethical toward an aesthetic, although in this movement the boundaries of both domains are radically transformed. The correspondences between Levinas's denunciations of the beautiful and Nancy's articulation of the sublime in terms of the infinite gifting (and disappearing) of the figure allow us to reorient the poethics of disappearing traces toward the works of art inspired by the Holocaust. Levinas rarely makes specific references to visual art, a trait in his work that can be attributed to Judism's interdiction of graven images, yet his allusions to particular artists are by no means uniformly negative. It is true that, for instance, he condemns Leonardo da Vinci's *Mona Lisa* for "its perfection in a world of suffering and evil" (quoted in Hart 2005, 128). However, his assessment of Charles Lapicque's paintings is favorable, and he remarks that, by effacing the content of the objects he is painting, the artist foregrounds open forms that do not "halt the play of erasures" (Levinas 1989, 147).

The "play of erasures" best describes the 1988 engraving by the well-known American artist Robert Morris, *Disappearing Places (Tarnapol)* (fig. 4.1).

This work is one of a series of lead reliefs in which the artist used oblique Holocaust imagery to, in his own words, "counter the pernicious amnesia that is already at work, softening the contours of this mark on our time" (quoted in Amishai-Maisels 1993, 359). The plates refer to small camps in Poland that have never been documented in photographs and therefore have been almost completely forgotten (the word *Tarnapol*, the name of one of the small camps, appears half-covered at the bottom of the panel), as if, in the words of Amishai-Maisel (1995a), "a curtain of oblivion were lowered over this site" (75). The impermanence of memory is also conveyed through the image of a phantom handprint sculpted on what seems to be a curtain: the indistinct grooves that look like a palm with outstretched fingers bring to mind the grip lines that victims clawed in the concrete walls of the gas chambers in their last agonizing moments. The proverbial heaviness of the medium in which the work was executed underscores the implacability of forgetting that has cloaked these places. *Disappearing Places* ponders this historical amnesia, but it also tries to "lift the curtain" and allow the traumatic inscription to break through the neutralizing, aestheticizing images that are trying to erase it. In that

Figure 4.1.   Robert Morris (American), *Disappearing Places (Tarnapol)*, 1988. Lead and steel. 36 1/8 x 46 3/8 x 2 in. 92 x 118 x 5 cm. Courtesy of Ileana Sonnabend Gallery.

sense, this blurry image of forgetting, which, like the name *Tarnapol*, seems to be both sinking into the lead and resisting the closure of its borders, signifies the journey of the trace into the future, while the contour of the outstretched hand interpellates the viewer.

Mordecai Ardon's (Max Bronstein) 1987 work *The Doll of Auschwitz* (plate 1) instantiates the poethics of disappearing traces on many levels. Ardon, a German Jew who fled to Palestine in 1933, painted the triptych in 1987, possibly inspired by the poem "My Doll in Auschwitz," which he heard recited on the street in Paris. In a way, the painting is a translation of this poetic work into a visual medium.[13] As in many of Fink's stories (such as "A Scrap of Time," "Traces," "The Key Game," or "The Garden that Floated Away"), Ardon's painting discloses a world in which a child is forced across the threshold of childhood into the knowledge of danger and impending death. In the first panel, the reality of the child's world—the row of colorful houses with the sun above the *shtetl*—begins to be engulfed

Plate 1. Mordecai Ardon (Israeli), *The Doll of Auschwitz*. Oil on canvas. 1987. Left panel: *At Home,* 116x81 cm; central panel: *The Road of Numbers,* 116 x 195 cm; right panel: *Darkness,* 116x 81 cm. Family J. Dimenstein Collection, Zurich. Courtesy of the Ardon Estate.

Plate 2. Mindy Weisel (American), *My Mother's Back (Memory in Blue)* (2003–2004). Oil on canvas. 91.4 cm x 91.4 cm Courtesy of the artist.

Plate 3. Bracha Ettinger (French Israeli), *Eurydice # 23*, 1992–2005. Oil and xerography, with photocopic dust, pigment, and ashes. Courtesy of the artist.

Plate 4. Ewa Kuryluk (Polish American), *Przy pracy, w chustce mamy* [At work, wearing Mother's scarf], 2001–3. Detail from the installation *Lecą żółte ptaki* [Yellow Birds Fly]. Drawing on silk. Courtesy of the artist.

by darkness and seems to be drifting away, while the doll cowers in a corner of the painting. The images are reminiscent of Marc Chagall's ominous portrayals of Jewish villages, with people, houses, and Torah scrolls floating in the air. They also correspond to Fink's (1996) account of the disjunction between the "old time" of peaceful childhood, which was "measured in an ordinary way" (6), and "the other time," uprooted from chronologies and syncopated with new, threatening words. In one of the stories, "The Garden that Floated Away," Fink's narrator metaphorically conveys this sense of spatiotemporal displacement: "Once I saw a garden float away. It was our neighbors' garden, just as beautiful and lush as ours. . . . I saw it float away, slowly and majestically, into the distance far beyond our reach" (11). In Ardon's painting, the disjunction is emphasized by the stark lines separating the panels. In the second panel of the triptych (titled "The Road of Numbers," in reference to cattle trains carrying their human cargo to the camps), the figure of the doll disappears, and only little doll hands stretch out from the abstractions of dark colors and broken lines, which, on closer inspection, are composed of concentration camp numbers, pointing to the train's inevitable destination. In the third panel, "The Shadows," the doll reappears, although, like a number of Fink's characters, it "has no face," indicating the anonymity of the child's death in the Nazi camp. It floats in the air, reminiscent of poet Paul Célan's incantation of "the grave in the air" in "The Death Fugue." The ascending six little stars correspond to the yellow star on the doll's jacket and contrast starkly with the dark background. Below are tiny footprints, pointing upward as well as toward the outside of the painting's frame, as evanescent and as indelible as Fink's footprints in the snow. The insistent unidirectionality of the footprints-indices seems to unborder the frame, leading the viewer beyond the image. The ominous "journey of no return" on the cattle trains to Auschwitz thus becomes a journey of memory, a "work" of imagination toward the time of the other, and a gift that, in Levinas's words, never returns to the same.

The spectral imprints of hands in both Morris's engraving and Ardon's painting lead us to reflect on the movement of the artist's own hand, suspended over visual representations of Holocaust victims, as in the works from the series *A Prayer for the Dead*, by Jewish Canadian artist Herzl Kashetsky. None of the painter's immediate relatives were directly affected by the atrocities of the Holocaust; yet for almost two decades Kashetsky felt a deep spiritual commitment to explore the

Figure 4.2.   Herzl Kashetsky (Canadian), *Mass Grave, Bergen Belsen* (detail), 1993. Oil on masonite. 81.3 x 106.7 cm. Courtesy of the artist.

Holocaust themes in his art. Following a trip to Europe in 1974, Kashetsky abandoned his former abstract stylistics in favor of photorealism. These first attempts to give visual expression to his reflection on the legacy of the Holocaust, such as his rendition of Margaret Bourke-White's well-known photograph of Holocaust survivors, in which he painted his own face into the scene, led him to further research and visit the camps as well as the sites of former Jewish communities in Poland. In a catalogue essay, curator Tom Smart describes Kashetsky's quest to find an appropriate medium to express his spiritual transformation as the process of discovering that "a work of art is a trace of the event" (Kashetsky 1997, 2). Most of Kashetsky's Holocaust art is realist and rendered in meticulous detail: it took him two years to sketch the diptych *Mass Grave, Bergen Belsen* (1993; fig. 4.2).

In this context, the viewer is struck by the canvas *Dark Remnants*, which seems to be executed in the style of abstract expressionism and thus appears oddly out of place (fig. 4.3). During the opening of the exhibition in Halifax (Canada) in November 2000, the artist explained that *Dark Remnants* was composed of scraps of cloth mounted on

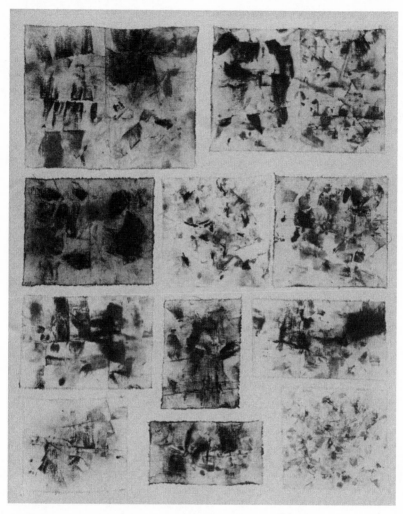

Figure 4.3. Herzl Kashetsky (Canadian), *Dark Remnants*, 1996. Oil on cloth on canvas. 66.0 x 55.9 cm. Courtesy of the artist.

canvas, several of many that were left over from what seemed to him like never-ending work on the diptych. The scraps were used to remove excess paint, and the artist could not bring himself to discard these material remains of his two-year labor on the horrifying image. The pieces of cloth, like Fink's "scraps of time," thus became the relics, recording the artist's journey toward the past in which the victims he was painting had suffered. In a way, the artist's efforts of sketching, wiping out,

Figure 4.4. *Star of David and Number,* carved in brick, exterior of Block 9, Auschwitz. Year unknown. Photo by Joseph P. Czarnecki. Courtesy of Grażyna Czarnecka.

and retouching the images of tangled human bodies in a mass grave express a journey in which, as in Levinas's (1986) evocative description, the other leaves a trace "in wiping out his traces. . . , divesting himself of the form which, however, manifests him" (357, 351). Ultimately, Kashetsky, from a generation that has not been affected directly by the Holocaust, becomes a witness, exposing himself without reserve to the other in vulnerability and pain, a process that, as he mentioned, was not without consequence for his health and sense of well-being.

In addition to Kashetsky's art, Morris's haunting work leads us to the images documented in a book by Joseph P. Czarnecki, *Last Traces: The Lost Art of Auschwitz.* The book contains photographs of etchings on the walls and ceilings in Auschwitz, with special attention to what the author calls epitaphs—carved initials, names, and prisoner numbers. For Czarnecki (1989), these "scratches" reflect "one of the most basic affirmative acts, a man leaves his name, by way of saying nothing more than 'I am,'" and they offer the prisoners a measure of solace that "one's passing would somehow be noticed" (155). An engraving of the Star of David with the prisoner number 130234 is a poignant example (fig. 4.4).

Like Kashetsky, who did extensive research for his Holocaust project, Czarnecki attempted to track down every "last trace," starting with the camp records. In the example above, he discovered that the number 130234 belonged to the prisoner Jan Wiater, who was brought to Auschwitz in 1943. Not all of the prisoners' identities could be established, but in many cases Czarnecki decrypted the engravings and was able to reconstruct the inmates' life stories, which he recounts in the book. These etchings have been subsequently covered or painted over, and the contemporary visitor to Auschwitz-Birkenau State Museum in Oświęcim is unaware of their spectral presence underneath the paint or behind the museum exhibits. Only by following in Czarnecki's "footsteps," as documented in *Last Traces*, can the reader recover the outlines, imaginatively reinscribing them back onto the ceilings and walls and retracing the journey of those whose hands left the marks. Particularly intriguing is the picture of the row of signatures that were found in a well, which is today located on a private farm near the former camp. As the author explains, the signatures were left by a well-digging commando: one member of the group had to lean down "into a still-wet cement pipe to leave the record of their existence" (Czarnecki 1989, 160). For decades, the traces of the group of men were interred under today's town of Oświęcim, until they were exhumed by the photographer and displayed in the book. In speaking of the trace, Levinas (1986) writes that when a stone scratches another stone, it leaves a mark, but the trace of the other's presence, perhaps of the person who held the stone, remains invisible. Yet, without the reference to that person, "this scratch is but an effect" (358). The traces preserved in Czarnecki's photographs, like the blurry photograph in Fink's story, are "scratches" that point far beyond their mere "effect." They are indices that have been obliterated by neglect on one hand and the official protocols of remembrance mandated by the museum on the other. Yet they are powerful memory traces of the men who passed through the world and left a mark.

The last example of visual poethics of disappearing traces is a bilingual edition of a collection of documentary photographs from Warsaw, edited by Jan Jagielski and Tomasz Lec, titled, in English, *The Remnants of the Warsaw Ghetto* and, in Polish, *Nie zatarte ślady getta warszawskiego* (The indelible traces of the Warsaw Ghetto). The authors describe their project as follows:

> The German occupants wanted to wipe out all traces of the mass murder of the inhabitants of the Warsaw Ghetto. . . . However, Hitler's troops did not manage to fulfil the order completely. Some material traces of the former ghetto were preserved, and this photo album is dedicated to them. . . . We would like our visitors to see a vivid

Figure 4.5.   Chłodna Street, 1942. *The Remnants of the Warsaw Ghetto.*
Courtesy of Jan Jagielski.

> picture of the history of the Warsaw Jews in the years 1939–1943
> during a few hours' walk following the indelible traces of the Ghetto.
> (Jagielski and Lec 1997, introduction; translation modified)

Each double page of the book contains a photograph taken in the
Warsaw Ghetto between the years 1939 and 1943, with a detail from
a map of Warsaw identifying the location, and a 1997 photograph of
the same location printed beneath. On the left-hand side are excerpts
from diaries and letters that pertain to the given location. Comparing the two photographs on each page, the viewer is struck by thick
crowds in the images from the ghetto, and by the distinct lack of human presence in the contemporary photographs (figs. 4.5 and 4.6).

In some of the pictures from the ghetto, the photographer captured
a close-up of a human figure—often lying on the street, against the
background of the architectural detail that makes the location easily
recognizable—although in the 1997 picture of the same location, the
place, again, is empty (fig. 4.7).

The juxtaposition creates a negative trace-image, through which
the outline of the human figure has been inscribed in the contemporary scenery. Like a chalk drawing on the pavement at the site of
an accident, it remarks the scene with the haunting memory of an

Figure 4.6.   Chłodna Street, 1997. *The Remnants of the Warsaw Ghetto.*
Courtesy of Jan Jagielski.

absent body, disturbing the landscape of today's Warsaw. In Fink's
(1996) story "Traces," the eyewitness recounting the annihilation of a
small-town ghetto marvelled, "The people are gone—their footprints
remain. Very strange" (137). Looking at the twin photographs, the
viewer experiences the same uncanny sensation—of an empty location inhabited by the absent figures, and of the doubling and overlapping of chronological frames, akin to Fink's splitting of time along the
dividing line of the first *Aktion* in the ghetto.

THE GIFT OF THE WORLD

The poethics of disappearing traces outlined above has been clasped
between two documentary testimonials: a scene from *Shoah*, a Holocaust documentary in the sense that it is a record of interviews in
the present rather than of cadres from the past, and Jagielski and
Lec's book of archival photographs, in which the shots of contemporary locations are juxtaposed with the photographs of the same
locations in the past. Perhaps the journey between the two documen-
taries, passing through Fink's literary texts, Ardon's and Morris's abstract art, Kashetsky's realist paintings, and Czarnecki's photographs

Figure 4.7.   Leszno Street, the Church of the Holy Mary's Birth, 1941. *The Remnants of the Warsaw Ghetto.* Courtesy of Jan Jagielski.

of etchings on the walls of Auschwitz barracks, when articulated as the movement of poethic tracing, renders the distinction between the document and the work of literature or art less preponderant. This equivocation is brought out in Czarnecki's book of documentary photographs: the author insists that these simple engravings, these "scratches" that he so painstakingly pursued with his camera, are the "art of Auschwitz." It is here that the gentle force of ethical imagination complements, enriches, and ultimately overflows the confines of the documentary frame, in the passage toward the time of the other.

Defending Levinas against charges that he rejects poetic imagination for the sake of ethics, Richard Kearney argues that the philosopher's suspicion of images "is not directed against the poetic power of imagination per se but against the use of such power to incarcerate the self in a blind-alley of self-reflecting mirrors." Through poetic imagination that reaches toward the other and allows the other to speak, Levinas's "face" "exceeds the plastic form of the image representing it" (Kearny 2002, 88).

In an attempt to develop a framework in which to situate Holocaust literature and art, I have argued that Levinas moves toward a different conceptualization of aesthetics. This "other" aesthetics is not concerned with representation, revelation, or dissimulation but with disturbance and interruption at the limit, where the image, the figure, the outline, open up to an outside. Levinas's notion of the trace, albeit an ethical figuration of unassumable alterity, signals therefore a possibility of aesthetic signification.[14] Within the poethics of disappearing traces, the other—ungraspable in an image or word—can attest to its existence from behind the figure, as an echo of what has been forgotten. The trace lacerates language or image, cutting deeply into its layers and rearranging its structures. In James Hatley's (2000) words, the modes of expression that are animated by the force of ethics (which he refers to as "prophetic witness") are ultimately "*dis-figuring*, that is to say, a figure is introduced only to be emptied out by the intrusion of a troubling excess that defies any space for a claim of mastery" (131). According to Levinas (1986), representation in the image, as understood by traditional aesthetics, allows for contemplative distance and mediation, which blunt the shock of the encounter with the other. Yet, he asks, "Whence comes to me this shock when I pass indifferent, under the gaze of another?" (350). Bearing witness is a continuing search for the disappearing trace, and it occurs in proximity with the other, where the impact of the other on my life is crushing. Ethical imagination carries the other toward the image, where the witness discovers its truth that is "not the truth of representation" (Levinas 1998b, 146). In that sense, a Levinasian art of disappearing traces radically calls into question traditional aesthetics: representation is undone by the trace, which interrupts, frustrates, and discomforts consciousness. At the same time, despite Levinas's insistence on the priority of ethics, the trace already carries the promise of a figure, as an aesthetic force of the ethical. To bear witness means therefore that what now emerges as an aporetic relation between the two forces registers itself in the vulnerability of the body, in the beating of the heart "exposed outside by breathing, by divesting its ultimate substance even to the mucous membranes of my lungs" (107). These striking expressions, again, resonate with Nancy's transvaluation of the sublime: for Nancy (1993), the sublime, the experience at the limit, is felt in the body and thus testifies to our capacity to be affected: "Suspended life, breath cut off—the beating heart" (46). At that limit—for Nancy, the limit of the sublime that, extending toward the outside, cuts across the body—"there is neither aesthetic nor ethics. There is a thought of offering which defies this distinction"

(49). The palpable breathlessness of Holocaust testimonials and the heavy stamp they leave on those who choose to respond mark them as a unique challenge to what Levinas condemns as the hold of representation over ethics in the West. As a witnessing subject—an artist, writer, viewer, or reader—I am being held responsible for the memory of the past since this challenge is inscribed in my own voice, the voice of the one who responds: "It is the pure trace of a 'wandering cause,' inscribed in me" (Levinas 1998b, 150), my very corporeality constituted by "the pain of the effort" (50). If National Socialism's ultimate crime was to obliterate the traces of the victims in order to make the atrocity unimaginable, *the poethic inscription of disappearing traces reveals itself as the movement in which the difference between the ethical injunction to remember and the aesthetic imperative of figuration is produced.* Bearing witness to this difference or *differend,* to use Lyotard's term, makes it possible to imagine the unimaginable and thus to produce works of remembrance.

The past, as it is usually measured by chronology, will eventually be assembled in the textbooks of history, but, as Levinas (1998b) insists, "When man truly approaches the other, he is uprooted from history" (52). Historiography abounds with examples of new generations appropriating for themselves the works of the dead and conquerors usurping the monopoly on historical truth, as Benjamin once stated.[15] "The judgement of history," says Levinas (1969), "is always pronounced *in absentia*" (242), and, although it is incumbent on us to learn, to know, and to understand, recorded history will continue as a series of betrayals. By contrast, what Levinas calls "justice" writes itself as traces, equivocation, and disturbance in the midst of evidence. Because ethics overflows recorded history, beings "can speak rather than lend their lips to an anonymous utterance of history. . . . Peace is produced as this aptitude for speech" (1969, 23). The task of Holocaust literature and art is to continue to write and rewrite history, so that the invisible can inscribe itself on its pages. This is not to reinscribe the opposition between the ethics of memory and the knowledge of history, but to insist, with Levinas, that the meaning of history is engendered by the moral obligations we have for one another. As Richard Cohen points out in his preface to Levinas's *Unforeseen History*, the meaning of recorded history comes to us from the future for which it is intended, from the time of the other, even though it is an account of past events. As such, in Levinas's (2004) apt phrase, it is "unforeseen" (*les imprévus de l'histoire*; 2004, xiii).

It is imperative that the storyteller passes on the account, even if she is always already dispossessed of her work by the other who has summoned her to pursue this task. Written in ethical language, her work is destined to "a history that I cannot foresee" (Levinas 1986, 227) because it goes toward the other in radical generosity, beyond aesthetic enjoyment or gratification. Levinas argues that justice requires representation in the Said, even if it betrays the alterity in a theme and immobilizes it in a figure; this is why we must strive to "postpone . . . the hour of treason." The works we have considered here actively labor to reduce that betrayal, but they also foreground the fact that it is their unique aesthetic force that brings us to them and holds us under obligation, thus making "infinitesimal difference between man and non-man" (Levinas 1969, 35).

The words from Talmud Sahendrin, "He who saves one person saves the world entire," have often been evoked in post-Holocaust contexts, especially in relation to the courageous deeds of the rescuers. In relation to the strife between memory and forgetting, the passage can be expanded to also mean that he or she who passes on the trace saves the world entire, rescuing it from oblivion one word, one detail, one "scratch" at a time. Each gesture is a unique event, in which the other has passed through the world, producing "fission of the same by the untenable other at the heart of myself; where disquiet disturbs the heart at rest" (Levinas 2000, 110–11).

CHAPTER FIVE

"Witnesses against Themselves"

Encounters with Daughters of Absence

The fragility of Eurydice between two deaths, before, but also after the disappearance . . . the figure of Eurydice seems to me to be emblematic of my generation and seems to offer a possibility for thinking about art.

—BRACHA L. ETTINGER, "Que dirait Eurydice?"

You are witnesses against yourselves.

—Joshua 24:15

DAUGHTERS OF ABSENCE: MEMORY IN BLUE

Already in 1998, historian Annette Wieviorka noted, with some trepidation, that traditional ways of representing history had been recently challenged by imaginative interpretations of the past. In contrast to objective and emotionally distant historical accounts, these representations often focus on transmitting sensory and emotive experiences, and on producing the effect of sympathy in the viewer. Visual works of art in particular have been increasingly accepted as legitimate forms of testimony. Indeed, they are even considered unique in their ability to evoke what falls outside of historical knowledge.[1] This final chapter looks back to the concepts of "the witnessing subject" and "disappearing traces," developed in previous sections of the book, in order to inquire what it means for visual works of art to "bear witness." It focuses on art created by the daughters of survivors and considers them as performative reenactments through which the witnessing subject constitutes itself by returning to and departing from the site of trauma. By examining the dialectic between inherited trauma, wounded memory and loss, and creative work oriented toward rebirth, promise, and restitution, I argue that it is by no means a coincidence that the interpretive shift in dominant modes of representing history, toward the privileging of imaginative works of art and literature, occurred at the same time that the children of survivors, the so-called second-generation, were coming into voice. The inquiry is also situated in the context of the feminist reflection on women's art, in relation to the culturally established role of daughters of survivors as "memorial candles."

Commenting on her childhood as a daughter of Holocaust survivors, second-generation artist Bracha Ettinger writes, "As a child, I was a witness to witnesses. When I paint or when I listen, I am that too" (quoted in Pollock 1995, 130). Unsurprisingly, such acts of witness are marked by a conflict between the obligation to the past (which these daughters never experienced yet whose traces they carry) and a desire to unburden themselves of traumatic memory, the tension being far more pronounced in the second generation than in the generation of survivors. These artists are thus often "witnesses against themselves," who resist the imperative to testify even though the positing of the witnessing subject is the prime impetus in the work. In Levinas's terms, such witnessing "occurs whether one wills it or not" (Hatley 2000, 94).

What is the *modus operandi* of these memory events if what they remember is someone else's memory, an unimaginable, inaccessible memory of "Over There"?[2] How do these "witnesses without the event" (Ettinger's phrase) testify to what Dori Laub and Shoshana Felman (1992) describe as an "event without a witness" (75)? Moreover, according to what criteria do we consider the authenticity of this "secondhand" memory work? To whom does this memory, which constantly transmutes the artwork into sites of mourning, belong? This chapter offers an exploration of the artists' intimate journeys through the memory of their parents' trauma, as it shaped their lives and work, yet at the same time it examines a larger social significance of the artwork as a witness to historical events in the past and a site of working through the community's unmasterable past. What emerges, therefore, is art's potential not only to represent but to fashion and even bring about new models of intersubjective, communal existence.

In critical analyses of art and literature of the second generation, scholars often draw attention to the writers' and artists' attempts to reference traumatic contexts in ways that problematize definitions of art as a means of representation. In Régine Robin's (2002) words, they look for ways to "transmit *otherwise* than in the fullness of representation" (135; translation and emphasis mine). In the context of an inquiry into the status of the visual work of art as witness and the artist as witnessing subject, it is important to underscore Robin's reference to transmitting memory *otherwise*, and to inflect it with an ethical sense that this peculiar adverb carries for Levinas.

Since the publication of Helen Epstein's (1979) groundbreaking study *Children of the Holocaust,* the generation that grew up in the shadow of the Holocaust has become recognized as a distinct social group.[3] At first, they were primarily seen as transferential recipients of their parents' emotional burdens, "bearing the scar without the wound" (Sicher 1998, 27) and embodying the irreparable loss and bereavement caused by events of which they had no direct memory. As Epstein intuited, traumatic symptoms in the second generation were produced not as much by the knowledge of the horrors recounted by the parents but precisely by the children's lack of such memory. As a result, the children's identities were shaped by that lacuna.[4] The scholars' interest in children of survivors reflected clinicians' diagnosis of impaired parenting skills of the first generation, attributable mostly to the caregivers' loss of their own parents at the transformative stage of their lives. The survivors' emotional unavailability, lack of empathy, overprotectiveness, and guilt-inducing behavior had debilitating effects on the family dynamic, often stunting the children's maturation and individuation process (Hass 1990, 43). Indeed, in various accounts, children of survivors amply documented the negative impact of the transferential dynamic, in which they had become projective screens of their parents' traumatic experiences and of their psychological struggle to cope with the past. This transference, that is, their "function as a repetition of their parents' encounter with death" (Grimwood 2007, 11) often led to overidentification and even obsession with the parents' experiences. Epstein (1979, 9–10), for instance, began her volume of interviews with children of survivors with a recollection of episodes in which she herself experienced such overidentification:

> I saw things [in my imagination] I knew no little girl should see. Blood and shattered glass. Piles of skeletons and blackened barbed wire with bits of flesh stuck to it the way flies stick to the walls after they are swatted dead. Hills of suitcases, mountains of children's shoes. Whips, pistols, boots, knives and needles. . . . The Seventh Avenue local became a train of cattle cars on its way to Poland. . . . There would be no burial. The passengers would vanish.[5]

According to Dominick LaCapra, the ultimate danger of such overidentification is not vicarious psychic wounding, which, in extreme cases, may lead to suicide, but the fact that the surrogate victim becomes immobilized in substitute suffering. Such passive submission is detrimental to the processes of working through since it prevents an individual from extricating herself from the past and engaging in future-oriented, meaningful ethical and political action. The artists discussed in this chapter, however, explore the processes of identification in a much more nuanced manner, as multiple strategies of dealing with the past, of becoming a self in the contemporary world, and relating to others.

In her work with children of survivors, historian Esther Faye (2001), herself also a child of survivors, argues that such recollections are not mere vicarious representations of events never experienced (and thus alienated from the 'real" historical event). Instead, they occasionally manifest the traces of deep memory (or a "somatic kernel") that bears a direct if perhaps inexpressible relation to the event (527).[6] This residue is unavailable to conscious recall and only resurfaces in the form of repetition compulsion. Yet it becomes a passage from "the failure to remember what is fundamentally impossible to remember" to testimony, and, as such, it can "bear witness to Shoah's truth."

The passage toward a witnessing subject articulated by Faye originates in the inherited trauma, but it also transcends the resulting pathologies. Epstein and Faye thus express a need for more holistic and affirmative perspectives on the transmission of traumatic memory. Agreeing with this viewpoint, Aaron Hass (1990), in his study *In the Shadow of the Holocaust,* reevaluates transgenerational interactions in survivor families to highlight survivors' determination and adaptability (as reflected in the high percentage of survivors who have moved on to lead successful lives). Instead of focusing solely on pathologies of survivors' family lives, he argues that this resilience was bequeathed to their offspring (22–23). Similarly, Efraim Sicher's (1998) edited volume *Breaking the Crystal* focuses on the second generation's positive attempts to "recover their personal story" from the narratives of their parents' lives, in which they have been imbricated (6). Both Hass and Sicher notice that, in many cases, the psychic need to search for "identity and memory" stemming from the inherited trauma has become a powerful creative force. Admittedly, many children of survivors pursued creative projects because they wanted to compensate their parents for their losses. Musician Patinka Kopec, for instance, speaks of her achievements as a way "to affirm the reason for my parents' survival" and to serve as "testament to their struggles" (quoted in Weisel 2000, 25, 30). But many also express feelings similar to those of one of Hass's interviewees: "I feel like my life was a gift so I don't waste it" (47).

American artist Mindy Weisel (2000) was born in 1947 in the Bergen-Belsen displaced persons camp. She undertook art as a form of therapy to cope with the pain of growing up with parents whose psychic wounds had made them emotionally distant and unavailable.[7] In painting, Weisel writes, she was able to express the feelings that had been stunted by her parents' perpetual sadness, and art became for her "a form of prayer, a form of dance, of song, of life itself" (xix). In the 1970s she began working on the series *Paintings of the Holocaust*, which were dark abstract canvases in watercolor or acrylic, overwritten with symbols of destruction, such as her father's concentration camp number (A3146) or Hebrew words that connote mourning.

The titles of the works served as unequivocal indices: *Barbed Souls*; *Ovens*; *Ani Maamin*. After a few years, however, Weisel began to introduce "passionate intense colors," especially a vivid blue that pushed through the stifling, mournful shrouds of dark paints. "The color blue," Weisel (2007) says, "my mother's favorite color, expresses the beauty and spirituality we were raised with." Having become a means of restoring broken family bonds, the color blue also allowed the artist to reengage with the Jewish tradition, since blue has spiritual significance in Judaism, as reflected in her painting *My Mother's Back/Memory in Blue* (plate 2).[8]

As representations, Weisel's canvases are indecipherable palimpsests, deaf and dumb witnesses whose referents recede into the thickness of paint. Yet, for the artist, they map her journey from traumatic reenactment of her parents' experiences toward healing and celebration of life. By chromatically inscribing the past in the present, Weisel literally "paints" her mother and herself out of darkness into the bright blue of beauty, spirituality, and love. Here, the color blue has become the badge of the witnessing subject, facilitating psychic recovery and a renewed sense of agency.

In her collection of interviews with daughters of Holocaust survivors titled *Daughters of Absence*, Weisel (2000) reflects, "Time supposedly heals all wounds. Does it really? Or do we take that time and take that loss and turn it into something else, something that takes the shape and the form of our loss. Is it perhaps the source of the deepest art?" (xv). Challenging the view that the debilitating effects of an inherited traumatic past are irreparable, Weisel's book serves as a forum for the "daughters of absence" to give testimony to complex interrelations between trauma and artistic creation. Weisel's objective is to celebrate the lives and artistic achievements of second-generation women. She is thus determined to give a positive answer to Efraim Sicher's question as to whether the Holocaust can be "a usable past" for the next generations, even if their embracement of life always takes place in memory of death (Sicher 1998, 9).[9] This affirmation is expressed in Weisel's (2000) dedication of the book, "To our dear family and friends, and those lost to us, may this book always serve as a reminder of the great miracle and beauty that is life," an homage much more celebratory in tenor than Emmanuel Levinas's (1998) epitaphic dedication in *Otherwise than Being*.[10] In their accounts in Weisel's interviews, the artists call on their creative work to reestablish continuity between the past and the present, and to recover a sense of wholeness and well-being. Although none of them tries to conceal the traumatic origin of their creative impulse, their focus is on what Robin (2002) describes as "the necessity to restore the connection beyond the rent, the reconstitution of the family tree, the need to find the traces" (129; translation mine).[11] In this view, the vicarious labor of mourning becomes a form of genealogical work in the process of which the artists attempt to stitch together the severed family ties and to forge connections not only to the murdered relatives (whom they never had a chance to know but whose names they often bear) but also to their living parents, some of whom have isolated themselves in their grief, unable to leave the past behind. Both in her artwork and in her book, Weisel underscores the central place of matrilinear genealogies in memory transmission, in the labor of mourning, and in creative processes. In a way, testimonies by creative women in Weisel's book perform a function akin to the chorus in a Greek tragedy: they are an assembly of female voices that mourn the dead, as women always have, and whose function is ultimately cathartic.

While embracing Weisel's perspective that emphasizes healing instead of dwelling on the wound, one needs to also remain mindful of James E. Young's and Dominick LaCapra's admonitions against the danger of creating "redemptive narratives" of the Holocaust, a risk certainly inherent in these life-affirming accounts.[12] Moreover, a scrupulous inquiry into the reasons for scholarship's shift of emphasis from trauma to reconciliation and psychic growth would require a larger examination of the social, cultural, historical, and political determinants that have shaped Holocaust memory, in recent decades, a task that exceeds the scope of my investigation.

In the following, I will engage with the artistic production of three "daughters of absence" who are not included in Wiesel's book: Lily Markiewicz (German British), Bracha L. Ettinger (French Israeli), and Ewa Kuryluk (Polish American). All are second-generation women artists, whose work has been profoundly influenced by their parents' experience of the Holocaust. Their works speak to one another at the intersections of witnessing, identity, and memory. Further, like Weisel, each of them has also produced written works that relate to their visual artistic production. Markiewicz wrote a volume of poetic reflections, which initiated one of her installation series; Ettinger, a prolific art theorist and psychoanalyst, has penned numerous interventions into art history that speak directly to her own art practice; and Kuryluk is a renowned art critic and novelist. While artists' books and written statements by artists are by no means unusual, they play a unique role in the art of second-generation artists. Finally, the subtitles in this chapter draw attention to the evocative color-coding of the artwork: Markiewicz's blue (which is also the dominant color of Weisel's canvases), Ettinger's violet, and Kuryluk's yellow.[13]

LILY MARKIEWICZ'S VISUAL POETHICS

While Weisel identifies herself unambiguously as "a daughter of absence" and refers to her art as a gift she has inherited from her parents, Lily Markiewicz's work manifests a more complex relation to her heirloom. As she states, her work is not about what happened during the Holocaust, but rather about its effects on her generation and the role it plays in the present.[14] Thus, although she describes herself as "a second-generation survivor" (Markiewicz 2002, 16), in many ways, her sophisticated statements on the paradoxes of inherited memory and the dilemmas of Jewish belonging echo those of Christian Boltanski. Boltanski was born in 1944 in France to a Jewish father and a Christian mother (the mother was hiding her spouse throughout the war). Although the artist admits that Judaism had a profound impact on his work, he refuses to equate his Jewish background with the Holocaust, and very few of his works make direct references to the Holocaust as a historical event, although they have often been read that way.[15] In one of the disclaimers, Boltanski says, "But my work is not about the camps, it's after the camps. . . . [It] is not about the Holocaust, it's about death in general, about all of our death" (quoted in Liss 1998, 51).[16]

Markiewicz was born in Germany, to parents of Polish Jewish descent. Her father survived the war in Russian labor camps after escaping from Poland, while her mother was hidden in a convent in Belgium. The artist currently resides in London, England, and works in a variety of media: performance, photography, film, video, and installation art. In her earlier works, Markiewicz explored Judaism and Jewishness as the site of self-definition, describing herself as a secular Jew.[17] In *I Don't Celebrate Christmas* (1990), for instance, she placed a mirror with the word "Jew" sandblasted across it at the entrance to the exhibition, imposing a startling identification tag on a visitor's chest. The interior space of the exhibition was divided into two rooms. In the first room, six mirrors were draped as a symbol of Jewish mourning (alluding to the prohibition of seeing oneself in the mirror during the shivah), with a spotlight illuminating the space in front of each mirror. Another mirror, suspended from the ceiling, reflected a text that was placed on top of a tall block. The text explained the Jewish custom of covering mirrors and made reference to Dumah, the angel in charge of the souls in the nether world. In the other room was a large panel with a photograph of the artist in the process of covering or perhaps uncovering one of the mirrors.[18] This self-reflective image hinted at the central theme of the work: the *unveiling* of the very processes of memory work and the emergence of the (veiling) subject, whom we see poised to announce herself in that space. In that sense, the multiplication of mirrors referenced but also questioned psychoanalyst Jacques Lacan's concept of the mirror stage. In the mirror stage, the divided subject, assembled from inchoate fragments of speech and body, is unified through specular (mis) identification. Within the space of Markiewicz's installation, however, such self-consolidation of the witnessing subject is denied. The other photographic panel in the room depicted a dark, semireflective surface of water, adding further symbolic layers, as well as evoking the Greek myth of Narcissus. In front of this image (and opposite the other photograph) were placed piles of cloth, neatly folded. As Monica Bohm-Duchen (1995b) notes, Markiewicz's use of the mirror surfaces hinted at the Western cultural symbol of female vanity, while cloth evoked traditionally female roles in the Jewish tradition, thus offering an artistic reflection on the construction of femininity in Judaism (138).

I Don't Celebrate Christmas thus provided a multilayered commentary on the complexities of the relation between artistic representation and the collective sites of mourning, the "layering" being visually expressed in the piles of folded cloth underneath the mirrors. As in the case of Boltanski's installations in which the artist used anonymous pieces of clothing (such as *The Clothes of François C* and *Canada*), Markiewicz's stacked cloth has been interpreted as an allusion to the mounds of clothes left behind by the murdered Jews in the Nazi camps (Bohm-Duchen 1995b, 138). They must be read, however, also more universally, as the artifacts of mourning in general, the clothes suggesting the absence and loss of their former wearers. Thus, through its rich symbolic dimension, Markiewicz's installation simultaneously encouraged more general interpretations, outside the scope of the Judaic tradition, yet prohibited them at the same time by branding the name "Jew" on the visitor's forehead and by including a description of the Jewish ritual of mourning. It also alluded to the violence of collective memory, which imposes group identity through naming and ritual. Innovative conceptual strategies developed for this installation allowed Markiewicz to fuse disparate interpretive frameworks, such as the psychoanalytic concept of structural trauma that the subject must work through in order to emerge as a unified entity; references to the Holocaust as part of family history; and the intersubjective and ritualistic contexts of collective memory. It also drew attention to the fragmentation of memory as it is intertwined with the processes of self-identification, and to the multiplicity of coordinates that orient these processes. Since installation art must be reassembled each time it is exhibited, it performatively aligns with the dynamic and fluctuating nature of memory, displaying it always anew, as an unrepeatable event.

Markiewicz's work is thus focused on the tense dynamic of the self's coming into consciousness as an artist and witness, referencing the historical trauma of the Holocaust only indirectly. Like Boltanski, Markiewicz (2002) resists being "subsumed into a Holocaust narrative" (15), although she did not object to her work being included in exhibitions that focused on the place of the Holocaust in cultural memory, such as *After Auschwitz—Installations* at the Imperial War Museum in London and *Art after Auschwitz*, curated by Monica Bohm-Duchen, both in 1995. As the artist explains, however,

Figure 5.1. Lily Markiewicz (British), *Places to Remember II*, 1995. Detail of the photo-sound installation. Courtesy of the artist.

her objective in participating in Holocaust-themed exhibits was to offer a counterperspective to the "usual striped-pyjamas images and the endless re-visitations of places of horror."[19]

This "scintillation of the Holocaust" (Sidra DeKoven Ezrahi's term, 1980) in Markiewicz's work was poignant in the installation *Places to Remember II*. The exhibit consisted of a rectangular white "room within a room," in reference to the Jewish holiday of Sukkot, which the artist constructed on site, with two large photographic panels mounted on opposite walls.[20] The first black-and-white photograph depicted what appeared to be sand pouring into a bowl, although the identity of both the grainy substance and the material of which the vessel was made were left deliberately ambiguous. The other was a triptych showing two black-and-white images of sand that were separated by a third color photograph of sand being sifted from hand to hand (fig. 5.1).

The images were accompanied by a voice recording that repeated lines referring to the themes of journeying and displacement. Here, the two hands poised in the gesture of pouring sand (salt? sugar?) in the middle of the triptych suggested the impermanence, perhaps even the emptiness, of memory. The arrangement of the hands seemed to symbolize openness, hospitality, and vulnerability, but could perhaps also mean the opposite: possession, might, and violence. It was unclear from what material the bowl was made: showing itself as a clay vessel, it evoked an ancestral memory that, like an oblation, both nourishes and provides an individual with a nameable place, although it also weighs one down with the burden of collective belonging. Metamorphosed into a metal bowl, however, it conjured, in Griselda Pollock's (2001a) words, "the memory of the battered tin bowl" from the Lager (16). The starkness of the suddenly visible grains of perhaps sand and the play of movement and stillness summoned the sensation of passing through a vast desert, as if trudging through a boundless

landscape of memory. Here Markiewicz alluded to the writings of
the Egyptian-born writer Edmond Jabès and his poetic evocations of
the Jew as a perennial figure of exile and archetypal stranger. Yet the
journey through those placeless "places to remember" was also an
exodus from a constraining framework of remembrance; here, also
in affinity with Jabès, the artist withheld direct references to "Auschwitz" and instead engaged in memory work as an infinite "distance
to travel" (Mole 1997, 176).

Prior to creating *Places to Remember II*, the artist wrote a book,
The Price of Words: Places to Remember 1–26. In the installation,
the white pages of the book would transform into white walls upon
which to hang up memory fragments, a textual narrative in a tense
parallel to the visual one. On each page of the volume, the artist inscribed a brief poetic reflection on memory, journeying, being in the
world and being-Jewish, homecoming, and displacement, each starting with a consecutive letter of the alphabet. The book was written
in the form of basic memory lessons from A to Z, a primer without
which one cannot begin the journey into the past. The text introduced
a personal dimension into the artist's work, the book's allusive, poetic aphorisms flickering like the flames of a memorial candle lit in the
memory of her parents: "I light a candle for this shadow, once so ea-
ger to abide by what was said: darkness, darkness; echoes in the hol-
low of my hands" (Markiewicz 1992, chapter W). In the counterpoint
of the two media and in their mutual tribute, Markiewicz thus set up
a creative dialogue between past, present, and future in which the images of grains of sand and marks of ink flowed together into the writing of memory. The solidity of the white walls echoed the durability
of the page, yet the images of shifting sands evoked forgetting and the
erasure of the referent in the act of writing.

In the poetic volume, the words were transformed into "places
to remember." They have "a price" because they come at the price
of painful recollection: the tongue is "charred" from holding them
inside one's mouth (chapter Q), as if they were themselves hot
and gritty grains of sand. At the same time, they are priceless in
their infinite capacity to carry an unbearable weight, and they are
cherished, even if they scorch and disfigure one's mouth. Under
the letter J, Markiewicz wrote, "As I trace the landscape of their
memory, bridging *Here* and *There*, *In* and *Out*, *Them* and *Us*, I
too have truly become a Wandering Jew" (J). Here, Markiewicz's
writing itself "wanders" in image- words, which are identified as

Figure 5.2. Lily Markiewicz (British), *Promise II*, 1997. Detail of the photo-sound-video installation. Courtesy of the artist.

"Jew-words." The text under the letter L, perhaps alluding to the artist's first name, states curtly, "(Always another place)" (L), offering a parenthesized acknowledgement of the condition of exile and displacement. Thus, similarly to her art, the words do not allow the witness to fully coincide with the act of witnessing. This perpetual dislocation of the witness indicates that one can never truly leave the wounding past behind, no matter how far one wanders away. This distance, however, also marks an opening toward a future whose meaning the words have not yet been able to capture, a future that will happen in another place, on another page yet to be written: "I carry memories to where there are none. . . . Places wedged in between, present only by virtue of not quite being there" (O). Perhaps the letter O, in the openness of its embrasure, designates this word-place yet to come. Markiewicz writes under the letter Y that forks like a crossroad, "I set my bundles down and build for them a place that will remember," but she also builds herself from that place, erecting the walls of self, both fragile and resilient, from the *matzevot* (tombstones) of these words/works that she has dedicated to her parents.

Markiewicz's next installation, *Promise II*, was composed of six blue light-sensitive dioline prints suspended from the ceiling, a video monitor embedded in the wall, and four speakers emitting the sounds of the public swimming pool and of rhythmic, underwater breathing (fig. 5.2).[21] The images, showing bodies of swimmers, would fade over time and eventually disappear, becoming white pieces of paper.[22] The installation simulated a visual, aural, and tactile environment, in which the images of moving bodies seemed frozen by the camera. Since, despite the white walls, the room was dark and cool, with only spotlights bringing out the large images, the installation exuded a cathedral-like solemnity, transforming the swimming pool into a temple. Here, the water and the darkness contrasted with the sand and bright light of *Places to Remember II*, situating the two works in a dialogue and underscoring their common themes of rituals of memory, coming into identity, nomadism, and searching for a home, and exploring the possibility of being Jewish "within a tradition which may also seem obsolete."[23] In *Promise II*, the artist created a space of self-encounter through the underwater descent into one's own body, thus countering the placelessness of trauma and the lacerating effects of traumatic memory. As she remarks in her artist's statement, "Whatever promise lies beyond the surface of the water, whilst immersed and observed by the unflinching eye of the goldfish, we come face to face with our own being" (2).

For Markiewicz (2002), this process of coming into consciousness is a precondition of becoming a witness (25). She comments, "If you think about witnessing, it means that you enter into a kind of relationship, first and foremost with yourself. You also, if you have been present in that moment of witnessing, will have the need to extend that out, toward others" (26). In the larger context of art by "daughters of absence," the cool blue of Markiewicz's swimming pool contrasts with the radiant blue of Weisel's canvases. While for Weisel blue was the color of memory and maternal legacy, for Markiewicz it evokes homelessness, uncertainty, and the vulnerability of the body in its proper mortality, as we become aware of it in the space of self-encounter. Yet what emerges in the spiraling columns of air that the swimmers breathe out, and in the taut lines of their bodies, is the strength that comes from that weakness. As in *Places to Remember II*, one panel shows the swimmer's open hand, projecting the confidence of the palm that needs not curl itself into a fist, as it would in fear or anger. The seriality of the six panels, corresponding to the six covered mirrors in *I Don't Celebrate Christmas*, seems to reenact traumatic repetition compulsion in the dark tunnels of memory. In the context of Jewish spirituality, constantly referenced by the artist even though she pulls away from its orthodox meanings, the number six is the symbol of connection, like the hooked letter *vav* [ו], the sixth letter of the Hebrew alphabet. This numerological reference in Markiewicz's work emphasizes the bond between the very different places that this memory connects. The taut, "*vav*-like" bodies of the swimmers in the six panels become powerful symbols of contrasting fragility and durability, pain and creative inspiration, all of which have shaped the dynamic between the first and the second generations. The transience of the materials included in the installation (water, sound, fading images) conveys the dichotomies of impermanence and continuity, creation and destruction, hypostasis of the self and its dissolution, which structure that relation and one's place within the "tradition." Markiewicz's installation is a theatre of memory seized with the terror of imminent disappearance, but it also offers a promise that it is possible to leave the traumatic landscape behind, to let it fade into history. This tension is played out in the body itself: by capturing her images in a disappearing medium and by creating, for a viewer, a sensation of being ungrounded, Markiewicz fashions a somatic experience of the dissolution of memory, where the body is a discursive site of working through trauma.

Markiewicz's conception of "promise" is derived from Jewish messianic thought, and she relates it to the view that the word is the only true homeland for a Jew. For Markiewicz, this promise of the word, by virtue of which one belongs to the Jewish people, is inseparable from the promise of coming home to oneself, of greeting oneself with joy, even if this event can never fully take place. In one of her talks, the artist remarked, "I seem to be building walls a lot," and *Places to Remember II* and *Promise II* involved a lot of building.[24] Yet both installations also drew attention to the fragility and impermanence of these identity-sheltering constructions. In *Promise II*, for instance, the walls suggested the safety and comfort of a maternal home, but they also receded into the darkness of the room, refusing to provide a foundation and a determined point of origin. The encounter with oneself is then always a missed encounter and a *méconaissance*. The intimacy of self-encounter evoked in the panels of *Promise II* posits a subject that emerges into time and space, yet this subject is also an addressee called upon by another who comes from the past; by the artist's parents whose voices have left traces in her work and summoned it into being. Reminiscent of Abraham's declaration "Here I am," which Levinas cites as the paradigm of unconditional submission to the call of the other, Markiewicz's self-encountering subject is also loosened from itself. Hence her perspective is also consonant with Levinas's view of the subject as constituted through the interpellation by the other. For Markiewicz, as for Levinas, just as I must speak, utter the Said, so that the Saying can trace itself in my voice, I must bear witness to myself so that I can leave a trace of bearing witness to the other.

In the panels of *Promise II*, the viewer becomes aware that human skin is the envelope that contains the self and safeguards its boundaries, protecting it from the outside world. Yet skin is also a sensitive, vulnerable membrane through which an individual comes into contact with others, and which is immediately affected by their actions. Along the surface of the skin, the self is vulnerability to touch: a site of pleasure and enjoyment but also of violence and pain. Skin is the body's outside layer, which often bears the marks of violent encounters in the form of scars. Levinas (1998) locates sensibility in the skin, since it is a tender and sensitive area of exposure to the other: "To be in one's skin is an extreme way of being affected" (89). Markiewicz's art evokes this double function of skin, and by provoking a somatic experience of art, she makes art "touch" the viewer, get under his or her skin. By engaging the viewer to the point of eliciting a somatic experience of trauma, the installation conjures up memory that is embodied and singular, and always intertwined with the processes of coming into oneself.

In the exhibition catalogue to *Places to Remember II*, art historian Griselda Pollock (2001a) writes that Markiewicz's work, "not *from* memory but *towards* the creation of the means of remembering, is a home-coming" (5), although this "home" is a place of continuous searching. The space of art is a construction site for the self to gather itself together as "a place to remember," both as a location where the rituals of memory are performed and as that which is to be remembered and borne witness to in order for the artist to "be." In *Promise II,* Markiewicz creates both a private space of reflection, healing, and self-discovery and a public place in which we can welcome one another. Her images, in their silent, controlled austerity, are reminiscent of Paul Célan's minimalist poetics and are inflected by Judaism's privileging of the invisible. They demand a new way of looking, a form of witnessing by means of visual hermeneutics. When Markiewicz (1992) asks, "Can you read this image?"[25] she proposes an aesthetic vision that shifts artistic practice into the realm of ethical commitment, of obligation to both the self and the other. This vision carries both a promise of legibility and a demand to try to understand, as announced in *The Price of Words*: "I ask you what you cannot read—read" (Z).

MEMORY IN VIOLET: BRACHA ETTINGER'S
MATRIXIAL GENEALOGIES

Born in Tel Aviv and currently working in Paris, Bracha Ettinger is an Israeli artist, psychoanalyst, and feminist theorist. The daughter of

Holocaust survivors, she has been searching for the means of expressing the psychic wound that her parents' trauma marked on her entire
being and impressed on her art. In her notebook, she writes, "My
parents are proud of their silence. It was their way of sparing others
and their children from suffering. But in this silence, all was trans-
mitted except the narrative. In silence nothing can be changed in the
narrative which hides itself. If being haunted is the direct testimony
of repression, the ceremony [art practice] is a testimony of testimony"
(quoted in Pollock 1995, 137).

Ettinger creates series of works in which she manipulates images from archival and family photographs in order to reflect on the
themes of memory, history, and exile. In series such as *The Eye of the
Compass* (1989–1990), *Mamalangue—Borderline Conditions and
Pathological Narcissism* (1989–1990), *Matrixial Borderline* (1990–
1991), *Infantile Autism* (1991), and *Autistworks* (1993–1994), her
signature technique is the photocopied reproduction and enlargement of documentary photographs and pictures from family albums,
the details of which she covers with India ink and charcoal. While
processing the photocopied images, she revisits the scenes of her family's life in prewar Poland and the sites of mass murder where many
of her relatives perished. In these reworkings, the old photographs
become infused with what French writer Henri Raczymow calls *la
mémoire trouée* (memory shot through with holes); their surfaces,
blotted with whiteness in the photocopied enlargements, are pierced
by absence.[26]

Mindy Weisel emphasizes the significance of matrilinear genealogies in the transmission of memory between generations by assuming
her mother's legacy in blue and augmenting it with testimonies from
other second-generation creative women. She refrains, however, from
overtly theorizing the gendered specificity of this bond. Ettinger, on
the other hand, presents her work in an explicitly feminist framework
and refers to her artistic interventions as "matrixial painting," intended to disrupt masculine modes of art practice and memory transmission. Further, Ettinger's work draws attention to the collusion between the erasure of feminine sexual difference and the foreclosure of
"the Jewish difference" in Western modernity. Commenting on her
work, Griselda Pollock (1995) writes,

> Ettinger allows intimacies to emerge between the predicament and
> possibility of both the feminine and Europe's historic other, the Jew-
> ish people. . . . Both woman and Jew foil modernity's dreams of order

by representing ambivalence—that which can neither be mastered nor assimilated to a phallic logic of the same, but must be rejected as Other. (131, 161)

Both in her artwork and in her theoretical essays Ettinger searches for an idiom through which to inscribe those sites of modernity's double forgetting in the drama of memory and witnessing.

In her theoretical writings Ettinger develops a theory of painting in the feminine, in which she argues for the ways of looking that are freed from masculine domination. In psychoanalytic theories, the gaze is construed as gender neutral, but it is still theorized in terms of masculine structures, whereby feminine difference shows up negatively, as a hole in the symbolic order. Against the phallic symbolic, founded on the Oedipal, male-oriented interpretation of the bond between mother and child, the artist conceives of a parallel psychic activity, which she calls the "matrixial sphere." Rather than a scene of Oedipal drama, the matrixial is an intersubjective zone of closeness and togetherness, in which fractured subjects continuously engage in what the artist calls "borderlinking": "always joining-in-separating with/from the Other" (Ettinger 2001, 90). In Pollock's (1995) words, Ettinger's matrix symbolizes "the coexistence in one space of several bodies, several subjectivities whose encounter at this moment is not an either/or but a co-mergence" (164). "Borderlinking" thus refers primarily to an affective immersion in the other's trauma, which then echoes the subject's own archaic traumas. For Ettinger (2001), the matrixial effect is an affective transcription of the erased memory of the missed encounter with the m/Other (Ettinger's formulation). The recovery of the forgotten yet indelible encounter thus occurs as a shared experience: "It conveys *traces of events* that cannot be born and carried alone" (112; italics mine). Ettinger (1999) writes, "In a matrixial borderlinking, traces of trauma in me are not 'purely' mine. Not only am I concerned by my own wound, and not only the encounter with the Other which is to me traumatic, but I am also concerned by the wound of the Other" (18).

From 1992 and continuing until today, Ettinger has worked on a series titled *Eurydice*, in which she transforms the details of a well-known documentary photograph in which a group of undressed women is being driven to the place of execution (fig. 5.3).[28]

The artist knew the photograph when she was a child, and when she later saw it displayed in Holocaust exhibits, she became haunted by a fantasy that it showed one of her lost family members. In her

Figure 5.3.   Undressed women, some of whom are holding infants, waiting in a line before their execution by Ukrainian auxiliary police. October 14, 1942, Mizocz, Ukraine. WS# 17877. Courtesy of the Unites States Holocaust Memorial Museum.

notebooks, Ettinger writes with emotion, "I want her to look at me! That Woman, her back turned to me. This image haunts me. It's my aunt, I say, no, my aunt's the other one, with the baby. The baby! It could be mine" (quoted in Pollock 1995, 158). Although the details from this photograph are also included elsewhere in the artist's works—indeed, the frequency with which this emblematic image reappears across the corpus of Ettinger's art is remarkable—I will focus on the series *Eurydice*, in relation to the artist's statement about the "Eurydicean" generation, as quoted in the epigraph of this chapter. Strikingly, Ettinger chose the images from that series to illustrate her seminal essay "Trauma and Beauty," as well as to accompany an excerpt from her conversation with Levinas titled *Que dirait Eurydice?*[27] Ettinger takes up the myth of Orpheus and Eurydice to challenge the paradigm of artistic creativity as located in the (masculine) gaze. She writes, "The gaze of Eurydice, starting from the trauma and within the trauma opens up, differently to the gaze of Orpheus, a place for art and it incarnates a figure of the artist in the feminine" (Ettinger and Levinas 1997, 30).

By rephotographing and recopying this unique *objet trouvé*, Ettinger creates an uncanny effect that transforms the photographic readymade into an artifact of mourning. In the enlargements, the liminal figures in *Eurydice #23* (plate 3) emerge as fragments of female bodies, their contours barely distinguishable, dissecting the gaze that has now replaced the eye of the camera. While Weisel's canvases and Markiewicz's prints in *Promise II* were dominated by the color blue, Ettinger covers the photocopies with layers of violet that bleeds into reds and oranges.[29] The images, overlaid with ambiguous shades, are insistent and indelible, while "Eurydice" both comes into view and disappears behind the screens of ink. Yet the indistinct silhouettes of condemned women bring the bodies into fluid togetherness. What Ettinger calls "borderlinking" is signaled in the painting itself, for instance, in one woman's torso leaning toward the back of the woman in front of her, in the intimacy of bodies touching one another.

The synergy of the matrixial gaze is related to the morphology of the female body, and Ettinger privileges the trope of the womb in late pregnancy, the "extimate" border zone of intimacy between the same and "the Stranger" that inhabits the woman's innermost space.[30] Similarly, Ettinger retells the myth of Orpheus and Eurydice as the memory of the intrauterine journey, of the passage through the womb/tomb. Orpheus's song can no longer pry itself away from the body of the woman from which it first emerged. The artwork, like Orpheus's song, can cross the threshold of death and leap into the light of the day only as the repetition of the return to the m/Other.[31]

The artist's deployment of the trope of motherhood (at the risk, as she realizes, of biological essentialism) is reminiscent of Levinas's use of the same figure to signify the intimacy of the ethical relation. For Levinas, motherhood is a striking metaphor for my responsibility to the other, which stems from the absolute nature of its need. The other resides "under my skin," like a child in a mother's womb, making the demand from within me. In invoking the child's fundamental, biological needs and the mother's unconditional giving, this metaphor, its abstractness dissolved into the intimacy of flesh, conveys the embodied nature of the subject's ethical indebtedness.[32] Levinas (1998) writes,

> The self involved in maintaining oneself, losing oneself or finding oneself again is not a result, but the very *matrix* of relations. The evocation of maternity in this metaphor suggests to us the proper sense of the oneself. . . . The psyche can signify this alterity in the same

> without alienation in the form of incarnation, as being-in-one's-skin,
> having-the-other-in-one's-skin. (104–5, 115; emphasis mine)

The echoes of Levinas in Ettinger's articulation of the matrixial are not coincidental: while living in France, the artist befriended the philosopher, with whom she conducted a series of interviews.[33] In *Que dirait Eurydice?* Ettinger acknowledges the affinity between her project and Levinas's ethics, and relates it specifically to the images in the *Eurydice* series. She draws on Levinas's description of the face of the other as vulnerable nudity, "the corporeity of the living being and its indigence as a naked and hungry body" (Levinas 1969, 129; quoted in Ettinger and Levinas 1997, 21) in order to speak of her own reworking of the haunting photograph of the undressed women being driven to death.

The ethically inflected "matrixial memory of the event" is the memory of the encounter with the other and the inscription in the self of the other's wound. The task of the artist as witness is to "transcribe" the traces of this event, which has not been consciously experienced, thus releasing "the unforgettable memory of oblivion" (Ettinger 1999, 18). The matrixial gaze is nourished by desire, not for the missing object but for jointness, for linking together. The connectivity occurs in the movement toward the threshold of the visible, opening up the possibility of "com-passionate wit(h)nessing," in which the painting produces an affective contiguity with the viewer's body. As conveyed in the neologism "wit(h)nessing," the space of bearing witness that opens up when the gaze is traumatized by the visual inscription of imminent death is always shared and experienced together with others. Art in the matrixial is an activity of remembering these encounters, and it carries the memory of becoming-subject together, in *"co-response-ability."* Thus the work reveals an alternative space of seeing, in which, to draw on Levinas's (1969) ethical theory of vision, the other "shines forth with [her] own light and speaks for [her] self" (14).

Reclaiming the matrixial sphere from within the phallic scenario has profound implications for the understanding of art. Reconceived in terms of matrixial "borderlinking," a work of art is that which allows a sensation of loss to surge to the surface and manifest itself as a powerful shock-effect in the viewer. When the operations of sharing and joining, imprinted in the psyche as traces of encounters with "the m/Other," are channeled to the edges of the visible/intelligible surface, a work of art, an *oeuvre*, becomes an *ouverture*—an opening onto a blind spot of memory and an invitation to the viewer to join in the journey toward that place.

Ettinger describes the movement of tracing, which in the work of art involves the interweaving of the artist's memory work with that of the viewer, as *Eurydician*. As in the myth of Orpheus and Eurydice, the shadow of Eurydice in the underworld symbolizes both the desire to see and the prohibition of looking. At the threshold of the visible, the apparition lures the gaze toward what it can never access. For Ettinger (2001), art draws us as close as possible to this threshold, "not by the image it presents but by the absence" (94–95). As in the tableau of *Eurydice #23*, the waxing and waning silhouettes of the women draw the viewer in and bring together the interwoven traces of the encounters between the artist, the viewer, and the missing women.

For Ettinger, reconfiguring subjectivity in terms of wit(h)nessing, that is, as an entity engendered in traumatic encounters with the other, corresponds directly to the traumatic weight of culture after the Shoah. As in Levinas's articulation of subjectivity, and, as we have seen, in Markiewicz's project, the archaic trauma of the self emerging into subjectivity through encounters with others is overlaid with historical and family trauma. The archaic "loss" of the mother, whom Ettinger seeks to reclaim from phallic scenarios, is inseparable from the "loss" experienced by the second generation, the literal loss of family genealogy.[34] Thus the canvases of *Eurydice* are at once the site of imaginary substitution and of working through traumatic overidenitfication with the murdered women, one of whom *could* have been the artist's mother.[35] Within that optics, the matrixial gaze crucially supports the structure of subjectivity as wit(h)nessing. Unlike the phallic gaze, which is based on the absolute absence of the object of desire, the connecting "look" can convey the dispersed traces of the Shoah. Moreover, matrixial borderlinking opens up the possibility of remembrance as a space in which memory transmission is a form of *sharing*: between the artist and viewer, and between one generation and another.

The silhouettes of female bodies in *Eurydice #23* begin to appear, already overlaid by the shadow of their imminent extinction.[36] The central figure's face is turned away, cast into darkness: Eurydice's eyes must remain withdrawn from gaze. Although she can never be properly "seen," Eurydice is "remembered" in the movement of the image being repeated and then traced in ink. This memory remembers "nothing" in terms of positive content, yet it preserves the traces of the missed encounter. In the catalogue essay for Ettinger's *Halala-Autistwork*, Jean-François Lyotard (1995a) remarks that the artist's tableaux testify to the feeling that "something is missing from or exceeding the sensible" (22). This sense of absence produces a memory event that occurs through embodied sensation, marked with feminine difference.

As Pollock (1995) reminds us, the female body, especially the nude female body, has been the erotic signifier of beauty in the (masculine) history of Western painting. In reference to Ettinger's tableaux, she asks, "What can the body signify after Auschwitz? After its terrible sufferings made known to us through a thousand chilling documentary photographs? Its coherence as a signifier was cremated there. The body can only now be painfully naked" (136). Importantly, for Ettinger, this does not mean the forbiddance of the beauty and sensuousness of the female body, although the artist takes an enormous risk by situating that body at the site of mass murder. Imbuing the canvas with violet inks, she also reinfuses it with a corporeality that has been obliterated in the medium of the documentary photograph deposited in an archive or on display in a Holocaust exhibit. Ettinger exposes this vulnerable body in her paintings, its utter destitution on the threshold of death, but also its beauty. In this way, feminine beauty, radically transformed in the space of wit(h)nessing, discloses the ethical within the aesthetic. It brings comfort and healing not through aestheticization of pain but by opening passages in which linking with other subjectivities becomes possible.

In *Eurydice #23* the photographic image has already annihilated the living body, whose faint contours are now dissected again by the photocopier (in Pollock's [1995] words, "the ultimate anti-auratic machine").[37] Yet the ritual of reproduction and enlargement exposes the fibers of paper and the grains of ink, and they become the living tissue of inscription that conveys the vulnerability of that trembling surface, now the image's skin. Ettinger often includes textual inscriptions in her works. A detail from *Mamalangue #4*, for instance, shows the French word "langueur" as if etched in the photocopied, grainy surface (fig. 5.4).

The word "languishes" at the bottom of the page, as if supporting the Hebrew words (all of which pertain to language) that cover the page, veiling the silhouette of a female body.[38] The outline of the decipherable word brings out the epidermis of the page and the coarseness of the surface of inscription. At the same time, the sacrilegious

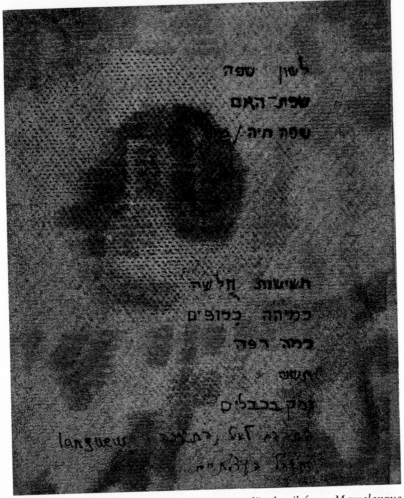

Figure 5.4. Bracha L. Ettinger (French Israeli), detail from *Mamalangue* #4, 1989–91. Oil, pen, and xerography, with photocopic dust, pigment, and ashes. Courtesy of the artist.

gesture of skin being tattooed with the word is chiseled into the surface of the image.

In the series *Mamalangue* (which can be translated as "mom-my-language"), Ettinger draws attention to the maternal phrasing that always leaves traces in the referential language of the Father. For her, the masculine inscription is intrinsically violent, although the material effect of the feminine cannot be made visible without recourse to a masculine symbolic. This imperceptible dialectic, "the becoming-skin" of language, is traced on the body.[39] The metaphor of "the wounds" and "scars" of memory thus becomes literalized in such corporeal inscription. Yet, for Ettinger, the skin-parchment is first and foremost the site of contact, vulnerability, and sharing, of sensuousness and touch.

Similar to Markiewicz's "countermonumental" use of photosensitive paper, Ettinger subjects the photographs to increasing degrees of "fading" through photocopying. In the process of endless repetition of the same photographic detail, she makes "visible" the effacement of memory. In her commentary on Ettinger's work, art historian Christine Buci-Glucksmann (1996) writes that Ettinger's works force the viewer "to gaze into the void in order to see again, as though the nothingness and quiver of these extenuated materials, cut up and reassembled, stood here for a failing of memory, faded and threatened by what it can see" (281). Against the technocracy of the era of mechanical reproduction (which, as Zygmunt Bauman argues in *Modernity and the Holocaust* [1989], was the enabling condition for mass extermination), Ettinger uses the instruments of technology to summon the "mystery of apparition" (Lyotard 1995, 23) or to visualize the invisible. At the same time, the dissolution of the photocopied image into the blankness of the page deposits the traces of what has been forgotten. The mechanical, back-and-forth movement of the photocopier evokes associations with traumatic repetition, yet these returns to the site of trauma are staged as the precondition of becoming-witness.

The journey of mechanicized oblivion is interrupted when the artist covers the effaced contours with the screens of violet inks and thus infuses the image with singularity and intimacy. Ettinger writes, "White, I tell myself could tell all about black and more. Violet cuts through them like a wound, or like a scar, depending on the moment. Wound-scar, evoking that perfection that has never been" (quoted in Pollock 1995, 158). Buci-Glucksmann (1996) asks, "Might these reddened lines and suddenly vivid purples testify, through their effect of discontinuity, against the effacement of the effaced?" (284). The painfully violet "skin of memory" (to recall Charlotte Delbo's [1995] phrase) is a bruised memory, memory in mourning.[40] Yet the reds and oranges that striate the surface of the image convey at once intensity or urgency of memory, and the joy in the memory's journey to recover what has been forgotten. The layers of colors both intensify the sense of remoteness from the image and from what it stands for, and bring it closer to the viewer at the same time. In the play of color, the image hovers in simultaneous proximity and distance, intimacy and inaccessibility.

Each of Ettinger's tableaux becomes a shelter for memory, a speechless witness that awaits an infusion of meaning. Each speaks of the forgotten origin of memory, the memory suffused with the trace of what cannot be retrieved in recollection. Ettinger's work both veils a familiar documentary image and brings it so close to the viewer's eye that it becomes almost indecipherable. Her canvases thus both preserve and question the status of this image as a historical document, transforming it into a memory event. The grainy texture of enlarged photographs turns the image into a nontransparent surface that is slowly eroding the past. The manipulation of the photograph draws attention to both the opaqueness and the intimacy of memory because the viewer is estranged from the familiar scene depicted in the image and immersed in it without reprieve, in smothering proximity.

In *Archive Fever*, Jacques Derrida (1996) explains that the term *arche* designates the principle that organizes an archival project. It names the law that institutes, imposes, and interprets the principles of how knowledge is organized and transferred. This process is not without violence: the archontic power must exclude anything that will not conform to the law in order to produce an intelligible whole and a meaningful history. By expropriating archival photographic material into a landscape of memory and transforming it into an intimate space of mourning and reflection, Ettinger's works confront the *arche*—the law that institutes and organizes memory. The matrixial gaze seeks to counter the effect of the archive's epistemic mastery, the way it dictates what constitutes the "content" of memory, by opening up the space of intimacy and sensuality in the experience of the image.[41] As the inscriptions of *la mémoire trouée*, Ettinger's images bring out the forgotten as it is embedded in the structure of the archive: the very necessity of the archive, its function in building and preserving historical knowledge, arises from the possibility of forgetting, that is, from memory's constitutive imperfection.

The documentary photograph that Ettinger glimpsed in a Holocaust exhibit and that triggered the memory of a picture she had seen in her childhood is an emblem of the problematic status of the archive in her work. If the archive stands for the body of procedures that dictate what constitutes the positive content of collective memory,

Ettinger's creative exposition of an archival artifact reclaims what the archive must exclude in order to make its claim to truth and knowledge: the female body in its materiality, sensibility, and vulnerability. Corporeality has been left out by official memory, either excised from the archive or reconstituted as a theoretical entity, a general concept divorced from the singularity of the lived experience. The artist's goal is thus to reembody the corpus that has been reduced to either documents of horror or tabooized object of remembrance. This process of embodying the image dislocates the documentary photograph from its properly "historical" time, although it also disturbs the time of the present in which the viewer tries to place it within the knowable and "memorizable." The artist thus seeks to recover the trace of that which we can never remember, which always eludes our efforts to chronicle and narrativize.

It is in this sense that Ettinger's work can be read as an inscription of the chiasmatic memory of the second generation.[42] In her tableaux, Ettinger (1999) reconceives the meaning of art with respect to traumatic memory: in light of her own family history, the idea of the beautiful must be "re-articulated in relation to wound." As she asks in "Trauma and Beauty," "If there is to beauty no other origin that the wound . . . whose wound is it? And what can we call today beauty?" (20). The artist produces the traces of trauma as both beauty and wound, and reenvisages transgenerational memory as the "conaissance" (being born together and coming into consciousness) of multiple subjectivities in the space of art. For Lyotard (1995a), a work of art is an entity that survives the moment of potential annihilation (144) because it bears witness to *Is it happening?* to what could not have been yet is occurring nevertheless. In Ettinger's work, the event of the work of art as "survival," the affective shock that *it is happening* rather than it is not, is also the event of memory journeying into the history of her parents' survival. The resurrection of the matrilinear genealogy, which the artist has imaginatively traced to the documentary photograph, is now effected through matrixial inscription on the surface of the painting.

Ultimately, art can be a form of witnessing that brings forth the traces of the "affective separateness-in-jointess" (Ettinger 1999, 22) of subjectivities indebted to each other in their innermost core. In the matrixial zone, ethics and aesthetics come together to radically transform the very scope of art. For Ettinger, it is this necessary conjunction of the ethical with artistic practice that makes witnessing (or, as she prefers, wit(h)nessing), possible. Or rather, Eurydice symbolizes the border zone of ethics and aesthetics, and she incarnates the beautiful as it occurs in close proximity to death. But at the same time, she is also an ethical trope of bearing witness to what will never pass through the threshold of the visible, although it must be born witness to. The effect of beauty, which is deeply rooted in the wound, is that the traces of unplaceable and "unrememberable" trauma are brought closer to the surface of memory. Ettinger's notion of the matrixial thus gestures to Levinas's distinction between language as ethical Saying and language as a plastic surface of words, although her work also implies that the ethical essence of language and memory is already infused with corporeality. As the voice of law, the ethical is gendered masculine. By showing how it always operates on the body, as the inscription of the feminine, Ettinger casts the *differend* between the ethical and the aesthetic in terms of sexual difference. Bearing witness to this *differend* is made possible as the effect of the feminine, as the matrixial affect, even if the dominant voice of the law, and of the archive, always threatens it with erasure.

MEMORY IN YELLOW: EWA KURYLUK'S SKIN/CLOTH ART

In his review of one of Kuryluk's exhibits, art critic Andrzej Wirth (2002) writes, "Kuryluk's is a partisan art of traces left in uninhabited landscapes or deserted interiors by conspiratorial strangers, ghosts descending from skies, propelled by winds, crashing randomly in the most unexpected places and disappearing underground." Kuryluk, a well-known Polish artist, art historian, and writer, left Poland in 1981 and has since lived in America and Paris, exhibiting her work internationally. Born in 1946, Kuryluk was long unaware that her mother, Maria Grabowska (Miriam Kohany), was Jewish, and that she had survived the war hidden in Lvov by her husband, Kuryluk's father, who later received a posthumous Righteous Among the Nations award. Kuryluk's other relatives on her mother's side, including her mother's sister Hilde and grandparents, Paulina Raaber Kahany and Hirsch Kahany, were "swept in the avalanche" (Kuryluk's metaphor for the Holocaust, which she borrowed from her mother). After her mother's death in 2001, Kuryluk found some photographs of her grandparents hidden in one of her mother's shoes tucked away in a closet. Kuryluk's mother, a talented pianist, suffered from schizophrenia (which was most likely triggered by wartime trauma), as did Kuryluk's brother, Piotr, who spent most of his adult life in a mental institution, until his death in 2004.

Kuryluk's photography and paintings have been exhibited world-wide. She is best known, however, for her "cloth art"—cutouts and sketches of human forms in cotton and silk.[43] Although she had been showing them since 1979, after her mother's death, these spectral figures began to tell the story of Kuryluk's family. The silhouettes of family ghosts first appeared in the installation *Yellow Birds Fly* (2001–3), the first of Kuryluk's "yellow" exhibits, which she dedicated to her parents. For Kuryluk, the color yellow resonates in multiple and ambivalent ways. As was blue for Mindy Weisel's mother, yellow was Miriam's favorite color—the color of canaries and Van Gogh's sunflowers, of survival and the sun's life-giving force.[44] Yet, at the same time, yellow was for Miriam the "Jewish" color of exclusion. As Kuryluk comments apropos another exhibit, *Air People* (2003), yellow marks the *Luftmenschen*: the uprooted, the outcasts, the Jews. The yellow color, the artist explains, has the same function as it did during the Holocaust: "It marks one as an outcast and denounces its wearer." In several of the images in the installation *Yellow Birds Fly*, the artist depicts herself at work, wearing her mother's favorite scarf with a print of Van Gogh's sunflowers. This heirloom, like the family photographs found in the closet, is now woven into the texture of her art (plate 4).

Shortly after her mother's death, Kuryluk wrote an autobiographical novel, *Goldi* (2004), in which she described the process of learning about her family's past and of growing up in a household full of secrets. Fragments of family history, incomprehensible at first, emerge gradually from Kuryluk's tales, intertwined with revelations about her Jewish ancestry and her mother's Holocaust past. In one episode, for instance, Kuryluk's brother instinctively panics when, on a stroll in the mountains, the family encounters a group of Austrian tourists with an aggressive German Shepherd. The book was followed by a companion art installation *Tabuś (Taboo)*.[45] As Kuryluk (2005) reflects, the real author of the exhibition was her mother, for whom "the horror that she had lived through became coded in the yellow color. She was seeing yellow birds and yellow snow. The yellow armband on my sleeve and the Star of David on my brother's sweater. . . . But she also loved Van Gogh" (15). In the installation, the artist hangs up curtains and drapes to create "evanescent rooms and air sculptures."

Figure 5.5. Ewa Kuryluk (Polish American),
Dziewczynka [A girl], 1995. Detail from the in-
stallation *Tabuś* [Taboo]. Paper and silk collage.
Courtesy of the artist.

In the center of the exhibit are the images of two children. One shows
her brother's face mounted on the figure of Anne Frank, from a picture that her mother once cut out from the newspaper. The other
is the artist's face as a child, mounted on the body of Anne Frank's
anonymous friend, from the same photograph (fig. 5.5).[46]

As in Ettinger's work, the sudden intrusion of an archival photograph (in both cases, the artists knew the images from Holocaust
exhibits as well as from their parents' drawers and closets) is shocking. The shock effect, however, depends on the viewer's complementary labor of memory because she must recognize the original image,
which has now been transformed (with the original figures decapi-
tated) and appropriated as part of family history. The other yellow

Figure 5.6. Ewa Kuryluk (Polish American), *Paulina na ławce* [Paulina on a bench], 1995. Detail from the installation *Tabuś* [Taboo]. Drawing on silk. Courtesy of the artist.

images in the installation are based on the prewar family photos of Miriam Kahany and Paulina Raaber Kahany that Kuryluk found in her mother's shoe (fig. 5.6).

Kuryluk's mother's choice of the hiding place for the family photographs is telling if we recall that, in numerous Holocaust memoirs, the author describes hiding family photographs in a shoe at the time of the deportation. The connotations with the metaphorical "skeletons in the closet" are obvious, while the fact that the shoe was hidden in a wardrobe brings to mind numerous stories of children who, during the Holocaust, were hidden inside or behind the wardrobes in gentile homes.[47]

In both *Goldi* and *Tabuś*, Kuryluk hides family tragedy behind loving memories of her family, which makes her legacy of silence and pain bearable. She refers to both works playfully as "an apotheosis of

little animals"[48]: Goldi is a hamster, a beloved family pet, and Tabuś
is the name of a little marmot from one of her mother's fables, who
lives in the mountains, the survivor of an avalanche. As the artist later
understood, for her mother, the marmot's name was an allusion to
the "taboo" of everything that she had once loved, lost, and repressed
(15). The warm, moving humor of Kuryluk's narrative in *Goldi* and
the cuddly euphemisms of the title animals in both the book and the
exhibit allow her to confront the taboo of Jewishness and to pass on
the stories that her mother could not even bear to remember. They
also help her reckon with family ghosts, which are always in cahoots
with the demons of Polish history. For Kuryluk, the burden of transgenerational memory has been compounded with the difficult process
of getting to know her family history, a process complicated by the
postwar history of Poland, marred with anti-Semitic violence. Overall, Kuryluk's heritage is her Jewish difference, which condemned the
family to outsider status, both during the war and in the difficult
reality of communist Poland. Yet Kuryluk is also the daughter of a
Righteous Among the Nations, with a claim to the proudest part of
Polish wartime history, and she tries to weave both of those threads
into her cloth art.

The characters of Goldi and Tabuś incarnate the family history of
perpetual secrecy and alienation, as well as the author's struggle to
define herself vis-à-vis conflicted memory and history. Yet they are
also the guardians of memory and inadvertent witnesses, a role that
Kuryluk also assumes, perhaps because her parents refused to do so.
In *Goldi*, for instance, Kuryluk (2004) imagines her mother to say,
"Fate appointed me to be a witness to history. But I copped out and
did not say a word" (146; translation mine). At the same time, the
processions of ephemeral cloth silhouettes in her exhibits serve as the
figures of mourning and of working through that difficult history.

Explaining the genesis of her artwork, Kuryluk points to the legend of Saint Veronica's shroud as an inspiration for her cloth art. In
her interpretation, however, the New Testament legend becomes overlaid with a traumatic memory of her brother's setting himself on fire,
after which "visions of burnt skin appeared before my eyes."[49] As she
said of her first textile installation in 1979, working with cloth meant
that "instead of skin, I was 'injuring' cloth." In Markiewicz's *I Don't
Celebrate Christmas,* mourning was emblematized in neatly folded
pieces of fabric, perhaps referring to the function of collective rituals
as a means to work through grief and to arrange the memories of the

dead loved ones into acceptable shapes so that they no longer rup-
tured the tranquility of the present. In Kuryluk's installations, however, the cloth is cut up, "torn," or wounded, as if in a performance of
keri'ah, the ritual tearing of one's clothes as a sign of mourning.[50] The
continuous repetition of the gesture of tearing and cutting indicates
the unremitting nature of intimate grief, even though, paradoxically,
the ambiance of Kuryluk's work, swathed in radiant yellow, seems
much more soothing than Markiewicz's cold blue.

Another inspiration for this unusual art is the tale of the Corynthian Maiden, in which a potter's daughter, stricken by grief after the
departure of her lover, traces his shadow on a wall and thus invents
painting. As art historian Lisa Saltzman (2006) argues, this myth is
especially productive for reflection on visual strategies of commemoration because it presents loss as the origin of art (2). While Ettinger's
work sought to recover Eurydicean art from within Orpheus's creation and release it from the patriarchal framework, Kuryluk looks to
legends in which young women themselves invent art through rituals
of remembrance that express grief and mourning. Kuryluk's elegiac
"yellow" art thus imitates the potter's daughter's gesture of capturing
shadows and Veronica's hanging up of shrouds, both of which convey
an image of the absent body. Here mourning is the foundation and
essence of art, while the color yellow and the ephemeral medium of
cloth symbolize an aesthetic of bereavement. As in the case of both
Markiewicz and Ettinger, moreover, the expression "memory-skins"
evokes Levinas's references to skin as the site where my responsibility
to the other is experienced as proximity. For Levinas (1998), ethics is
the "exposedness of skin prior to my intention," which turns me inside out, like a "concave without a convex" (49), and it is experienced
as a raw shock of unmediated exposure to the other. As with Levinas's sometimes shocking, even monstrous, figures of speech, Kuryluk's epidermal/textile art reveals a fascinating paradox: her shadowy
figures are soft, pliable, and tenderly executed, while their spectral
presence on the curtains, drapes, and the furniture in the installations
is unassuming, unthreatening, and welcoming. Yet they are also "cut-
up," maimed, and stitched together from disparate fragments, drawing attention to the unavoidable violence of such memory-cutting and
"skinning." As in Ettinger's paintings, they reveal the somatic layers
of memory, its vulnerable "skin" exposed to pain, as if clad in Nessus's tunic.[51]

MEMORY CARVED IN THE FLESH OF THE WORLD

In her work on trauma, Cathy Caruth (1996) wonders if it is possible at all for survivors of the Holocaust to work through the trauma so that they can truly bear witness to it as a historical event. She concludes, "It may only be in future generations that 'cure' or at least witnessing can take place" (136). If she is correct, children of survivors could be privileged witnesses to the Shoah, although they are secondary witnesses who substitute themselves imaginatively, often with reluctance and "against themselves," for the primary witness. In her important contribution to second-generation literature, writer Eva Hoffman (2004), the author of *After Such Knowledge*, comments, "The second-generation after each calamity is the hinge generation, in which the meanings of awful events can remain arrested and fixed to the point of trauma; or in which they can be transformed into new sets of relations with the world, and new understanding" (103).

The artists of the second generation continue to explore traumatic landscapes, bound by the double imperative to "never forget" and to leave behind the haunted ancestral halls (and ghettos). For each of the four artists discussed here, art is an uncertain territory, where the difficulties of dealing with parents' memories are compounded by the difficulties of growing up in a household that has not been able to perform its rites of mourning properly. Yet the forms of art that the "daughters of absence" have taken up become a conduit through which they bring themselves into existence as subjects and witnesses in their own right. Their works tell life stories in a way that foregrounds performative acts of memory (re)construction, in which the flow of color or an unexpected gesture in the space of an installation breaks through the barriers of psychic resistance and repression.

The work of "daughters of absence" reveals the gift and the onus of second-generation memory that is not the artists' own, although it intrudes in their everyday lives, invades their mental spaces, and deposits a somatic residue of insomnia, anxiety, and distress. The imperative "Remember!" constantly threatens to subsume their art, and it is a source of both inspiration and struggle. As a consequence, these works exude an uncanny feeling of dislocation from familiar landscapes of memory, tracing figures of displacement and exile that obliquely reference the parents' traumatic past. Yet this destination in the past, toward which they travel and from which they flee in their works, also promises a form of homecoming and a new geography of the present. Constructing rather than reconstructing the memory of an uninhabitable and therefore "unrememberable" past, they also journey, as Markiewicz (1992) writes beautifully, toward the place "beyond the scattered ashes of demanding souls" (W), outside the scorched landscapes of memory.

The imaginative vitality of these works certainly confirms that the second generation must also be considered beyond the framework of disabling pathologies. Rather, they can be seen as a companion project to what I describe in chapter one as Levinas's philosophical transvaluation of trauma. As I have tried to show, "the daughters of absence" revalue their parents' traumatic experiences by registering the processes of working through on the somatic and visual level, an effect intensified by the works' chromatic coding. Blue is the color of Zyclon B—the inevitable association for anyone who has seen the images or visited the sites of former death camps. Yet in Weisel's work blue has surfaced as the color of Jewish spirituality and her mother's love of beauty. In Markiewicz's installation, blue is the color of life-giving water and the journey of self-discovery. Ettinger's violet is similarly transformed: it is the hue of mourning and wounding, of memory bruised by horror; yet it also becomes the color of feminine intimacy and sharing, especially when it begins to seep into oranges, and it is emblematic of what the artist calls wit(h)nessing. Finally, Kuryluk's yellow is the color of fear and death, of mental illness and social isolation, but also of survival, family bonds, sunlight, creative energy, and warmth.

For the second generation in particular, memory arrives from elsewhere, like an echo whose source they cannot identify (to return to Levinas's evocative metaphor): it is most intimate yet never properly theirs.[52] Following Levinas, no memory fully belongs to me, since I am always a witness to the existence of the other. Even the most intimate memory arrives from an elsewhere that the self cannot remember, and it bears a trace of this primary ethical indebtedness. If we consider that memory is a matter of sociality in a Levinasian sense, that is, it refers to a unique ethical relation between the self and the other, these works also posit what may appear counterintuitive: that it is necessary to assume responsibility before the other for the ways one works through trauma, and even through one's most intimate grief. This art demands what Levinas once described as the "eye that listens," a curious metaphor in which the eye becomes the organ through which the command to remember is obeyed.[53] Insofar as the visual experience registers in the fibers of the body, it is also a feeling, sentient eye. As in Markiewicz's *Promise II*, the sensations of the eye fall in unison with the beating of the heart, animated by the rhythm of the breath, which is how the artwork calls upon the viewer's ability to respond, her response-ability as a "secondary witness."

How can a memory that is not mine constitute me as a witnessing subject? In many ways, the artwork of the second generation embodies what has been referred to in chapter one as the Levinasian structure of subjectivity as witnessing. It conveys the ethical truth that the subject, in its very constitution, is indebted to the other and to the other's memory, which it absolutely cannot know or possess. For the "daughters of absence," this ethical injunction is inseparable from the somatic experience of the imagined content of their parents' memory. The second generation embody "in the flesh" the Levinasian trope of the immemorial past whose traces they carry.

What these works propose is a visual exegesis of the haunting stories that have (not) been told to the artists by their parents. The fact that all of these artists have supplemented their artwork with textual commentary (in various forms and genres) encourages their interpretation as a modern-day, post-Holocaust Haggadah; that is, they can be read in terms of collective memory, identity building, and ritual, even if these are very intimate and singular works of memorialization. In that sense, this art, which "takes root in the wound" (Derrida 1978, 66) and unceasingly revives it, also affirms the legacy of pain and seeks to transform it into a possibility of the future, a future which may also include the forgetting of its traumatic origins. It is possible to say then that these works bear witness to the future more so than to the past. As Christian Boltanski (Boltanski and Gumpert 1994) remarks, apropos his own Holocaust-inflected art, "Art is always a witness, sometimes a witness to the events before they actually happen" (37).

The instability between private and collective memory staged in these works also begs the question about the ethical implications of the art gallery's role as the site of an uncertain encounter with trauma and as a simulacral space of bearing witness. What happens when a photographic document migrates from the archive to the gallery? Or when the number on the camp inmate's forearm is calligraphed onto an abstract painting? To an extent, artists cannot avoid the danger that artistic gestures will jeopardize memory by turning its referents into auratic art objects or even fetishes. This is the case especially when they engage images that have been sacralized by collective rituals of memorialization. Yet the art gallery becomes the site where memory is being produced rather than merely evoked, where it speaks to the present and is accountable to the present. It allows for the experience of "working through" to play itself out in intersubjective contexts between the artist and the work, and it invites the viewers to step in and become empathetic witnesses.

Although the works by these four artists engage in rituals of collective remembrance and mourning, they also challenge official narratives of the past by exposing the untenability of the boundary between private and collective remembering. As the second-generation artists are well aware, their personal recollections, imbued with grief, have been intertwined with public memory. Their private rituals of bearing witness are being transformed into physical as well as metaphorical sites where the community's memory is stored. Obviously, the images, objects, and materials that the artist has chosen as vehicles of expression are related to her location within social, historical, and cultural circumstances, which continue to influence her recollection. Paying attention to this interrelation of private and collective processes of memory has deep ethical implications. The four artists I have engaged with here situate their memory-work in larger ethical and even political contexts, embracing responsibility for the way collective memory is produced and invested with value-laden significations. As foregrounded in the work of "the daughters of absence," art has the capacity to expose the multilayered mechanisms of recollection and remembering, and to probe the ways in which we construct the meaning of what we have remembered. Mindy Weisel (2000) asserts that the word "talent" comes from the Greek, and it connotes responsibility (xx). While I have not been able to find evidence of the Greek word's association with "responsibility," it is most pertinent that this is how Weisel interprets the word's etymology.[54] Weisel's emphasis on responsibility also coincides with Pollock's (2001b) observation that art "can transport the viewer beyond the immediate to invent a place that is the point of an ethical encounter between past and present, between absence and presence, between artist and witness/viewer" (9).

Finally, insofar as they succeed, if one can speak of success here, the works by "daughters of absence" reveal that the very scene of representation is structured by the wound that has not been experienced or remembered. In that sense, they also expose the trauma of representation itself; as Saltzman notes in her interpretation of the myth of the Corynthian Maiden, loss, dispossession, and mourning constitute art's primal scene. Visual art that foregrounds its function as a ritual of commemoration thus reinscribes this fundamental absence at the heart of representation. In the end, the post-Holocaust art of memory shows us that art is always inflected by an ethical necessity to bear witness to loss, and, conversely, that these testimonial processes always depend on an aesthetic moment. Markiewicz remarks, "Primarily my work is engaged in finding a language for something that is fundamentally either silent or without a clear conceptual framework."[55] Entertwined with the experience of the sublime as articulated by Lyotard (see chapter three), witnessing entails the paradoxical mixture of pain, in this case stemming from traumatic recollection and pleasure, the pleasure of inventing a new idiom in which the inexpressible is, after all, expressed.

Epilogue

"To Write Another Book about the Holocaust . . ."

As I was working on the final paragraphs of this book, a colleague of mine commented, "Let's be honest: who wants to read another book about the Holocaust?" The question stirred up a deep-seated anxiety. I know that my desire to read books about the Holocaust is not shared by the majority of the population in North America today. In light of my colleague's remark, the title of this book, *Disappearing Traces*, which refers primarily to the model of ethical and aesthetic strategies for representing the Holocaust, acquires another, perhaps opposite, meaning. The traces of the Holocaust are gradually disappearing from contemporary public consciousness, and its place as a cultural phenomenon and the main historical event of the twentieth century is no longer a given. Only a decade ago, art theorist Griselda Pollock (2001a), writing about an exhibit of Holocaust art, expressed a wish that the voice of every single Holocaust witness be given hospitality, be it in art exhibits, oral testimony archives, publishing houses, or classrooms. But is the time for such hospitality running out?

The proliferation of Holocaust representations in the eighties and nineties has been often attributed to an urgency to remember before the disappearance of the last witness. Yet already in the midnineties we began to hear about the saturation of culture with Holocaust memory, the need to leave it in the past and "move on." Writing in 1995, Andreas Huyssen ascribes the increasing unwillingness of contemporary culture to engage in active remembrance to changing conceptions of time in the age of the simulacrum. He thus sees the contemporary obsession with museumification and other techniques of preserving the past as the obverse side of the culture of amnesia. Hence, the responsiveness of the public to Holocaust productions in a variety of media, including popular culture, is, paradoxically, a symptom of the desire to forget: to confine this historical trauma to museums, history books, libraries, and video collections. It is not surprising that, although new Holocaust monuments are still being erected, sections on the Holocaust are tacitly eliminated from school curricula. Further, it has been argued that it is necessary to pry ourselves away from the Holocaust to make room for the memory of more recent traumatic events. As a result, representations of the Holocaust are now evaluated and displaced by other, competing narratives of identity-shaping disasters and global conflicts.

Those of us who consider the memory of the Holocaust to be central to how we understand the contemporary world and ourselves—and this group is not limited to survivors and their descendants—find it difficult to accept the arguments that we should "move on." The fatigue resulting from reading too many books about the Holocaust will likely never befall us because we have a spiritual, ethical, and political commitment to *Zakhor!* that we feel and experience very deeply. And yes, we are anxious about the prognosis that the Holocaust is bound to disappear into "mere" history or become a popular myth, the backdrop for another episode of the superhero epic *X-Men*.[1] In recent years, I have often experienced an uneasy disjunction between the community that "remembers the Holocaust," with which I identify, and my colleagues, friends, and neighbors, who define themselves in relation to different historical reference points, and cultural and moral paradigms.

Yet my determination to "write another book about the Holocaust," despite my colleague's warning, goes beyond personal reasons and a loyalty to the community of Holocaust rememberers. In continuing to write about the Holocaust, I have drawn encouragement from comments by students in my Holocaust courses. As one of them has remarked, "It is strange, but after taking this class, I can't quite read the newspaper headlines in the same way." Historian Annette Wieviorka (2006) writes that her own task as a Holocaust scholar is to study the role of testimonies in the construction of history and collective memory, and she adds that this inquiry will allow us to illuminate processes at work with respect to other historical periods" (xiv). My student's comment makes it clear that the "historical period" in which the lessons of the Holocaust are most relevant is our own.

As a scholar of Polish Jewish descent who has been researching the history of Polish Jewish relations during and after the Holocaust, I am aware of the alternative histories that are now being written in the countries behind the former Iron Curtain. Since 1989 fresh perspectives have come into view, stemming from changes in the politics of memory in the countries of the so-called New Europe. The prolific Holocaust scholarship that is now taking place in these countries has been made possible by the opening of archives that were previously inaccessible, such as the Soviet KGB archives or, more recently, the International Tracing Service archive in Bad Arolsen, in former East Germany. These developments in Poland, Hungary, Ukraine, Estonia, the Czech Republic, and elsewhere have precipitated the emergence of new historical narratives, cultural paradigms, and modes of social coexistence in the territories where, after all, the tragedy of European Jews took place. As contemporary Polish artist Elżbieta Janicka remarks, in Poland, unlike in America or Israel, "There are ashes floating in the air. We breathe that air. And the wind, clouds, the rain? The ashes are in the earth, in the rivers, in the meadows and forests—always being recycled. . . . We are the sarcophagi—absorbing those remnants from everywhere and in many ways" (quoted in Cichowicz 2006, 1).[2] It is only now that this deeply traumatized landscape is being surveyed, often by scholars with deep connections to these places, whose parents and grandparents still remember the Jews who suddenly disappeared from their neighborhoods. This is a very different memory of the Holocaust, fraught with complexities that have not yet entirely crossed the radar of American scholars, not to mention of the North American general public. At the moment, the Eastern European Holocaust problematic occasionally appears in the spotlight, as happened after the publication of Jan T. Gross's books *Neighbors* (2000), about the murder of the Jews in the town of Jedwabne by their Polish neighbors, and *Fear* (2006), which dealt with Polish complicity in the murder of the Jews during and immediately after the Holocaust; during the production of the film *Defiance* (2008), about the Jewish partisans in the Eastern part of Poland;[3] and when news of the discoveries of mass graves in Ukraine by Father Patrick Desbois's research team made the headlines.[4] These moments, however, only reveal a continuing disjunction between perceptions of the Holocaust in North America and in former Eastern Europe, as if, when it comes to that topic, the Iron Curtain were still hanging. In the area of Holocaust studies, much remains to be done in terms of cultural dialogue and global academic partnership. To an extent, the way in which discussions about the Holocaust, its aftermath, and its significance in the present enter into that dialogue is a litmus test determining whether such culturally sensitive, open-minded exchange is possible. Recognizing the Holocaust as a common cultural and historical landmark is a crucial step in a dialogue the goal of which is to clear up mutual misconceptions, clichés, and prejudices. One of the signs that such dialogue is already happening was a multilateral protest, in 2009, against the restoration to priesthood of bishop Richard Nelson Williamson, a Holocaust denier, by Pope Benedict.[5] All of this goes to show that many more books about the Holocaust still remain to be written.

At present, comparative approaches to the Holocaust have been increasingly supplanting earlier beliefs about the uniqueness of the Holocaust, which often excluded such perspectives. Significant challenges to the view of the exceptional place of Holocaust memory, which came to light in North America during the debates around the construction of the United States Holocaust Memorial Museum on the Washington Mall,[6] stem from a concern that the uniqueness claim has dehistoricized the Nazi genocide of the Jews while at the same time deemphasizing and even erasing the histories and cultural identities of other groups that have struggled for recognition of the atrocities they have endured. Further, as race theorist Charles Mills (1997) cogently argues, the insistence on the exceptionality of the Jewish genocide has been predicated on "white amnesia" about the historical record of genocides of nonwhite peoples. In Mills's view, the horror and significance of the Holocaust will by no means be diminished by the recognition that it occurred within a historical trajectory of colonial conquest and that Hitler applied to Europe colonial procedures of oppression and mass murder that had been successfully practiced elsewhere.[7] What enabled the large-scale mass murder of European Jewry, therefore, was the racialization of the Jewish other that had been made possible only within the epistemological, political, and moral bounds of what Mills calls "the racial contract" (102–5).[8]

Many scholars have recently expressed concern that the uncontested prominence of the Holocaust in public memory creates a hierarchy of suffering and a morally suspect competition of martyrdoms. Yet, as Alan S. Rosen had already written in 1996, we must recognize that "no determinate group's suffering ought to be consigned to perpetual misconception, insignificance, invisibility, or silence" (3). The emphasis on one group's history of persecution must not diminish another group's claim to the historical importance of its suffering. This is why Michael Rothberg, in *Multidirectional Memory* (2009), proposes an alternative to a competitive and adversarial model of memorialization. Examining the intersecting legacies of the histories of the Nazi genocide and European colonialism, he shows that the conflicting memories can be fruitfully rethought as "multidirectional," that is, as a productive intercultural dynamic of cross-references and negotiations that have the potential to "create new forms of solidarity and new visions of justice" (5). An exploration of overlapping historical and cultural memories can both deepen our understanding of the Holocaust, especially of its forgotten aspects, as well as bring into visibility other instances of genocidal violence, both before the Holocaust (such as the extermination of the Native people of North America, the atrocities of the Atlantic slave trade, the murder of 1.5 million Armenians by the Turkish Ottoman Empire, and the starvation of millions of Ukranians by the Soviet regime), as well as those that occurred in very recent history and are unfolding in front of our eyes right now. As Rothberg also notes, the undeniable benefit of the massive interest in the Holocaust has been the development of conceptual tools and theoretical frameworks that can now be successfully implemented to uncover and bring to light other instances of atrocity, oppression, and injustice. Thus the widespread presence of the Holocaust in public consciousness may provide a point of departure and legitimization for the claims to recognition by other groups that have suffered violence.

In the summer of 2010, newspapers in Europe and North America carried headlines about the forced deportations of the Romanian and Bulgarian Roma in France, triggered by a clash between the Roma and the police in the town of Aignan. Although mass expulsions of the Roma had been taking place for years in post-1989 Europe (and also in countries such as Norway, Sweden, Germany, and Poland), the brutal actions of the Sarkozy government gained notoriety and were condemned by the European Parliament, which had found the administration in violation of the European Union antidiscrimination and freedom of movement laws, including the European Union Charter of Fundamental Rights. Yet what struck me the most in the Halifax *Chronicle Herald* reprint of the August 20 *New York Times*[9] report on the expulsions was that, rather than photographs of roundups, liquidations of the encampments, and forced deportations, the article included a picture of a Romany woman smoking a cigarette while holding a very young child. The caption read, "Roma Mariana Sasz smokes a cigarette while holding her child after arriving in Bucharest, Romania, from France on Thursday." Instead of images of the violence perpetrated on a minority group, the readers were served, somewhat incongruously, a not-so-subtle portrayal of irresponsible Romany motherhood.

According to the polls, the Roma continue to be the most discriminated-against minority and the most despised ethnic population in Europe. Unlike anti-Semitism, whose public expressions draw outrage and condemnation, and, in some European countries, can carry a legal penalty under the provision of hate crimes, "anti-Gypsyism" seems to be socially acceptable, even in the most polite circles. Current popular sentiments often echo the early twentieth-century view of the Roma as "a plague against which countries must unflaggingly defend itself" (quoted in Hancock 1996, 52), fuelling neo-Nazi violence, house burnings, lynching, and local pogroms in countries such as Romania and Bulgaria. As the Roma scholar Ian Hancock bitterly notes, the Roma and the Sinti seem to be holding lesser stakes in the ranking of human abuse. Hancock points out a troubling analogy between the removal of the Roma from the streets of Barcelona (to the Camp de la Bata outside the city) before the 1992 Summer Olympics, and a roundup of the Roma in Berlin in 1936 before the prewar Olympic Games. Writing in 1996, Hancock criticizes the unwillingness of Holocaust scholars to recognize the true scope of Nazi violence against the Roma and the fact that, like the Jews, they were targeted primarily on racial grounds. Hancock quotes a 1949 statement from the secretary of the Gypsy Lore Society, herself Jewish, that "these two people shared the horror of martyrdom at the hands of the Nazis for no other reason that they were—they existed" (quoted in Hancock 1996, 39). Although in recent years scholars have paid more attention to the "final solution of the Gypsy question," while the murdered European Jews have been mourned and their martyrdom commemorated, the Roma victims are still awaiting this rightful honor. The site of the Gypsy concentration camp at Lety in the Czech Republic (almost all Czech Roma perished during the war), not far from the memorial museum in Theresienstadt, is host to a pig farm, an industrial enterprise built by the Czech government in 1972. In 1995 a small memorial with no names was erected, and it has served as a place of annual commemorations of O Parrajmos. Despite intensive efforts by Roma activists and condemnation from some European countries, as

well as from the Simon Wiesenthal Center for Tolerance, the pig farm
has not been relocated (on the grounds of maintaining economic vi-
ability and job security for the local workforce).

In Canada, the country I now call home, the case in question at
the moment is a call by First Nations leaders, scholars, and activists
to recognize as "cultural genocide" the government's policy of forced
assimilation of aboriginal people. Starting in the second half of the
nineteenth century and lasting until 1984, when the last institution
was closed, the policy was implemented through a system of manda-
tory Indian residential schools that were funded by the government
and run by the churches. The mandate of the schools was, in the
words of Duncan Campbell Scott (1920), the deputy superintendent
of Indian affairs, "To get rid of the Indian problem. . . . Our objective is to continue until there is not a single Indian in Canada that has
not been absorbed into the body politic and there is no Indian question."[10] In practice, an estimated 150,000 aboriginal, Inuit, and Métis
children were forcibly removed from their communities and placed in
substandard living conditions, where they were severely punished for
speaking their language or practicing Native traditions, and subjected
to rampant physical, emotional, and sexual abuse, with a large number of children dying from disease or during failed escape attempts.[11]
In 2007 the government of Canada announced a compensation pack-
age for the victims; in 2008, a Truth and Reconciliation Commission
was established, and the prime minister of Canada, Stephen Harper,
offered an official apology to the former students.

The tragic legacy of the attempted "final solution of the Indian
problem"[12] has been the destruction of the aboriginal identity and
the annihilation of Native cultures and languages, resulting today
in severe social pathologies of substance abuse, health problems,
high suicide and infant mortality rates, and much lower levels of
education among the First Nations. The scope of the devastation
and the continued conspiracy of silence in Canada has led some
of the First Nations spokespersons to seek recognition under the
provisions of the UN genocide convention. The convention defines
genocide as not only an intent to kill, in whole or in part, the members of a group but also as "b) causing serious bodily and mental
harm to members of the group; c) deliberately inflicting on the
group conditions of life calculated to bring about its physical destruction in whole or in part; and e) forcibly transferring children
of the group to another group" (quoted in Chrisjohn and Young
1997, 150–51). A common strategy to legitimate the claim that the

violence against the aboriginal groups had genocidal proportions and to bring it into visibility has been to draw on the work of Holocaust scholars and to pursue analogies with the Holocaust. In *The Circle Game*, for instance, aboriginal scholar Roland Chrisjohn supports his demand for the recognition of "the genocide by cultural obliteration" by pointing out similarities between the Canadian government's stated goal of "killing the Indian in the child" and the genocidal intentions of Hitler's regime; the analogies between the machinations of the government agents charged with removing the children from their communities and "Goering, Hess, and friends" (Chrisjohn and Young 1997, 49); and comparisons between the misguided attempts at appeasement and reconciliation by the Canadian government and US president Ronald Reagan's symbolic visit to the Bitburg cemetery (58). Even if some of these comparisons may be exaggerated (if we insist on comparing the number of victims and the scope of the violence), this has been an effective strategy to advance a very legitimate goal of giving prominence to individual narratives (in the form of publications by reputable publishing houses and inclusion in school curricula), and of developing nationwide practices of commemoration that could counter the culture of amnesia that has been so successfully cultivated by mainstream Canadian society.

In his book on Levinas, *Vigilant Memory*, literary theorist Clifton Spargo (2006) concludes that the "lesson" of the Holocaust for today is that *any* violence upon a human being is inadmissible, political contexts notwithstanding (250). According to Levinas, human suffering is always ultimately useless, and it cannot be converted into systems of meaning, the systems that are often used as political agendas to justify inflicting violence on others. From a Levinasian standpoint, the ethical recognition of the purposelessness of human suffering and the unconditional "Thou shall not kill" is the minimal condition of "politics after Auschwitz." Such politics resists any identitarian (nationalist or other) discourses, due to which I only feel obligated to care about the suffering of the members of my own community or group. According to Spargo, the obligating status of *any* injustice is the only way in which "the memory of injustice becomes interchangeable with a question about why we care for the suffering of the other in the present" (261). My greatest wish for this book is that some of the strategies for discussing the literary, artistic, and philosophical representations of traumatic history I have proposed will be taken up to further develop ways of remembering that are dedicated to countering all forms of injustice.

Responding to Adorno's dictum that one cannot write poetry after Auschwitz, Imre Kertész (2004), whose work has been discussed at length in the first two chapters of this book, once said, echoing Paul Célan, that "after Auschwitz, one can only write poetry about Auschwitz" (40; translation mine). This postulate is diametrically opposed to my colleague's skepticism about the need for yet another book on the subject, although we must now recognize the hyperbolic and ethical import of Kertész's statement. What the writer has in mind is that, while the Holocaust caused widespread and irreparable destruction, it has also been "a source of a new culture" (44) in the decades after the war and continuing today. Since he is convinced that the Holocaust never "goes away" and always eventually catches up with us (67), Kertész hopes that memory of the disaster will continue to be a cultural need that grows out of the rebellion against historical amnesia, permeating the present and reaching far into the future, beyond its immediate historical context. This is why he proposes that, despite the destruction, the legacy of the Holocaust is ultimately affirmative. He writes, "The Holocaust carries with it great values. Hidden behind it, are great moral values." If the Holocaust is the central trauma of Western civilization, it is really up to us whether it will be "a continuous (and destructive) source of neurosis or a creative element" (216). In relation to Spargo's reading of Levinas, I interpret Kertész's remarks to mean that such cultural transformation must be founded upon the ethical precept of compassion and receptivity to the suffering of the other, *any* particular other.[13]

In his post-Holocaust reflection in the last section of *Negative Dialectics*, Adorno (1983) reformulates Kant's categorical imperative as "to arrange one's thoughts and actions so that Auschwitz will not repeat itself, so that nothing similar will happen" (365). Adorno himself did not envisage a way to overcome the collapse of meaning-making systems brought about by Auschwitz.[14] Although Levinas never explicitly discusses Adorno in his work, we can hypothesize that his own ethical philosophy is an attempt to overcome the impasse of Western thought that the German philosopher articulated in such stark terms. For Levinas, an exit from the cul-de-sac of history leads through the realm of the interhuman, in which the suffering of the other is never justifiable. For Levinas, to respond to Adorno's new categorical imperative means that I remain non-indifferent and that my vigilance knows no rest. This is how I understand his remark, in an interview, that "for me, the Holocaust is an event of still inexhaustible meaning" (2001, 260). In another interview, explaining the impact of the Holocaust on his life and work, Levinas (1987b) says, "The work of memory does not mean clinging to the past but renewing the past by new experiences, new circumstances, new wonders or horrors of the lived life. And in that sense, it is the future that is important and not a pure past. . . . It is important to maintain the memory of what happened for the truth of the Shoah. But the essence is to always find the actuality of the lessons of the Shoah with respect to new experiences" (14; translation mine).[15]

But how can we make sure that these "new experiences" are not a repetition of the old ones? Throughout this book, I have argued for the power of imagination to preserve the memory of the Holocaust. As a number of readers of Holocaust literature have now attested, imaginative explorations of the Holocaust not only deepen our historical understanding but also "help restore the uniqueness of the human spirit . . . and breathe new life into the materiality of victims and survivors" (Schwarz 1999, 37). In *The Origins of Totalitarianism*, political philosopher Hannah Arendt (1958) states that imagination—the power to create new things and new scenarios—is annihilated under the conditions of total domination. For Arendt, the *Muselmänner* in the Nazi camps, human beings that only passively responded to stimuli, without consideration for the future, were the most horrifying example of totalitarianism's destruction of the faculty of imagination. Without imagination, writes Arendt, there can be no new beginning, no future, and certainly no better future. She postulates therefore that imagination, "with its incalculability, is the greatest of all obstacles to total domination" (456), and it must continue to be opposed to totalitarian forces. Not only the artist but also the intellectual "after Auschwitz" has an obligation to exercise this faculty to its full potential because only "the fearful imagination of those who have been aroused by the events but have not themselves been smitten in the flesh" can afford to keep thinking about horrors and thus "dread the camps as the possibility in the future" (441).

We can conclude therefore that Holocaust testimonials posit a duty to imagine, without which a duty to remember is only an empty phrase. The literary, artistic, and philosophical works on the Holocaust with which I have engaged here provide an important addendum to that statement: in order to imagine a better future, one must first be able to imagine the past. Thus it is my hope that, for the reasons that have just been outlined, the "poethics of disappearing traces" developed in this book—the ethically inflected imaginative strategies of bearing witness and working through traumatic history—will serve to offer a measure of resistance against the erasure of the Holocaust, both from collective memory and from our hearts, so that its traces do not disappear after all.

INTRODUCTION

1. For more recent, extensive discussions of Adorno's dictum and its impact on the debates about the limits of representation "after Auschwitz," see, for instance, Josh Cohn, "'The Ever-Broken Promise of Happiness': Interrupting Art, or Adorno," in *Interrupting Auschwitz* (New York: Continuum, 2003), and Michael Rothberg, "After Adorno: Culture in the Wake of Catastrophe," in *Traumatic Realism: The Demands of Holocaust Representation* (Minneapolis: University of Minnesota Press, 2000).

2. Binjamin Wilkomirski, *Fragments: Memories of a Wartime Childhood*, trans. Carol Brown Janeway (New York: Schocken Books, 1995). In the wake of revelations that Binjamin Wilkomirski's book was not based on personal experiences, *Fragments* became downgraded from the category of Holocaust memoir to that of a "fake" or "forgery," and the ensuing controversy prompted the publishers, first in Germany, and then in the United States, to withdraw it from print. For a well-balanced account of the controversy, see Stephen Maechler's investigation into Wilkomirski's life, *The Wilkomirski Affair: A Study in Biographical Truth*: New York: Schocken Books, 2001).

3. See Norman Finkelstein, *The Holocaust Industry: Reflections on the Exploitation of Jewish Suffering* (New York: Verso Books, 2000).

4. See the exhibit catalogue *Mirroring Evil*, ed. Norman L. Kleeblatt (New York: Jewish Museum, 2001).

5. See, for instance, David H. Hirsch, *The Deconstruction of Literature: Criticism after Auschwitz* (Providence: Brown University Press, 1991); Elizabeth Bellamy, *Affective Genealogies: Psychoanalysis, Postmodernism, and the "Jewish Question" after Auschwitz* (Lincoln: University of Nebraska Press, 1997); and Richard Wolin, *The Seduction of Unreason: The Intellectual Romance with Fascism: From Nietzsche to Postmodernism* (Princeton, NJ: Princeton University Press, 2004).

6. See especially James Hatley's *Suffering Witness: The Quandary of Responsibility after the Irreparable* (2000) and Clifton Spargo's *Vigilant Memory: Emmanuel Levinas, the Holocaust, and the Unjust Death* (2006).

7. See, for instance, Tokarska-Bakir's influential essay "Jedwabne: History as a Fetish" (in Glowacka and Zylinska 2007). Tokarska-Bakir is the author of, among others, *Legendy o krwi: Antropologia przesądu* [Blood legends: An anthropology of prejudice] (Warsaw: Wydawnictwo WAB, 2008), and *Rzeczy mgliste* [Foggy matters] (Sejny: Pogranicze, 2004), in which she uses trauma theory and postmodern ethics to examine the phenomenon of anti-Semitism.

8. The impact of the Holocaust on philosophical thinking in general has been recognized and convincingly argued by philosophers Alan Rosenberg, James Watson, and Alan Milchman. See, for instance, *Contemporary Portrayals of Auschwitz: Philosophical Challenges,* ed. Alan Rosenberg et al. (Amherst NY: Humanity Books, 2000), and *Echoes from the Holocaust: Philosophical Reflections on a Dark Time,* ed. Alan Rosenberg and Gerald E. Myers (Philadelphia: Temple University Press, 1988).

9. Regarding the theoretical framework of the book, I have also relied on the debates about the distinction between memory and history, initiated by Pierre Nora's influential book *Sites of Memory,* in which he conceives of memory and history as antagonistic, whereby history, a representation of the past, seeks to subsume memory, which is "always a phenomenon of the present" (1996, 3).

10. Eaglestone, for instance, dedicates separate chapters to the discussion of literary testimony, historical interpretations of the Holocaust, and philosophical responses to the Holocaust. However, in staging encounters between these different genres and disciplines, he shows how such conversations can help to mutually illuminate their various claims as well as their often unacknowledged presuppositions.

11. I am mindful of art curator Jill Snyder's comment that "from the beginning of the century, modern artists have tapped a rich vein that flows between the visual and verbal realms" (1994, 5). My readings draw on the potential of that "rich vein" in Holocaust contexts.

12. Within the so-called Western tradition, at least since Plato's symbolic gesture of expelling the poets from the Republic, art was considered in terms of mimetic representation and viewed as subservient to ethics (conceived, after Aristotle, in terms of what constitutes good life). In the seventeenth century, with the emergence of the discipline of aesthetics (in the works of Alexander Baumgarten and, later, Immanuel Kant), art began to emerge as an autonomous domain, independent of ethics or politics. For a summary of the traditional relationships between ethics and aesthetics, and of postmodern challenges to that paradigm, see the introduction to Glowacka and Boos's *Between Ethics and Aesthetics* (2002). See also Kaplan's introduction to *Unwanted Beauty* (2007) for a brief overview of the emergence of the discipline of aesthetics and its central concepts of the beautiful and the sublime.

13. Kant's categorical imperative states that a man ought to act so that any one of his actions could be made into a universal law that binds all mankind.

14. "L'authenticité de l'art doit annoncer un ordre de justice."

15. Deguy writes, "Continuons d'appeler (poétique) une certain invention de la circonstance, une manière d'emporter le morceau; l'intrusion de la

parole deplacée qui, de la déplacer, inscrit 'le moment'" (1978, 35). I would like to thank Christopher Elson for this reference and for his translation of Deguy's term.

16. "Aesthetics of remembrance" is a term used by Lisa Saltzman in her influential study *Making Memory Matter: Strategies of Remembrance in Contemporary Art* (2006).

17. Karyn Ball argues that the discourse of the unspeakable (in postmodern thinkers such as Lyotard and Blanchot, or in art historians such as James E. Young) is indebted to Adorno's indictment of lyrical poetics (2008, 9–11).

18. A similar demand for factual knowledge in examining the mechanisms that lead to the atrocities informs nonphilosophical critiques of works about the Holocaust, such as Tim Cole's *Selling the Holocaust*, in which the author protests against the commodification of the Holocaust, and Norman Finkelstein's *Holocaust Industry*, where the author exposes its political instrumentalization. Both authors consider the focus on knowledge and understanding to be a remedy against such excesses.

19. In "Narrative Ethics and Incommensurable Discourses," Amit Marcus writes, "His [Lyotard's] commitment is to an ethics that is never complacent, that constantly (re)examines its own discursive conditions, practices and boundaries, and attempts to give itself an account of the wrongs that it helps to prevent in comparison with the wrongs that it generates or perpetuates" (2008, 4).

20. Agamben supports his refutation of the unspeakable with archival research. In the appendix he quotes from the memoirs of the *Muselmänner*, that is, those who, by Agamben's own definition, were suspended between the human and the inhuman because they could not speak: "I am a *Muselmann*" (Edward Sokół); "I too was a *Muselmann*, from the beginning of 1942 to the beginning of 1943. I wasn't conscious of being one" (Jerzy Mostowski); "In my own body I lived through the most atrocious kind of life in the camp, the horror of being a *Muselmann*" (Bronisław Gościnski; quoted in Agamben 1999, 67). Agamben believes that by giving the *Muselmänner* "the last word" (165), he has proven that "the unspeakable" can and indeed must be spoken.

21. See, for instance, my treatment of "the intranslatable" as a trope for the necessity of communication (in chapter two), and of "silence" as a rhetorical figure that institutes the labor of memory and calls for future commentary (in chapter three).

22. Faurisson advances his spurious claim about the nonexistence of gas chambers in his book *Mémoire en defense* (Paris: La Vielle Taupe, 1980). The book appeared with a preface by Noam Chomsky, in which the American linguist and neoliberal public intellectual defended Faurisson's right to express his views on the grounds of the freedom of speech.

23. Similarly, Karyn Ball argues that Lyotard's thesis about "unpresentability" performs two *rhetorical* functions: protecting the specificity of traumatic experience against the claims of empirical knowledge and providing an opportunity to "theorize the aesthetic conditions of the Holocaust's reception as a trauma to and of language" (2008, 137).

24. Reflecting on the genesis of the term "the Holocaust," Derrida writes, "A word, unfit even to name the cinder in the place of memory of something else" (1991, 71). In his text *Shibboleth: For Paul Celan* (included in the volume *Sovereignties in Question*), Derrida apologizes for his indirectness in referring to the Holocaust: "Forgive me if I do not name, here, the *holocaust*, that is to say literally, as I chose to call it elsewhere, the all-burning [*le brûle-tout*], except to say this: there is certainly today the date of that holocaust that we know, the hell of our memory; but there is a holocaust for every date, and somewhere in the world, for every hour" (2005, 46).

25. Agamben finds the association between "crematoria and altars," as implied in the term "Holocaust," to be abominable. Further, his research shows that the provenance of the term is predominantly Christian, and, from its inception, has been burdened with the legacy of anti-Semitism. "That is why," says Agamben, "we will never make use of this term" (1999, 31). For an extended discussion of the genesis of the word "Holocaust" and its religious connotations, see Zev Garber and Bruce Zuckerman, "Why Do We Call the Holocaust 'The Holocaust'? An Inquiry into the Psychology of Labels" Modern Judaism 9, no. 2 (1998): 197–211.

CHAPTER ONE

Wiesel quoted in "From the Ashes: Elie Wiesel in Conversation with Roy Bonisteel," in Man Alive *(Canadian Broadcast Corporation, 1973), 28 mins. Child survivor quoted in Wieviorka (2006, 147). Spivak quoted in Spivak (1996, 186).*

Note: *A preliminary version of this chapter appeared in Emory's comparative literature e-journal* Reading On *1 (2006), "Trauma, Memory, Testimony."*

1. Leitner and her two surviving sisters were the first Holocaust survivors to disembark in the United States, on May 8, 1945. See, for instance, David Patterson, "Isabella Leitner," in *Encyclopedia of Holocaust Literature*, 104–6 (Westport: Oryx Press, 2002).

2. The books appeared, respectively, as Isabella Leitner and Irving Leitner, *Saving the Fragments: From Auschwitz to New York* (New York: NAL Books, 1985); Isabella Leitner, *The Big Lie: A True Story* (New York: Scholastic Inc., 1992); and Isabella Leitner and Irving Leitner, *Isabella: From Auschwitz to Freedom* (1994). The award-winning film *Fragments of Isabella* (1989), directed by Ronan O'Leary, with music by Carl Davis, was made with the support of the Amnesty International. The stage production by Irving Leitner premiered in St. Petersburg in 1993.

3. See also Filip Müller, *Eyewitness Auschwitz: Three Years in the Gas Chambers* (Chicago: Dee, Ivan R. Publisher, 1999).

4. By pointing out that "the writing of history cannot take place without testimonies . . . that is, without traces that make that writing possible," Wieviorka (2006, 5) challenges the methodology of historians such as Lucy Dawidowicz and Raul Hilberg, who reject eyewitness testimony as a credible

source of historical knowledge. In the epilogue of her book, however, Wieviorka is troubled by the increasing separation between testimony and history, and between individual memory and historical memory, which she attributes to a growing demand for the display of feelings and emotions in popular culture. In a word, as LaCapra notes, she is unwilling to admit the place of affect in the writing of history (LaCapra 1998, 144).

5. The essay is a commentary on the novella "Yosl Rakover Talks to God," by Israeli writer Zvi Kolitz. It was originally given as a talk on the French radio program *Ecoute Israël* and then published in 1963. The essay first appeared in English in 1990: *Difficult Freedom: Essays on Judaism* (Baltimore, MD: The Johns Hopkins University Press, 1990).

6. Philosopher Howard Caygill (2002) writes that Levinas's two major philosophical works are veiled "works of mourning for the victims of National Socialism" (5). Gad Soussana (2000), in a short essay, "Entre mémoire et archive: La langue de témoignage" (Between memory and the archive: The language of testimony), arrives at a similar conclusion. He states that Levinas's double epigraph situates his philosophical work in the place of testimony, haunted by the echoes of incessant in memoriam: "Un autre mémoire donnant à notre intériorité dévasté le sens de sa survie: le témoignage de la mort de l'autre, insurpassable témoignage de l'autre en moi" (Another memory that gives my devastated interiority a sense of survival: a testimony to the death of the other, the unsurpassable testimony to the other in me; 137). Soussana does not comment on the differences in content between the two versions of the epigraphs or on the intimate, as well as religious, dimension of the epigraph in Hebrew.

7. "May the great and ineffable name of the Lord be exalted and sanctified in the world." When Wiesel and Levinas once met in person, Levinas praised Wiesel's work by describing it as "kiddush hashem" (the sanctification of the Lord's name). Incidentally, the two had the same teacher of the Talmud, Mordechai Chouchani. I would like to thank Joseph Rosenberg for sharing with me his ideas about the Kaddish in relation to Levinas's ethics.

8. See chapter 2 for a discussion of the disjunction between a more general statement in French and its intimate, untranslated Hebrew equivalent.

9. Agamben situates his inquiry within a larger framework of a "new" ethics, which he describes as "an ethics of a form of life that begins where dignity ends," an ethics founded on the inclusion of unprotected bare life, emblematized in Agamben's (1999) work by the figure of the *Muselmann* (69). Agamben does not elaborate on the details of this new "cartography" of ethics (13). He insists, however, on the need to distinguish between juridico-political and ethical frameworks, and reproaches Levinas for reducing the legal dimension of responsibility to ethics.

10. Noting the overemphasis on testimony in contemporary theory, Bob Plant speaks of a veritable "testimony industry" today. Yet the testimonial imperative, he argues, has inhered in the Cartesian epistemological paradigm from its inception and thus has always been present in the structure of the Western subject. Plant insists on the centrality of the epistemological question of truth in the problematic of testimony, against Levinas's emphasis on

the primordial "ethical" truth of testimony, whereby the self-signification of the face is the very foundation of truth. Plant is concerned with the danger of divorcing testimony from the question of knowledge-based truth claims, and his prime examples of such a hazard are Zvi Kolitz's fictional account and Binjamin Wilkomirski's pseudomemoir, to which Plant refers as false witnesses. The confines of this chapter do not allow me to engage in a polemic with Plant's compelling thesis; let me remark, however, that to argue his point about the philosophical relevance of testimony, Plant also turns to examples of Holocaust memoirs (albeit, in this case, negative ones). Even his phrase "testimony industry" immediately brings to mind Norman Finkelstein's "Holocaust industry," thus indirectly referring Plant's entire discussion to Holocaust contexts. Those contexts, however, render problematic Plant's distinction between "epistemological truth" and the "truth of testimony": Agamben (1999), for instance, despite his insistence on the "knowability" of "Auschwitz," questions traditional parameters of knowledge. The main aporia of the death camps in relation to the problem of truth, he argues, is the disjunction between reality and facts: "Facts so real that by comparison nothing is truer; a reality that necessarily exceeds its factual elements" (12). A challenge to cognitive regimens of truth in relation to "Auschwitz" is at the center of Lyotard's formulation of *the differend* (see chapter three).

11. In *Testimony: Crises of Witnessing in Literature, Psychoanalysis and History*, Laub (Laub and Felman 1992) writes, "Not only, in effect did the Nazis try to exterminate the physical witnesses of their crime, but the inherently incomprehensible and deceptive psychological structure of the event precluded its witnessing, even by its victims. . . . This loss of capacity to be a witness to oneself and thus to witness from inside is perhaps the true meaning of annihilation, for when one's history is abolished, one's identity ceases to exist as well" (80, 82).

12. In Agamben's view, the process of acquiring factual knowledge about the events has now been completed, even if the details are still accruing. Agamben's assertion is questionable if we take into account that, since 1989, an entirely new set of historical data has been emerging in former communist countries such as Poland, Ukraine, Lithuania, Estonia, and Romania (see the epilogue). The opening of the Soviet archives and a dramatic shift in the politics of memory and history have affected the countries of the "new" Europe in ways that cannot be accounted for in terms reducible to a mere accumulation of knowledge. In many cases, such knowledge coincides with a radical upheaval in the nation's self-conception and with a paradigm shift in its historical self-understanding, thus necessitating a reformulation of the general framework for thinking about the Holocaust, against Agamben's (1999) assertion that such a framework has already been established (11).

13. For a discussion of the relation between the notion of *teshuvah* in Judaism and Levinas's conception of the witnessing subject, see Dorota Glowacka, "Negative Witnessing and the Perplexities of Forgiveness: Polish Jewish Contexts after the Shoah," in *Essays on Levinas and the Law: A Mosaic*, ed. Desmond Manderson, 180–99 (Hampshire: Palgrave Macmillan, 2009).

14. While Levinas does not investigate the etymology of the word "witness" (*témoin*), Wieviorka, Agamben (1999, 26–27), and Derrida (2005, 75), in very different contexts, draw attention to the genesis of the word "witness" in the Greek designation for "martyr" (*martus, marturion*). Thus the fact that "a witness is associated with the destiny of the one to whom he witnesses" (Wieviorka 2006, 33) is inscribed in the very word that designates it. When Agamben points out that, etymologically, the word "martyr" is linked to "witnessing," he shifts the semantic field of "martyr" from referring to a justification, even a glorification, of another's death to bearing witness to that death.

15. In explaining the etymology of the word "responsibility" (from *spondeo*, "the guarantor of something for someone"), Agamben traces it to the archaic Roman concept of "hostage," which meant consigning oneself as a hostage to guarantee the fulfillment of a legal obligation.

16. In making the case for "empathic unsettlement" in the study of history, LaCapra (2004) similarly explains why responsibility toward the other can never be fully assumed. He writes that "desirable empathy" (as opposed to transferential identification) "involves virtual not vicarious experience—that is to say, experience in which one puts oneself in the other's position without taking the place of—or speaking for—the other or becoming a surrogate victim who appropriates the victim's voice and suffering" (135).

17. *Dasein* is Heidegger's term that refers to the ontologically primordial structure of subjectivity. It is derived from the German expression *da-sein*, which means "being there/here." For Heidegger, *Dasein* is prior to the subject, that is, to the entity that relates to objects and that can be defined in terms of consciousness. Being-in-the-world is a fundamental mode of *Dasein's* existence, which means that *Dasein* is always situated in a network of relations with other entities in the world, toward which it always comports itself with care (*Sorge*). Another such existential mode is *Dasein's* Being-toward-death: *Dasein* always appropriates the possibilities of its existence in the face of its mortality. See Martin Heidegger, *Being and Time*, trans. John Macquarrie and Edward Robinson (Oxford, UK: Blackwell, 1997).

18. As Wieviorka points out, a similar idiom of testifying by proxy emerged at the Eichmann trial. She quotes Haim Gouri, who stated that "the numerous witnesses . . . were the very center of the trial, because they served as faithful proxies of the Holocaust. They were the facts" (quoted in Wieviorka 2006, 85). Based on Haim Gouri, *Facing the Glass Booth: The Jerusalem Trial of Adolf Eichmann*, trans. Michael Swirsky (Detroit: Wayne State University Press, 2004).

19. See chapter three.

20. In Hebrew, the name "Gabriel" means, literally, "the strong man of God," Gabri-el. The figure of Gabriel as a messenger from God first appears in the book of Daniel, where he interprets Daniel's dream and prophesizes the apocalypse ("Understand, son of man; for the vision belongs to the time of the end").

21. Wiesel (1966) underlines the radical nature of temporality lived by his character, outside of linear chronologies: "He was living in the time of

war, outside time" (4). The division of the novel into four chapters, "Spring," "Summer," "Autumn," and "Winter," highlights the cyclical movement of repetition. It also reorients the understanding of temporality in terms of messianic time, which I reinterpret here as the ethical time of the other. For an extensive discussion of temporality in *The Gates*, see Joyce B. Lazarus, "Expanding Time: The Art of Elie Wiesel in *The Gates of the Forest*," Modern Language Studies 24 (Fall 1994): 4:39–46.

22. In tracing the etymology of the word "author" to the Latin *auctor* (which, among other designations, also meant "witness"), Giorgio Agamben (1999) points out that authorship always entails an act of witnessing "insofar as testimony always presupposes something—a fact, a thing or a word—that preexists him" (149).

23. For Levinas, Jewish suffering at the hands of the Nazis is the paradigm of gratuitous human suffering. For an extensive discussion of Levinas's injunction against post-Auschwitz theodicy in "Useless Suffering," see Leonard Grob, "Some Fundamental Doubts about Posing the Question of Theodicy in the Post-Holocaust World," in *Fire in the Ashes: God, Evil, and the Holocaust*, Pastora Goldner Series in Post-Holocaust Studies, 189–200 (Seattle: University of Washington Press, 2005), and Clifton Spargo, *Vigilant Memory: Emmanuel Levinas, the Holocaust, and the Unjust Death* (2006, 166–72).

24. Agamben also speaks of "nonsense" at the very core of speech (in relation to the hypostasis of the subject), but he situates it at the intersection of linguistics and ethics. Recalling Hurbinek, a little boy in Levi's narrative who could not speak any language and only repeated "uncertain and meaningless" clusters of sounds (*mass-klo, matisklo*), Agamben (1999) comments, "To bear witness, it is therefore not enough to bring language to its own nonsense, to the pure undecidability of letters. It is necessary that this senseless sound be, in turn, the choice of something or someone that, for entirely other reasons, cannot bear witness" (39).

25. Polish director Andrzej Wajda included this episode in his film *Korczak* (1990).

26. Ashley Brett Kaplan (2007) discusses chronological structures in Semprún's narratives in relation to Marcel Proust's conception of involuntary memory, that is, a sudden eruption of memory that markedly transforms the present moment of recollection. This analogy has been suggested by Semprún's own references to Proust in *The Long Voyage* (54–76).

27. In this section, Semprún describes at length the communist network's resistance activities in the camp. Since a number of French political prisoners worked in the *Arbeitsstatistik* office and had access to the inmates' files, they used their powers to save the prisoners they considered worthy of rescue, most often their own comrades. These practices were also described in Levi's *The Drowned and the Saved*, in the notorious chapter "The Grey Zone," and Semprún makes it clear that he was himself aware of the moral ambiguity of these acts of rescue.

28. Maurice Halbwachs (1877–1945) was a prominent French philosopher and sociologist, best known for his groundbreaking study *The Collective Memory* (*Les cadres sociaux de la mémoire*, 1925).

29. In 2004 the novel was retranslated by Tim Wilkinson and appeared as *Fatelessness* (New York: Random House, 2004).

30. Although Kertész's descriptions of his life as a survivor resonate remarkably closely with Terence Des Pres's (1976) characterization of the survivor's existence as the "small, additional, added on life" (24), they lack Des Pres's affirmation of the value of biological survival.

31. These narratives confirm clinical observations by psychologists who have worked with survivors. Dina Wardi writes, for instance, that "some of the survivors still do not believe that they have really remained alive" (quoted in Grimwood 2007, 9).

32. In his Nobel address, Kertész recounts receiving a copy of the document from the former camp of Buchenwald confirming that "inmate number 64-921, Imre Kertész" died. Kertész (2004) states, "So I died once, but probably in order to live, and this is my true story" (217). Charlotte Delbo (1995) recalls a similar experience of learning about her death in Auschwitz: while attending a commemorative ceremony, she heard her own name being read among those of the dead (xviii).

33. In *Fragments of Isabella*, for instance, Leitner (1980) rejoices, "Mama, Mama, the shadow of the madman is fading! We have another son, Mama. . . . He is the sound of your soul. He is the voice of the six million. He is Richard" (81). Kertész is not alone, however, in pondering the wisdom of begetting children after Auschwitz. On several occasions, Wiesel mentions how difficult it was for him to arrive at a decision to have a child (his son Elisha).

34. Although trained in philosophy, Kertész (1997) is unsparing in his condemnation of German philosophical tradition. He writes, "The history of the world is the image and deed of cognition. . . . Thus spoke H. again, not H. Führer and Chancellor but H., larger than life-sized visionary, philosopher, court jester, headwaiter of select delicacies to all Führers, Chancellors, and other sundry titled usurpers" (29). "H." most likely stands for Hegel, although Heidegger seems indicted in this initial as well. Numerous passages in *Kaddish* betray Kertész's familiarity with Heidegger's philosophy of being, although the acerbic tone of these reflections reveals his disillusionment with the German philosopher's existential analyses.

35. The following lines from Célan's (1988) poem are tacitly woven into the narrative of *Kaddish for a Child Not Born*:

we dig a grave in the breezes there one lies unconfined
A man lives in the house he plays with the serpents he writes
he writes when dusk falls to Germany your golden hair Margarete
he writes it and steps out of doors and the stars are flashing he whistles
his pack out
he whistles his Jews out in earth has them dig for a grave
he commands us strike up for the dance
. . . .

He calls out more sweetly play death death is a master from Germany
   he calls out more darkly now stroke your strings then as smoke you
will rise into air. (61–62)

36. Here I disagree with Lee Congdon's (2003) conclusion in his other-wise excellent discussion of Kertész's work, informed by his reading of Mau-rice Blanchot's *The Writing of the Disaster* (2005), that the protagonist's childhood rather than Auschwitz is the underlying trauma of this narrative, "the [true] site of the disaster" (7). I argue that the narrator now remembers his childhood through the prism of his Auschwitz experience. In fact, my reading of Kertész's novel as an assertion of the intractability of Auschwitz, its having engulfed "all," even the events that happened before it, seems to better elucidate the meaning of Blanchot's notion of the "disaster"; Blanchot (1995) writes, "*The disaster takes care of everything*" (3).

37. Kertész (1997) writes, "And please stop saying . . . that Auschwitz is a product of irrational, incomprehensible forces, because there is always a rational explanation for wrongdoing: it's quite possible that Satan is himself, like Iago, irrational; his creations, however, are rational creatures indeed; there every action is as soluble as a mathematical formula" (31).

38. My reading of *Kaddish* as emphasizing the structure of witnessing and an address to another, the novel's bleak general tone notwithstanding, differs significantly from, for instance, Robert Eaglestone's interpretation. For Eaglestone, *Kaddish* epitomizes Kertész's "choice of discontinuity and the end of community," in contrast to other writers' attempts to recreate a community and adhere to the tradition in the wake of the disaster (2004, 97–98).

39. Agamben (1999) writes, "The authority of the witness consists in his capacity to speak solely in the name of an incapacity to speak—that is, in his or her being a subject" (158).

40. In his essay on Levinas's notion of substitution titled "At This Mo-ment, in This Text, Here I Am," Derrida (1991) expresses the proleptic di-mension of the ethical subject's obligation by the phrase "Il y aura obligé" (He will have obligated).

41. Agamben (1999) also draws on the idiom of trauma when he states that "subjectification, the production of consciousness in the event of dis-course, is often a trauma from which human beings are not easily cured" (123).

42. Michael Kigel (among others) draws an analogy between Levinas's own experience of the historical trauma of the Holocaust and his evocation of traumatic encounters with the other in the ethical relation. Kigel argues that the philosopher's notion of ethical temporality as "immemorial past," as it relates to his central concept of the "trace," is marked by "the no time of Auschwitz"; as such, it can be "compared to the classical definition of trauma as a wound in memory" (in Malka 2006, xix). It is on ethical grounds, how-ever, whereby the traumatic encounter is first and foremost an affirmation of the existence of another human being, that I would defend Levinas's transvaluation of trauma against, for instance, LaCapra's (2007a) criticism of philosophical positions that posit foundational trauma "as the basis for identity" (168). LaCapra's concern stems from cases such as Wilkomirski's, where the contentious author has sublimated a memory of deprived child-hood into an identity-affirming story of Holocaust victimization (LaCapra

2007a, 168; 2004, 81; and elsewhere). As Derrida (1999) explains, Levinas reconceives trauma in ethical terms, as the trauma of the encounters with the other that allows the self to emerge as an ethical subject. My reading is congruent with Derrida's characterization of Levinas's conception of trauma as "happy traumatism" (11).

43. In *Suffering Witness*, James Hatley finds an excellent illustration of Levinas's radical precept in one of the harrowing episodes in Tadeusz Borowski's short story (1976) "This Way for the Gas, Ladies and Gentlemen" (in the volume of the same title). After a recent transport of prisoners has been unloaded on the ramp of Auschwitz-Birkenau, the members of the Canada *Sondercommando*, including Borowski's protagonist Tadeusz, clean out the corpses of infants left behind in the wagons. When the SS man threatens to shoot the women who recoil in horror when asked to take the dead infants, one woman steps out and offers to carry the bodies. Then she turns to Tadeusz, who is screaming at the women in intoxicated rage, and, gazing into his eyes and smiling at him, she whispers, "My poor boy" (40). In offering compassion to her tormentor instead of hate and fear, and pitying her persecutor (and this is who Tadeusz, also a prisoner at Auschwitz, has become), as if taking his deed upon herself, the nameless woman enacts the movement whereby the suffering by the other's hand passes into pity and suffering for the other, even if he is a persecutor.

44. Perhaps the most powerful expression of the witness's affliction of breathlessness is the title of Sarah Kofman's veiled reflection on the death of her father in Auschwitz, *Smothered Words* (*Paroles suffoquées*), trans. Madelaine Dobie (Evanston: Northwestern University Press, 1998; originally published in 1987). Kofman writes, "Knotted words, demanded and yet forbidden . . . , which stick in your throat and cause you to suffocate, to lose your breath, which asphyxiate you, taking away the possibility of even beginning" (39).

CHAPTER TWO

Note: This chapter has been inspired by the stories told to me by my father, Wiktor Jassem, who survived the war in different hiding places on the "Aryan side." As all survivors, my father often marvels at the sheer miracle of his staying alive while so many around him perished. Yet, during the war, the knowledge of different languages, which he had been ardently learning from an early age, saved his life on many occasions (to which he refers as his "great escapes"). When my father had to move between hiding places, he carried with him, on a little trolley, a gramophone and his collection of analog records with language lessons. After the war, my father became a professor of linguistics.

1. Notable exceptions can be found in the works by Berel Lang, Alan Rosen, and Susan R. Suleiman, and in some commentaries on Célan's poetry.

2. Abraham Levin wrote *Mi-pinkaso shel ha-moreh mi-Yehudyah*, which was translated into English as *A Cup of Tears: A Diary of the Warsaw*

Ghetto, ed. Antony Polonsky (Oxford: Blackwell, 1989). Yitzhak Katznelson was the author of an elegy lamenting the destruction of Eastern European Jews, *Dos lid funem oysgehargetn yidishn folk,* translated into English as "The Song of the Murdered Jewish People," trans. and annot. Noah H. Rosenbloom (Israel: Hakibbutz Hameuchad Publishing House: 1980).

3. Engelking (1994) writes, "The problem of the language of testimony is extremely important. In what language should the story of war experiences be told? . . . Survivors often had to talk about the experiences in languages that they learnt only after the war. Could they find, in those languages, the words that described experiences about which they were thinking in another language? . . . I am convinced that it is easier to talk about war experiences in the language one was using at that time, in which one was naming that world" ("Niezwykle ważny jest moim zdaniem także problem języka przekazu. W jakim języku powinny być opowiadane doświadczenia wojenne? . . . Ocaleli często musieli opowiadać o swoich przeżyciach w językach, których nauczyli się dopiero po wojnie [np. po angielsku]. Czy mogli znaleźć w tych językach słowa opisujące rzeczywistość, o której myśleli w innym języku? . . . Jestem przekonana, że łatwiej jest opowiadać o doświadczeniach wojennych w języku, którego się wówczas używało, którym nazywało się tamten świat" 247–48; translation mine).

4. Suleiman focuses on memoirs written in English by survivors who immigrated to the United States from Hungary. Most of these texts were written many years after the war, when the authors had already attained competence in their second language.

5. See chapter one for the discussion of Kertész's *Kaddish for a Child Not Born* and the protagonist's condition of existential homelessness.

6. Kertész describes his trade as a translator in many of his novels, such as *Kaddish* (see chapter one), *The Other, Liquidation,* and *Fiasco.*

7. "Then said they unto him, Say now Shibboleth: and he said Sibboleth: for he could not frame to pronounce it right. Then they took him, and slew him at the passages of Jordan: and there fell at that time of the Ephraimites forty and two thousand" (Judges 12:6; King James Bible).

8. Adorno made the comment, "To write poetry after Auschwitz is barbaric" in 1949, in his essay "Cultural Criticism and Society," later included in the volume *Prisms* (Adorno 1967, 34).

9. In the original: "Lass uns sie waschen/lass uns sie kämmen" (Célan 2001, 68).

10. In Poland, during the war, the "translation" of Jewish names into Polish-sounding ones was common (such as writers Sonia Landau/Krystyna Żywulska and Jerzy Nikodem Lewinkopf/Jerzy Kosiński, or child educator Henryk Goldszmidt/Janusz Korczak). Many survivors chose to keep their Polish names after the war.

11. In the last two decades, the receptiveness of national Eastern European languages (Polish, Ukranian, Estonian, and Hungarian, for instance) to the idiom of Holocaust testimony has become a litmus test of a given country's attitudes to the past, as well as a significant indicator of transformations in the politics of memory.

12. The full title of Kurt Lewin's memoir is *Przeżyłem: Saga Świętego Jura spisana w roku 1946* [I survived: A saga of Saint Yur written in the year 1946] (Warsaw: Zeszyty Literackie, 2006).

13. For instance, some of Fink's stories were included in the first anthology of women's writings about the Holocaust, *Different Voices,* ed. Carol Rittner and John K. Roth (St. Paul: Paragon House, 1993).

14. Ida Fink was born in 1921 in Zbaraż, today's Ukraine. Before the war, she studied at the musical conservatory in her hometown. She escaped from the ghetto, with her younger sister, in 1942, and, equipped with a fake birth certificate obtained by her father, volunteered for work in Germany. She described her wartime ordeal of double identity, betrayals, and constant fear of being discovered in *The Journey* [*Podróż*], trans. Joanna Weschler and Francine Prose (New York: Farrar Straus Giroux, 1992). Fink immigrated to Israel in 1957. Despite international acclaim (among others, she received the Anne Frank Award and the Alberto Moravia Award, and two films, Pierre Koralnik's *The Last Hideout* (2003), and Uri Barbash's *Spring 1941* (2008), were based on her texts,) prior to the fall of communism, her writings were relatively little known in Poland, and their reception there was lukewarm. In 2003 Fink's short stories and plays were first published in Poland in the collection *Odpływający ogród* (A floating garden) to much critical acclaim. For an analysis of Fink's short stories and plays, see chapter four.

15. In a conversation in New York in 2003 with journalist Giovanna Borradori, Jacques Derrida comments (in English, which is neither his nor the interviewer's first language) on the need to consider the violence of the English language's global hegemony. He states that "the world order that felt itself targeted through this violence [the 9/11 attacks] is dominated largely by the Anglo-American idiom that is indissociably linked to political discourse that dominates the world stage, to international law, diplomatic institutions, the media, and the greatest technoscientific, capitalist, and military power" (Borradori 2003, 88). Although this conversation took place in the aftermath of the events of 9/11, the philosopher's comments are pertinent to the issues of translation and linguistic hegemony in general.

16. Similarly to Leitner's narrative, Olga Lengyel's *Five Chimneys* was written in her native Hungarian immediately after the war, but it was first published in a French translation in 1946 and translated into English in 1947. To the best of my knowledge, neither Leitner's nor Lengyel's memoir has appeared in the authors' native Hungarian.

17. In contrast to the writer's or translator's effort to conceal the mark of strangeness and to weed the foreign accent out of the survivor's narrative, several accounts written by children of survivors foreground the traces of foreignness in their parents' Holocaust speech. Art Spiegelman's exaggerated transcription of his father's heavily accented English in *Maus* is perhaps the best-known attempt to record a parent's linguistic displacement. Another masterful inscription of the translation *differend* by a child of survivors is Debbi Filler's rendition of her father's speech in her one-woman comedy show *Punch Me in the Stomach* (1997), directed by Francine Zuckerman. Filler's performance is riveting, since she transforms herself on stage into her

father, vicariously recreating his experience through the cadences of her father's accented speech. Parts of a written transcript of Filler's "translation" appeared in a volume of interviews with daughters of survivors, *Daughters of Absence*, edited by artist Mindy Weisel (see chapter five).

18. In an earlier short story, "A Tale for Hollywood," Krall (1996) describes being hired by Izolda to turn her extraordinary story into a novel, which could then serve as a script for a Hollywood movie. She completely fails to meet Izolda's expectations, however; she complains, "All my despair, my heart, my tears—and in your version? A few sentences. Is that really all?" (178). The story appeared in Polish in the volume *Hipnoza* (Kraków: Wydawnictwo a5, 2002).

19. The other eye witnesses whom Lanzmann interviews in English are Rudolf Vrba, a former prisoner in Treblinka, and Jan Karski, an emissary of the Polish government in exile, and a member of the Polish Home Army.

20. Bomba's harrowing attempt to protect himself from pain with a buffer of English is in sharp contrast with the most prominent appearance of English in the film, namely, historian Raul Hilberg's expert commentary. As Alan Rosen points out, most of the important histories of the Holocaust were written in English, including the first influential comprehensive accounts, Gerald Reitlinger's *The Final Solution* (1952) and Hilberg's *The Destruction of European Jewry* (1961).

21. "Szymek" is a diminutive of "Szymon," and the fact that the inhabitants of Grabów greet him in this way indicates a certain warmth: they are genuinely happy to see him and learn of his survival.

22. The disregard for the Polish language in the published screenplay *Shoah: The Complete Text of the Acclaimed Holocaust Film* is shocking. First of all, although the practice of omitting diacritical signs has become customary in works about the Holocaust, considering that the proper names of the death camps are themselves the sites of memorialization, even small inaccuracies in the spelling of "Sobibór" or "Chełmno," for instance, are problematic. Some other errors in the transcription of Polish words also show an astonishing lack of care (e.g., "Orkrobek" instead of what, to the Polish ear, clearly sounds like "Orchówek," or translating "Mrs." as "Pana" instead of "Pani," a basic word in both languages).

23. Several scholars have commented on Lanzmann's lack of attention to the nuances of Polish peasants' utterances and his propensity to make generalizations about their behavior, based on his perception of widespread Christian anti-Semitism among Polish villages. Jean-Charles Szurek (2007), for instance, writes, "In a more general sense, there is no communication between the director's universe and the peasants' because, however important it is to comprehend their relationship with the Jews, when their words are translated, they have been emasculated as they cross the language barrier" (153).

24. Translatory struggles in *Shoah* can be contrasted with the famous "translation" scene in Roberto Benigni's *Life Is Beautiful,* in which the Babelian chaos of the camps is thrown into comic relief, and the deathly threat of incommunicability disarmed by laughter and comic reversal. The main character's lack of knowledge of German ultimately enables his son's survival.

This masterful burlesque can therefore be read as a parable of a redemptive narrative of survival by means of overcoming the translation *differend*.

25. See Marek Wilczyński's (1994) comparative analysis of Fink's stories and their translations into English.

26. The change of titles during the publication history of Primo Levi's camp narrative also bespeaks the tension between hegemonic appropriation and palliative distance afforded by the English language. *Se questo e un uomo* was first published in the United States in 1959, by Orion Press, under the title *If This Is a Man*, and it received little attention. It was then republished in 1979 by Penguin as *If This Is a Man and The Truce*. It became widely read only when, on the recommendation of the well-known American writer Philip Roth, Levi's book was reissued in 1993, bearing the title of *Survival in Auschwitz*. The new title in itself seemed to "translate" Levi's anguished reflection on the essence of humanity after Auschwitz into a redemptive narrative of survival.

27. As Rosen notes, Levi's later use of spoken German—his coarse pronunciation and inappropriate use of colloquialisms—also carry a "linguistic tattoo" of his Auschwitz experience with that language.

28. As Leslie Morris (2001) argues, such "sounds of other languages are the sounds of memory that can be a tangible recording of how the event is remembered. They release an acoustic echo of prior sounds" (368), producing a material imprint of the Holocaust in the language of testimony.

29. See chapter one.

30. The book was also published in England in 2004, under the title *Landscapes of Memory: A Holocaust Girlhood Remembered* (London: Bloomsbury, 2004). For a comprehensive comparison of the versions in English and in German, see Schaumann 2004. Some of the changes in the English text were a result of the feedback Kluger received from the readers of *weiter leben*. They included replacing fictional names in the German version with the real names of Kluger's German and American friends. Also, after the first version was already published, Kluger learned that her father had not been gassed in Auschwitz but most likely was shot during a transport to the East—information she was trying to process while writing the book in English. Another significant change is the addition of "Girlhood" in the title of the English version, which reflects a more explicit feminist agenda in *Still Alive*.

31. Suleiman (1996) refers to English, which she herself learned as a child when her family emigrated from Hungary immediately after the war, as a "kindly stepmother tongue" (645), the expression that also aptly describes Kluger's warm and appreciative relation to the language of her adopted country.

32. The delay in publishing the version in English was dictated by personal reasons. Since the memoir presented an unflattering portrayal of the author's mother, Kluger (2001) was hoping her mother would never read the book. Unfortunately, although Alma Hirschel usually stayed away from "anything German," she came across her daughter's memoir and was "badly hurt" (210). Kluger published the novel in English only after her mother's death.

33. Linda Schulte-Sasse contends that American audiences were unresponsive and even hostile to Kluger because she challenged the American "high drama" version of the Holocaust and American readers' tendency to interpret its events in redemptive terms.

34. In her study of the effect of the German language on survivors for whom their mother tongue was also the language of the genocide, Canadian Holocaust scholar Karin Doerr speaks of the difficulty for those survivors of dealing with their "language memories," triggered by words associated with death and fear, such as *Umschlagplatz* or *Selektion*, the words that, in memoirs, appear untranslated regardless of the language of the testimony. To illustrate the affective ambivalence toward German on the part of survivors who grew up speaking that language, Doerr (2009) cites the example of second-generation artist Ruth Liberman's language-art piece *Word Shot*. Liberman, a child of Holocaust survivors, who grew up in postwar Germany, stages a confrontation with the German words that she hates by shooting at them (while they are mounted on boxes) with a pistol and then taking photographs of the words riddled with bullets (53).

35. For instance, an ethnic Pole will provide a different axiological interpretation and therefore representation of the fact that he or she did not help a Jewish neighbor (fear of reprisals) than a survivor who interprets this failure of neighborly solidarity as ultimate betrayal rooted in Polish anti-Semitism (Lang 1988, 343).

36. Drawing on Talmudic commentaries, David Patterson (2006b) explains that the objective of the tale of the Tower of Babel was not, as is usually thought, to explain the genesis of the multiplicity of languages. The name Babel literally means "confusion," and it conveys the emptiness of manmade words and the presumptuousness of the people who believed that they could themselves create words and infuse them with meaning, beyond the realm of divine creation. I find Patterson's theological reading illuminating with respect to Benjamin's view of language as the transcendent horizon of communicability, whose essence is its heteronymous relation to what exceeds its concrete manifestation in the words of particular languages.

37. The first version of "Die Aufgabe des Übersetzers" was published in 1923, as a preface to Benjamin's translation of Charles Baudelaire's *Tableaux parisiens*.

38. In her commentary on "The Task of the Translator," Carol Jacobs (1975) writes, "Translation does not transform a foreign language into one we may call our own, but rather renders radically foreign the language we believe to be ours" (756).

39. Describing his first encounter with Levinas at the ENIO, L'École Normale Israélite Orientale, where the philosopher held the post of the principal, Malka (2006) recollects that the students made fun of his French "because of its heavy Slavic accent" (xxxiv). One of Levinas's students recalls that "his language was certainly interesting . . . , a bit fantastical, behind which lay Russian, German, and Hebrew" (152).

40. See chapter one.

41. According to the cabalistic legend, in the act of divine creation, the emerging forms could not support the weight of divine energy and light.

When the angels dropped the vessel in which the light was being carried, it shattered, and the particles of light dispersed across the universe. *Tikkun* refers to the process of gathering the dispersed fragments, of the reparation, restoration, and mending of the original being of things, in order to hasten the coming of the Messiah.

42. Benjamin's theory of translation can be seen as anticipating his messianic view of history, which he outlines in his later essay "Theses on the Philosophy of History." In "Theses," Benjamin (1969) envisages modernity's condition of fragmentation against what he calls a weak messianic promise, as embodied in the apocalyptic figure of Angelus Novus (253–64).

43. For Fackenheim's discussion of *tikkun olam*, see chapter four of *To Mend the World* (1994), "Historicity, rupture, and *tikkun olam*."

CHAPTER THREE

This chapter is dedicated to Mrs. Helena Jockel, whose account of her ordeal in Auschwitz has touched me as well as many of my students to whom she has spoken. Despite the horrors she endured, Helena always finds beauty in the world around her and in the many people she meets. Her love of life and her passion for literature (Franz Kafka, Gogol, Toni Morrison . . .) continue to "save the honour of thinking."

Note: A short version of this chapter appeared under the title "Lending an Ear to the Silence Phrase: Lyotard's Aesthetics of Holocaust Memory," in Minima Memoria: Essays in the Wake of Jean-François Lyotard, ed. Claire Nouvet et al., 49–66 (Stanford: Stanford University Press, 2007).

1. I am using the term "phrase" to be consistent with the English translation of the French *la phrase*, which in *The Differend* means both "a sentence" and "a phrase" (which could be a musical phrase, for instance).

2. See introduction, notes 1 to 3.

3. For Lyotard (as for Levinas), Western conceptions of knowledge culminated in Hegel's speculative dialectic. Its logical operator is the concept of *Aufhebung*, that is, sublation or dialectical elevation (the word is derived from the German verb *aufheben*, which means "to cancel," "to preserve," and "to lift"). In the movement of *Aufhebung*, a concept or term acquires a "higher" meaning through a dialectical interplay with another term or concept, that is, through the movement of double negation that results in the synthesis of opposites. Lyotard (1992) objects to attempts to subsume "Auschwitz" under speculative dialectics because the suffering of Holocaust victims cannot yield higher meaning, and no "profit" can be derived from it (364). Further, speculative discourse erases disagreement and thus does not allow for genuine discussion, oriented toward the discovery of new idioms. For Lyotard, Faurisson's relative success in putting forth his spurious claim is a result of manipulating speculative logic. In that case, asks Lyotard, "Is it possible that some kind of discourse, some kind of logic, sprung from the anonym 'Auschwitz' would be maintained 'afterwards' which would not be

its speculative result?" (366). *The Differend* is the philosopher's own attempt to answer this question in the affirmative. For an in-depth discussion of Lyotard's critique of speculative logic in "Discussions, or Phrasing 'After Auschwitz,'" see Karyn Ball (2008), chapter 3, "'Auschwitz' after Lyotard."

4. Andreas Huyssen (1995), in contrast, singles out Lyotard's "sweeping indictment of Western modernity" (252), and he underscores the ethical foundation of the philosopher's thought, that is, his plea (in *The Differend* in particular) for the need to recognize marginalized and repressed life histories, in defiance of the Western politics of exclusion and domination.

5. Some of Lyotard's best-known essays on the sublime include his manifesto "Answering the Question: What is Postmodernism?" the essay "The Sublime and the Avant-garde," and a number of texts on the Jewish American painter Barnett Newman. Lyotard's most extensive and detailed exposition on the sublime is his book on Kant's *Critique of Judgment, Lessons on the Analytic of the Sublime,* trans. Elizabeth Rottenberg (Stanford: Stanford University Press, 1994).

6. For an extensive discussion of Lyotard's *differend* in relation to the unpresentable, see Gasché (2007, 317–22). As Gasché argues, the notion of unpresentability in Lyotard must be seen as a primarily ontological problematic, rather than as a question pertaining to knowledge.

7. The texts included in Levinas's *Quatre lectures talmudiques* (1968) appeared in English in the volume *Nine Talmudic Readings,* translated by Annette Aronowicz (Bloomington: Indiana University Press, 1990). As described in chapter one, Levinas's frequent example, indeed, a model of such unconditional listening, is Abraham's response "Here I am" to God's calling of his name. It indicates Abraham's absolute readiness to follow God's command, even if he does not know yet what he will be asked to do.

8. In Judaism, the name of God must be concealed since the believer is forbidden to pronounce it.

9. "Mamusiu! Ja przecież byłem grzeczny! Ciemno, ciemno!"

I woła woła jedno miejsce puste
Wy którzy się mnie nie boicie
bo jestem mały i wcale mnie nie ma
nie wypierajcie się mnie
zwróćcie mi pamięć po mnie
te słowa pożydowskie
te słowa poludzkie
tylko tych siedem słów
(Ficowski 1988, 24).

10. Choć pamięć blednie/nie ze zgrozy/tak od trzydziestu blednie lat (Ficowski 1988, 23).

11. Compare with the translation of the original text in the Hebrew Bible:

Hear, Israel, the Lord is our God, the Lord is One.

Blessed be the Name of His glorious kingdom for ever and ever.
And you shall love the Lord your God with all your heart and with all
   your soul and with all your might.
And these words that I command you today shall be in your heart.
And you shall teach them diligently to your children, and you shall
   speak of them when you sit at home, and when you walk along the
   way, and when you lie down and when you rise up.
And you shall bind them as a sign on your hand, and they shall be for
   frontlets between your eyes.
And you shall write them on the doorposts of your house and on your
   gates.
And it shall come to pass if you surely listen to the commandments to
   love the Lord your God and to serve him with all your heart and all
   your soul,
That I will give rain to your land, the early and the late rains, that you
   may gather in your grain, your wine and your oil.
And I will give grass in your fields for your cattle and you will eat and
   you will be satisfied.
Beware, lest your heart be deceived and you turn and serve other gods
   and worship them.
And anger of the Lord will blaze against you, and he will close the
   heavens and there will not be rain, and the earth will not give you its
   fullness, and you will perish quickly from the good land that the Lord
   gives you.
So you shall put these, my words, on your heart and on your soul;
   and you shall bind them for signs on your hands, and they shall be
   for frontlets between your eyes.
And you shall teach them to your children, and you shall speak of them
   when you sit at home, and when you walk along the way, and when
   you lie down and when you rise up.
And you shall write them on the doorposts of your house and on your
   gates.
In order to prolong your days and the days of your children on the land
   that the Lord promised your fathers that he would give them, as long
   as the days that the heavens are over the earth.

                                                —Deuteronomy 6:4–9

12. The number seven is a general symbol of mankind's association with
God, and it is the favorite religious number in Judaism. Seven, for instance,
is the divine number of completion; the menorah has seven arms; and seven
refers to the day of rest, the Sabbath. Wiesel's reference is specifically to the
Seven Seals of Revelation, that is, the prophesy of disasters that will befall
mankind (wars, famine, disease, and persecution) before it is redeemed by
the coming of the Messiah.

13. In her careful reading of Lyotard, Karyn Ball (2008) interprets
Lyotard's argument to mean that scientific facts, which purport to be

objective, "do not in themselves justify moral imperatives, which modify reality by guiding social and political actions" (97).

14. The play "The Table" was based on Fink's experiences when she worked as an interpreter and clerk of the court during the trials of Nazi criminals in Israel. She explains her motive for writing the play: "I realized that the way the interrogation is conducted changes that interrogation into the theatre of the absurd. *The Table* is a protest against the law that judges genocide according to the standards conceived for trivial crimes" (Orski 1994, 97; translation mine). *The Table* is one of Fink's best-known pieces: it was broadcast as a radio play and filmed for a television play in Germany, Poland, and Israel.

15. Longinus's real name is unknown, and it is estimated that he lived between the first and third centuries CE. He writes, "The silence of Ajax in the *Nekuia* is great and more sublime than any speech." Longinus, *On the Sublime*, trans. James A. Arieti and John M. Crossett, ix, 2:53 (New York: Mellen Press, 1985).

16. See chapter two.

17. Gertrud Koch (2007) describes *Shoah* as a cinematic exploration of the limits of representation. Through the elision of documentary images, Lanzmann underscores "the boundary between what is aesthetically and humanely imaginable and the unimaginable dimension of annihilation" (130).

18. The harshest criticisms concerned Wajda's christological interpretation of the Holocaust (for instance, the portrayal of Korczak framed him as a Christian martyr, with legible allusions to the figure of Francis of Assisi). The critics were also sceptical of the director's depiction of Polish-Jewish relations during the Holocaust, with emphasis on Polish rescue of Jews. Lanzmann, on the other hand, accused Wajda of having produced Holocaust kitsch. See Ginsberg 2007.

19. Petr Ginz's notebooks containing the diary, as well as some of his drawings, were found by the owner of an old house in Prague, who, "for some inexplicable reason" (Pressburger 2007, 4), decided to keep them and then forgot about their existence. The man remembered about the notebooks when the name of Petr Ginz was announced on Czech television in connection with the tragedy of the space shuttle *Columbia* in 2003. Ginz's painting *Moon Landscape* was chosen by Israeli astronaut Ilan Ramon to accompany him on the space flight. The shuttle exploded reentering the Earth's atmosphere, and all the crew members perished. Petr's sister, Chava Pressburger, who is also the editor of *The Diary*, describes her feelings when she saw the pages of her brother's writing: "When I saw them, I felt as if Petr hadn't actually died. It seemed to me that he was alive somewhere in eternity and was letting me know by sending this particular message" (5).

20. "Odysseus' Scar," in *Mimesis: The Representation of Reality in Western Literature*, trans. Willard R. Trask. (Princeton, NJ: Princeton University Press, 2003).

21. See the introduction for the discussion of the recent backlash against the notion of the unspeakable and the unpresentable.

22. Friedlander and LaCapra discuss the dangers of evoking the "high" idiom of the sublime in Holocaust contexts. Friedlander (1993) argues that

what instigated the atrocities—especially mass executions committed by the special battalions in the East—was what he refers to as *Rausch*, the sense of growing elation precipitated by "the staggering dimension of killing" (111). Since this sensation corresponds closely to Kant's "mathematical sublime," for Friedlander the sublime carries a negative connotation with the Nazi ethos of power. LaCapra (1994) also notes National Socialism's appeal to the rhetoric of the sublime, and he views Nazi "distorted secular religiosity involving scapegoating and victimization" to be the culmination of what he calls the "immanent" (or this-wordly) sublime (14). Both Friedlander and LaCapra quote Heinrich Himmler's notorious 1943 Posen speech to upper-level SS officers as an example of the rhetorical expression of sublime elation. Himmler's speech made it clear that *Rausch* was inseparable from the moral sense of fulfillment of the highest duty (the Führer's will). As Thomas Trezise (2001) also notes, Himmler's injunction to the German troops "to have kept our integrity, that is what has made us hard. In our history, this is *an unwritten and never-to-be-written* page of glory" is the highest expression of the sanctioning of the unspeakable (51; the author's emphasis).

23. Alluding to Lyotard in her introduction to the catalogue of the exhibit *Impossible Evidence: Contemporary Artists View the Holocaust,* art historian and curator Andrea Liss writes, "The articulation of new idioms is precisely the task that faces the artists represented in this exhibition" (Liss and Snyder 1994, 11).

24. In her response to Agamben, Karyn Ball (2008) points out that in his assumption that witnessing arises from a lacuna that is in itself unwitness-able, Agamben depends on the same rhetoric of unspeakability for which he condemns Lyotard (14).

25. Wiesel's distinction between his truthful biographical accounts such as *Night* or his later *Diaries,* and his novels (such as *Dawn* or *The Gates of the Forest*) proves untenable on closer scrutiny. A revealing moment in Wiesel's oeuvre is the discrepancy between the details regarding his leg injury in January 1945, as first described in *Night* and later repeated in *All Rivers Run to the Sea.* In *Night,* Wiesel (1982) recalls injuring his foot in Auschwitz, for which he was hospitalized and which caused him agony during the death march to Buchenwald. He writes, "Toward the middle of January, my right foot began to swell because of the cold. I was unable to put it on the ground. . . . I could not sleep. My foot felt as if it were burning" (74, 79). Yet in his memoir written forty years later, Wiesel (1995) remembers that it was his knee that caused him such agony: "A doctor glanced at my knee, touched it. I stifled a scream. 'You need an operation,' he said. 'Immediately'" (90). This minor yet perplexing discrepancy jeopardizes Wiesel's "truth" claim (and therefore his sharp distinction between autobiography and fiction).

26. Kaplan argues that, for many Holocaust survivors (and she uses examples of Célan, Delbo, and Semprún), "beauty" was a self-avowed defense mechanism that sustained them during their ordeal in the Nazi camps and later became a means to work through trauma.

27. See chapter five for the discussion of Markiewicz's work.

28. In "Answering the Question: What Is Postmodernism?" Lyotard cites Duchamp's *Nude Descending a Staircase* (1912) as an example of the sublime postmodern moment. He references Stein's *How to Write* (1931) in the "Gertrude Stein" notice in *The Differend*, the only passage in this ostensibly philosophical work dedicated to a literary figure.

29. Lyotard (1990a) writes, "Claude Lanzmann's film, *Shoah*, is an exception, perhaps the only one. Not only because it rejects representation in images and music, but because it scarcely offers testimony where the unpresentable of the Holocaust is not indicated, be it for a moment, by the alteration in the tone of voice, a knotted throat, sobbing, tears, a witness fleeing off-camera, a disturbance in the tone of the narrative, some uncontrolled gesture" (26).

30. Another example of a fabricated Holocaust memoir that has garnered attention is Misha Defonseca's *Misha* (1997). It tells the harrowing story of a little girl's survival in the woods as she travels across Europe and lives with the wolves. Defonseca, who, like Wilkomirski, is not even Jewish, has defended her book: "There are times when I find it difficult to differentiate between reality and my inner world," she said. "The story in the book is mine. It is not the actual reality; it was my reality, my way of surviving" (Abel 2010). Similarly, the publication of Laurie Friedman's book *Angel Girl*, based on Herman Rosenblat's tale of meeting his future wife at the barbed wire fence at Buchenwald, where she was throwing him apples and bread to keep him alive, was cancelled by the publisher after Rosenblat admitted to having fabricated the story ("Children's Holocaust Book Pulled," *Halifax Chronicle Herald*, December 31, 2008).

31. Andreas Huyssen (1995) restates this paradoxical relation between memory and forgetting as follows: "Is it not the case that each and every memory inevitably depends both on distance and forgetting, the very things that undermine its desirable stability and reliability and are at the same time essential to the vitality of memory itself?" (250)

32. Lyotard (1990a) quotes Wiesel's epigraph in *The Gates of the Forest* in his discussion of Holocaust memory in *Heidegger and "the Jews"* (47).

33. As an infant, Jerzy Ficowski's wife Elżbieta Ficowska was carried out of the Warsaw ghetto in a toolbox, one of the hundreds of children rescued by Irena Sendlerowa and the organization Żegota, whose mandate was to aid the Jews in the Warsaw ghetto. Her identity was established thanks to a small, engraved silver spoon that was placed in the box next to the infant. See Agnieszka Mieszkowska, *Matka dzieci Holocaustu: Historia Ireny Sendlerowej* [The mother of Holocaust children: Irena Sendler's story] (Warsaw: Warszawskie Wydawnictwo Literackie MUZA SA, 2005).

34. See excerpts from Dr. Kremer's diary in "The Good Old Days," in *The Holocaust as Seen by Its Perpetrators and Bystanders*, ed. Ernst Klee et al., trans. Deborah Burnstone (Old Saybrook: Konecky & Konecky, 1991).

35. For an extensive description of the four clandestine photographs of the *Sondercommando* burning corpses in Auschwitz-Birkenau when the capacity of the crematoria was exceeded, see Didi-Huberman 2008. The album with the photographs of the SS functionaries, which belonged to

SS-*Sturmführer* Karl Höker, was given to Paul Shapiro, the director of the Center for Advanced Holocaust Studies at the Unites States Holocaust Memorial Museum (USHMM), by a former US Army officer, sixty years after he found it in Frankfurt in 1946. See for instance, a picture of the SS female auxiliaries who, after an outing on July 22, 1944, show with mock sadness that they have finished eating their blueberries. From the USHMM collection, document #34769. For the discussion of "ordinary men" and the "banality of evil," see, respectively, Christopher R. Browning, *Ordinary Men: Reserve Police Battalion 101 and the Final Solution in Poland* (HarperCollins Publishers, 1992), and Hannah Arendt, *Eichmann in Jerusalem: A Report on the Banality of Evil* (New York: Viking Press, 1963).

CHAPTER FOUR

Note: A preliminary version of this chapter appeared as "Disappearing Traces: Emmanuel Levinas, Ida Fink's Literary Testimony, and Holocaust Art," in Between Ethics and Aesthetics: Crossing the Boundaries, *ed. Dorota Glowacka and Stephen Boos, 97–14 (Albany: SUNY Press, 2002).*

1. In Irit Amiel, *Podwójny krajobraz* [A double landscape] (Warsaw: Prószyński i S-ka, 2008).

2. Malka (2006) writes, in a short interlude following the chapter on Levinas's wartime ordeal: "A trace that comes from who knows where. A trace without a past. Or yet a trace whose past can never reveal a presence, but only testifies to that which can never be said. A trace like a retreat. A trace like an ancient promise. A trace that one can feel only as that which has always been missing.

Whence is it drawn, this notion that is so strange and so beautiful?

From Proust, perhaps, and the passage of the 'missing Albertine' where the memory of forgetting itself becomes suffering?

Or rather, as one might suppose, from the beginning, from Exodus 33, where God is manifest in his trace alone?" (83).

3. In Exodus 33:20, when God's covenant with the Israelites is confirmed at Mount Sinai upon Moses's receiving of the commandments, the prohibition of seeing the divine face, on the pain of death, coincides with the pronouncement (and the inscription on the tablets) of the divine law: "And he said, Thou canst not see my face: for there shall no man see me, and live . . . , and thou shalt see my back parts: but my face shall not be seen."

4. James Hatley (2000) explains the veiled nature of Levinas's references to the divine: in speaking of the revelation of God in the neighbor and stranger, Levinas privileges the vulnerability of the human existent over the figurations of God (83).

5. David Patterson (2006b) elaborates, "To harbor the image of the divine is to seek the presence of the divine through a relation to our fellow human being that is expressive of a higher relation." This paramount reflection of the divine in the human, to whom I am therefore unconditionally obligated, is expressed in biblical interpretations. Patterson cites *Pesikta de-Rab*

Kahana 12:6: "Only when you are My witnesses, am I g-d, but when you are not My witnesses, I—if I dare speak thus—am not G-d" (48).

6. In *Altered Readings*, Jill Robbins (1999) proposes that a recourse to aesthetics is inscribed in Levinas's own texts and in his use of language that, in itself, interrupts traditional philosophical vocabulary. Although the philosopher ostensibly privileges philosophical works over literature, he frequently relies on citations and literary allusions (from Shakespeare or Russian and French literature, for instance) to convey the message of the primacy of ethics. Robbins also pays attention to Levinas's use of metaphors and evocative figures of speech, despite his exhortations against rhetoric in general (xxii). The face of the other, for instance, a central concept in Levinas's work, functions rhetorically as a synecdoche, which stands for the other's radical alterity as well as for the ethical force of language. Similarly, the ambiguity of the visual connotations of the face, even though Levinas insists that the face withdraws from vision and is primarily conveyed in speech, allows us to conceive of images and literary tropes that would not consume its alterity. Thus, even on the performative level, Levinas's writings point to a need of conceptualizing the ethical and the aesthetic together, and subsequently of conceiving of the transcendence of the other in a literary text or in a work of art.

7. In *Given Time*, where he explains the logic of absolute gift (the event of giving that lies outside the economy of exchange and cannot be captured within the symbolic order), Jacques Derrida (1992b) draws on the same trope of Ulysses's journey back to his home in Ithaca: "*Oikonomia* would always follow the path of Ulysses" (7).

8. For an account of the misunderstanding surrounding Zvi Kolitz's novella, see Paul Bedde, "Zvi Kolitz," in "Yosl Rakover Talks to God" (Levinas 1999, 27–77). For years, the text was believed to be an authentic document, found in the ruins of the Warsaw ghetto. As indicated in his essay "Loving the Torah," Levinas correctly took the story to be a work of fiction, and he recognized its merits as such.

9. See note 24, chapter three.

10. Fink recounts that an Israeli poet criticized her way of writing about the Holocaust because she talks about what she saw in a quiet voice, as if whispering: "He said that I open the window just a little and look at the world through the crack, while one should open the window wide and shout very loudly!" (Sobolewska 2003, 3).

11. For further discussion of the trope of silence in Fink's stories, see Wilczyński (1994) and Horowitz (1997, 217–25). See also chapter three of this book.

12. In reconfiguring Levinas's notion of the trace as an ethico-aesthetic concept, which allows us to understand Levinas's notion of the face as the trace-structure but which also opens up the very possibility of the distinction between ethics and aesthetics, I am indebted to Jacques Derrida's notion of arche-trace. In deconstructing the privilege of presence in Western metaphysics, Derrida introduces the term *différance*, "a concept without a concept" since it denotes the originary play of differences that opens up the possibility of conceptualization. The movement of *différance*, through which

binary oppositions between terms and thus signification are produced, is a simultaneous temporalization and spacing of presence, whereby a sign is always hollowed out by the past that constitutes it and the future in which it will be repeated, as well as separated in a spatial sense from what it is not but from which it demarcates itself in order to appear as a presence. For Derrida, therefore, the origin is always divided by the space and time of the interval. In *Of Grammatology*, Derrida (1976) writes, "*The (pure) trace is différance. It does not depend on any sensible plenitude, audible or visible, phonic or graphic. It is, on the contrary, the condition of such plenitude. Although it does not exist, although it is never a being-present outside of all plenitude, its possibility is by rights anterior to all that one calls sign (signified/signifier, content/expression), concept or operation*" (62). As in Levinas's thinking of the trace of the other, the archetrace cannot be derived from an origin or an empirical presence that would subsequently leave a mark.

13. The poem "My Doll in Auschwitz" is by Erich Fried. See Erich Fried, *Children and Fools* (New York: Serpents' Trail, 1995).

14. Reflecting on Levinas's use of figurative language, Clifton Spargo (2006) cautions against ascribing to it "a simply determinative influence on the philosophical speculation in which it participates." At the same time, like Robbins, Spargo recognizes that Levinas's philosophical argument in favor of the priority of ethics always performs at the level of richly figurative language. To negotiate this paradox, Spargo proposes the term "ethicofigural language," to signify a mode of expression that posits ethics as prior to acts of imagination and cognition "through which the ethical situation is conceived and acted upon." Ethicofigural language is juxtaposed to the figurative language that for Levinas is always suspect because it coincides "with the fault of aesthetic imagination" and betrays the immediacy of the face-to-face" (209).

15. In "Theses on the Philosophy of History," Benjamin writes that traditional historians always side with the victors, and "all rulers are heirs of those who conquered before them. Hence empathy with the victors invariably benefits the rulers." Benjamin (1969) argues that "all civilizations are monuments to barbarism" (256), and he calls for a way of writing history that would give voice to the oppressed.

CHAPTER FIVE

This chapter is dedicated to the memory of Stephen C. Feinstein, whose pioneering work on the art of the second generation has inspired the reflections below in every respect.

Note: I have borrowed the term "daughters of absence" from the title of Mindy Weisel's (2000) book, Daughters of Absence: Transforming the Legacy of Loss, *in which the artist refers to female children of survivors. When a more general reference is required, I will speak of the works by "the second generation," although I use this term in a narrow sense, referring specifically to children of Holocaust survivors, rather than to a larger group of those who were born after the war and who identify with the subject matter of the Holocaust, as in Efraim Sicher's (1998) broad view of the second generation, or to both children of survivors and children of perpetrators (and others of their generation), as in the studies by Marita Grimwood (2007) and Erin McGlothlin (2006). The term "second generation" continues to be a contested terrain.*

I would like to thank Mindy Weisel, Lily Markiewicz, Bracha Ettinger, and Ewa Kuryluk for permission to reproduce images of their work, and for their kindness and helpful comments during the process of revising this chapter.

1. For an extensive discussion of the shift in dominant modalities of Holocaust representation, see the introduction.

2. The simple yet powerful descriptive "Over There" to indicate the second-generation survivors' relation to the imaginary site of their parents' trauma was coined by Israeli novelist David Grossman, *See Under: Love*, trans. Betsy Rosenberg (New York: Noonday Press, 1989).

3. Appearing in *New York Times Magazine* in 1977, Helen Epstein's groundbreaking article "Heirs of the Holocaust," in which she issued an appeal to the generation of children of survivors to come forward, provoked an overwhelming response. Israeli psychoanalyst Dina Wardi's influential work on "memorial candles" appeared in Hebrew in 1990 and was translated into English in 1992. The first full-length study of second-generation texts, Alan Berger's *Children of Job: American Second-Generation Witnesses to the Holocaust* (Albany: SUNY Press, 1997), was published in 1997, followed by a volume edited by Alan Berger and Naomi Berger, *Second Generation Voices: Reflections by Children of Holocaust Survivors and Perpetrators* (Syracuse, NY: Syracuse University Press, 2001). In her 2007 study of second-generation literature, Marita Grimwood speaks of a veritable "outpouring" of children of survivors' accounts in the 1990s, and she identifies this literature as a distinct genre within the canon of survivor literature.

4. Epstein (1979) writes, "I knew I carried slippery, combustible things more secret than sex and more dangerous than any showdown or ghost. Ghosts had shape and name. What lay inside my box had none. Whatever lived inside me was so potent that words crumbled before they could describe" (9).

5. In his novel *Un cri sans voix* (published in English as *The Book of Esther*), Henri Raczymow (1985) explores the limits of such overidentification. Raczymow, himself a son of survivors, describes Esther's inability to cope with her parents' wartime experiences. Transgenerational transmission of trauma manifests in her identification with the women who were murdered in the Warsaw ghetto, eventually leading to her suicide: "Elle était comme coupable de vivre. . . . Elle était malade du passé qu'elle n'avait pas connu et qui la poursuivait" (109, 119). Esther seems to be inhabited by a dibbuk, by "un morceau en lui étranger, autonome, qui vie de sa vie propre," and she even speaks in the voice "qui est la sienne et n'est pas la sienne" (137). In biblical mythology, however, the righteous Queen Esther thwarts Haman's

scheme to annihilate the Jewish people, thus becoming a symbol of Jewish survival and healing, the role eventually assumed in the novel, through "substitution," by Mathieu, Esther's brother.

6. The theoretical framework of Faye's (2001) discussion is Jacques Lacan's conception of traumatic real. The real, for Lacan, is the psychic reality that marks the limit of what can be symbolized and is therefore always "missed." Although the real resists symbolization, it persists in the psyche as continuously effaced memory-traces that recur in the subject's speech in the form of unconscious repetitive registrations (528–29).

7. The motif of taking up painting as a form of therapeutic healing appears in the recollections of numerous artists who are Holocaust survivors, the prototype of which were perhaps artist Friedl Dicker-Brandeis's remarkable therapeutic art workshops with child inmates in the Theresienstadt family camp. According to Amishai-Maisels (1993), Samuel Bak's childhood art, which was first exhibited in Vilna in 1942 when Bak was only nine years old, served the purpose of coping with the reality of living in a ghetto under the Nazi occupation (132). Avigdor Arikha's early works were created in therapy sessions after he arrived in Israel from a labour camp in Transnistria (Romania) at the age of fifteen, although he made his first sketches in 1943, when he was still in the camp (Amishai-Maisels 1995b, 32, 272).

8. In the Torah the Israelites are commanded to dye one of the threads of their *tallit* (prayer shawl) with blue dye, which is to remind them of the blue sky and thus of God above them. The blue dye (*Tekhelet*) corresponds to the color of divine revelation (Midrash Numbers Rabbah xv).

9. Weisel's book focuses on personal stories of healing, and its intention is celebratory. By contrast, Sicher's aim is to provide a broader perspective, which takes into account the way personal stories of coping with the parents' past through artistic creativity have been embedded in larger collective narratives of culture and identity.

10. For the discussion of Levinas's epigraph, see chapter three.

11. "La nécessité de refaire lien par-delà le déchirure, la reconstitution de l'arbre généalogique familial, le besoin de retrouver des traces."

12. See, for instance, James E. Young, "Between History and Memory: The Uncanny Voices of Historian and Survivor," *History and Memory* 9 (1&2): 47–58, and Dominick LaCapra (2001 and 2004).

13. The "color-coding" of memory appears in artwork by other children of survivors. Italian Israeli artist Lena Liv, for instance, has titled her mixed-media work *Memoria di nero e blu* [Memory of black and blue]. See Lena Liv, *Memoria di nero e blu* (1991), in Bohm-Duchen (1995).

14. The artist's comment in private correspondence, December 12, 2010.

15. Boltanski (1994) writes, in the section "Artist's Writings," "He only admitted it much later on, but already back in the 1970s I was telling him that the Holocaust and more generally his relation with Judaism had a crucial influence on his work. A piece like 'The Clothes of François C' relates directly to those images of piles of clothing in the concentration camps" (137). It is curious that Boltanski offers this autobiographical note in the form of a dialogue between his two "selves," one of which appears in the

third person. Boltanski's use of this grammatical device underscores the fact that he conceives of his art as an act of discovering himself as a witnessing subject.

16. For a detailed account of Boltanski's ambiguous understanding of his work's relationship to the Holocaust, see Kaplan (2007, 127–47).

17. For a commentary on this work, as well as on some other earlier pieces by Markiewicz—such as a mixed-media work *Keeper of Accounts* (1987) and an art video *Silence Woke Me Up Today* (1989)—, which explore more directly the issue of Jewish belonging, see Feinstein (1998). See also the exhibit catalogue for *I Don't Celebrate Christmas*, with the catalogue essay by Carole Enahoro (London: Camerawork, 1990).

18. The artist rearranged the space of the gallery by setting up a wall with a mirror (with the word "Jew" on it) at the entrance to the gallery. The viewer then had to decide to enter the gallery through a narrow space on either the left or the right of the wall. The interior space of the gallery was divided into two subspaces.

19. The artist's comment in private correspondence, December 12, 2010.

20. Sukkot is a seven-day Jewish festival that commemorates the forty years of Israelites' wondering in the desert and living in temporary shelters. It involves building a booth or *Sukkah* (as prescribed in Leviticus 23:42: "You will dwell in booths for seven days, all natives of Israel shall dwell in booths" (http://www.jewfaq.org/holiday5.htm). Judaism 101, "Sukkot." Accessed December 15, 2010.

21. Pollock (2001a) points out that the Talmud instructs parents to teach their children to swim, so that they can survive in an environment in which they would otherwise drown (6), while Neumark (2001) draws attention to the importance of the rituals of submersion in the *mikveh* (23).

22. As the artist explains, her work can be considered in tandem with the German school of Holocaust countermonuments, such as Jochen Gerz and Esther Shalev-Gerz's *Monument against War and Fascism and for Peace* in Harburg (1986) and Jochen Gerz's *Stones against Racism* in Saarbrücken (1997). For an excellent discussion of countermonuments, see James E. Young, *The Texture of Memory: Holocaust Memorials and Meaning* (New Haven, CT: Yale University Press, 1993), and *At Memory's Edge* (New Haven, CT: Yale University Press, 2000).

23. The artist's comment in private correspondence, December 12, 2010.

24. Artist's talk at the Nova Scotia College of Art and Design, Halifax, July 10, 2002.

25. In a private conversation, July 10, 2002.

26. Speaking of his own experience as a child of survivors from Poland, Raczymow (2003) uses the phrase *la mémoire trouée* to describe his memory of a past devoid of content, a "nothingness" that he nevertheless feels compelled to express, even as he continues to ask himself "*by what right* could I speak." He writes, "My books do not attempt to fill in empty memory. They are not simply part of the struggle against forgetfulness. Rather I try to present memory as empty. I try to restore a non-memory, which by definition cannot be restored or recovered" (413–14).

27. Ettinger's gesture of providing the anonymous women, who are most likely Jewish, a name from the Greek mythology might be seen as problematic, but this cultural translation is not uncommon, and perhaps it is inevitable: viz., Weisel's recourse to the Greek etymology of the word "talent" to describe Jewish women artists, or my own comparison of Weisel's book to the Greek chorus. In reference to chapter two, "The Tower of Babel: Holocaust Testimony and the Ethics of Translation," this peculiar instance of *traduttore traditore* eventually aims to immortalize and universalize the murdered Jews in post-Auschwitz Western modernity.

28. The description of the photograph from the USHHM website states, "According to the *Zentrale Stelle* in Germany (Zst. II 204 AR 1218/70), these Jews were collected by the German Gendarmerie and Ukrainian *Schutzmannschaft* during the liquidation of the Mizocz ghetto, which held roughly 1,700 Jews. On the eve of the ghetto's liquidation (13 October 1942), some of the inhabitants rose up against the Germans and were defeated after a short battle. The remaining members of the community were transported from the ghetto to this ravine in the Sdolbunov *Gebietskommissariat*, south of Rovno, where they were executed. Information regarding this action, including the photos, were acquired from a man named Hille, who was the *Bezirks-Oberwachtmeister* of the *Gendarmerie* at the time. Hille apparently gave the five photos (there were originally seven) to the company lawyer of a textile firm in Kunert, Czechoslovakia, where he worked as a doorman after the war. The Czech government confiscated the photos from the lawyer in 1946 and they subsequently became public. That the photos indeed show the shooting of Jews in connection with the liquidation of the ghetto was also confirmed by a statement of *Gendarmerie-Gebietsfuehrer* Josef Paur in 1961." http://inquery.ushmm.org/uia-cgi/uia_doc/query/8?uf=uia_EtwMJH.

29. The intense violet hue is obtained through mixing oil paint with the pigment from the dust and ashes collected from the photocopy machine when it was stopped halfway through the reproduction process.

30. The term "extimate" (which Ettinger uses as well) is Lacan's, and it refers to the phenomena that cut across the inside/outside binary.

31. In her critique of Lanzmann's *Shoah*, Marianna Hirsch (Hirsch and Spitzer 2007) evokes the myth of Orpheus and Eurydice to demonstrate the erasure of women's voices in the film. Lanzmann's primary interlocutors and collaborators are male eyewitnesses, while women appear on the periphery of the film, their faces virtually unseen (they are mostly multilingual translators of the male voices, "the midwives of male creation"; 186). The mythic force of Lanzmann's "Orphic creation" therefore largely depends on the exclusion of the female modes of survival and forms of remembrance.

32. For an excellent discussion of Levinas's use of the trope of motherhood, see Lisa Guenther, *The Gift of the Other: Levinas and the Politics of Reproduction* (Albany: SUNY Press, 2006).

33. The exchanges with Levinas took place between 1991 and 1993. The first edition of the text that later appeared as *Que dirait Eurydice?* titled *Time Is the Breath of the Spirit*, was published in 1993 by the Museum of Modern Art at Oxford. In this work, Ettinger tried to make a feminist intervention

into Levinas's ethics, arguing for the ethical irreducibility of feminine difference (without, unfortunately, being able to convince the French philosopher).

34. This sensation is best conveyed by Helen Epstein's (1979) mournful
words "Our family tree had been burnt to a stump" (11).

35. Incidentally, Raczymow (1985) also evokes the name of Eurydice: "Ne
pas s'attarder, ne pas se retourner. Ne pas se retourner sur Sodome-Auschwitz
ou sur Eurydice, comme Orphée" (133). For Raczymow, Eurydice is the figure
of impossible, forbidden, and lethal vicarious memory of the Holocaust.

36. Didi-Huberman (2008) writes, apropos the clandestine photographs
of the Sonderkommando in Auschwitz-Birkenau, that "an image is not 'the
denial of absence' but, rather, its very attestation" (163).

37. Pollock is alluding to Walter Benjamin's influential thesis that, in the
era of mechanical reproducibility, the work of art loses its "aura."

38. Some of the words inscribed in the painting, possibly a quotation
taken from a poem, are:

"Lashon Safah" (Language/Tongue Language)
"S'fat H-aem" (Mother Tongue)
"Safah Chayah" (Living Language)

39. In her book on second-generation literature, Erin McGlothlin (2006)
writes that, in an affective sense, "the legacy of Holocaust survival is inscribed into the back of the child, a mark that is sensed intensely but nevertheless remains unknown and inaccessible" (8).

40. See Charlotte Delbo, "Days and Memory," in *Different Voices:
Women and the Holocaust*, ed. Carol Rittner and John K. Roth, 329–30 (St.
Paul: Paragon House, 1990).

41. Writing about Boltanski's post-Holocaust installations, van Alphen
(1997) comments that the artist's strategy of "mimicking" archival research
is intended to problematize historians' approaches to the Holocaust. Instead
of providing information, the expropriated photograph "lures" the viewer
into the event itself, allowing for a direct even if unnaratable experience:
"We are no longer listening to the factual account of a witness, to the story
of an objectified past. Rather, we are placed in the position of being the subject of history. We are subjectively living it" (10). Van Alphen's remarks are
undoubtedly relevant to Ettinger's work.

42. In her curatorial essay "Fifty Years On," Monica Bohm-Duchen
(1995b) argues that Boltanski's manipulation of archival photographs has the
effect of countering the "saturation" with Holocaust imagery in recent decades, caused by audiences' overexposure to the images of horror. This argument also applies to Ettinger's use of the photograph in a way that seeks to restore the image's capacity to move the viewer (rather than merely to shock her).

43. An illustrated collection of essays on Kuryluk's work, which appeared in 1987, was *The Fabric of Memory: Ewa Kuryluk's Cloth Works,
1978–1987*, edited by Ewa Kuryluk and Jan Kott (Wilmette, IL: Formations,
1987). Kuryluk's other works often include references to skin, such as *Cotton
Skins* (Edmonton, Canada, 2001), an outdoor installation *Skin* (Princeton,
NJ, 1984), and *Skin/Sky—Red/Blue* (New York, 1990).

44. Based on the artist's statement on Ewa Kuryluk's website, http://www
.kuryluk.art.pl, in the "Installations" section. Accessed December 18, 2010.

45. *Tabuś* (Taboo) was first exhibited in 2005, in the Artemis Gallery in
Kraków, which is located in the former Jewish district of Kazimierz. The installation was featured at the Jewish Cultural Festival.

46. The artist also included the text in which she explains her photographic references:

"Ulica w Amsterdamie/Ann Frank ze skakanką i koleżanka z kółkiem./
Po przeciwnej stronie Auschwitz-Birkenau:/Kobiety i dzieci w drodze
do krematorium./Kopie zdjęć wyrwanych z gazet/i znalezionych przeze
mnie/w papierach mamy po jej śmierci./Dopiero wtedy zrozumiałam,/
co miała na myśli mówiąc/'Miałaś takie samo kółko/jak koleżanka
Anny./A Piotruś taką samą skakankę'" (A street in Amsterdam/Anne
Frank with a jump rope and her friend with a hoop./On the opposite
side Auschwitz-Birkenau:/Women and children on the way to the
crematorium./Copies of pictures torn out of newspapers/which I found /
in Mother's papers after her death./Only then did I understand/what she
had meant by saying, /"You had the same hoop/as Anne's friend./And
Piotruś the same jump rope").

47. See, for instance, Polish Jewish writer Hanna Krall's (1985) semiautobiographical account in *Sublokatorka*, translated into English as *The Sub-
tenant* (Evanston, IL: Northwestern University Press, 1992).

48. www.kuryluk.art.pl. One of the artist's most recent installations,
Golden Ship (2007), dedicated to her brother—"the ultimate shipwreck"—
continues in the yellow, thus chromatically inscribing Piotruś's history of
growing up as a *Wunderkind*, followed by a nervous breakdown and mental
illness, into the realm of significations announced by that color.

49. From the artist's statement on Ewa Kuryluk's website, http://www
.kuryluk.art.pl, in the "Installations" section. Accessed December 18, 2010.

50. During the Jewish period of mourning, shivah, the relatives of the
deceased tear their clothes and wear the torn garments as an expression of
grief, in substitution for cutting or marking their bodies, a gesture that sym-
bolically substitutes for self-mutilation.

51. I am drawing here on Levinas's evocation of the myth of Nessus's tunic to express the vulnerability of the self that is exposed without recourse in
the ethical encounter with the other.

52. See chapter one, "'Like an Echo without a Source': Subjectivity as
Witnessing and the Holocaust Narrative."

53. Levinas (1998a) writes, "But then light presents itself in light, which
latter is not thematic, but resounds for the 'eye that listens,' with a resonance
unique in its kind, a resonance of silence" (130).

54. The word "talent" originally described an ancient weight or money
used for the payment of goods and services. It derived from the Greek word
talanton (Τάλαντο), which means balance, sum, or weight.

55. The artist's comment in private correspondence, December 12, 2010.

EPILOGUE

1. The opening scene of the feature film *X-Men* (2000, directed by Bryan Singer) takes place in a Nazi concentration camp. The Holocaust episode implies that the evildoing of the supervillain in the film (Magneto) is related to his incarceration in the camp and to what he witnessed during the Holocaust.

2. "W powietrzu krążą popioły. My tym powietrzem oddychamy. A wiatr, chmury I deszcz? Popioły są w ziemi, w rzekach, na łąkach i w lasach—poddawane nieprzerwanemy recyclingowi. . . . My jesteśmy sarkofagami—absorbującymi te szczątki zewsząd i na różne sposoby." Elżbieta Janicka is one of several contemporary Polish artists who recognize the Holocaust as central in the Polish cultural and historical consciousness. Among others works, she is the author of the award-winning conceptual project about the Nazi death camps, *Miejce nieparzyste* (The odd-numbered place). The title is a reference to the government policy of separate seating for Jewish students at Polish universities in the 1930s.

3. *Defiance* (2008), starring Daniel Craig and directed by Edward Zwick, is a story of the Bielski brothers, who led a group of Jewish partisans in Poland (now Belarus) during World War II. The film provoked an outrage in Poland because of historical inaccuracies, especially ignoring what Poles view as the Bielski partisans' crimes against the local populations.

4. See Father Patrick Desbois's *The Holocaust by Bullets: A Priest's Journey to Uncover the Truth Behind the Murder of 1.5 Million Jews*, trans. Catherine Spencer (New York: Pallgrave Macmillan, 2008). To date, in collaboration with the United States Holocaust Memorial Museum staff, Father Desbois and his team of researchers have identified about 800 (of an estimated 2,000) locations of mass executions of Jews in Ukraine.

5. In 1988 Richard Nelson Williamson was excommunicated by the Holy See due to his prior unauthorized consecration as a bishop by Archbishop Marcel Lefebvre. Pope Benedict XVI lifted his excommunication in January 2009, apparently unaware of the reports accusing Williamson of Holocaust denial. As a result of widespread protests, the Vatican ordered Williamson to distance himself from his views on the Shoah before being readmitted to episcopal functions within the Church. See Richard Owen and Ruth Gledhill (2009).

6. For an account of the controversies surrounding the mandate of the USHMM, see, for instance, the second volume of Elie Wiesel's *Memoirs* (Wiesel was one of the founding members of the committee appointed by US president Jimmy Carter). See also, for instance, Harold Kaplan, *Conscience and Memory: Mediations in a Museum of the Holocaust* (Chicago: University of Chicago Press, 1994); Michael Berenbaum, *After Tragedy and Triumph: Modern Jewish Thought and the American Experience* (Cambridge: Cambridge University Press, 1990); and Peter Novick, *The Holocaust in American Life* (Boston: Houghton Mifflin, 1999).

7. For a book-length analysis of this claim, see Enzo Traverso, *The Origins of Nazi Violence*, trans. Janet Lloyd (New York: The New Press, 2003).

8. Borrowing conceptual tools from social contract theories as they emerged from the political philosophies of Hobbes, Rousseau, and Kant, Mills argues that Western epistemology (in so far as it defines what counts as knowledge), moral theory (as it specifies who counts as an autonomous moral agent), and political theory have been predicated on the subordination and exclusion of nonwhite subjects.

9. See http://www.nytimes.com/2010/08/20/world/europe/20france.html. Accessed April 10, 2011.

10. Quoted by Daniel N. Paul, "We Were Not the Savages," http://www .danielnpaul.com/IndianResidentialSchools.html. Accessed April 10, 2011.

11. See, for instance, accounts by survivors of the Shubenacadie Indian residential school Isabelle Knockwood and Daniel N. Paul. Shubenacadie, near Truro, Nova Scotia, was one of the most notorious among about 130 Indian residential schools that operated between 1922 and 1968 for the children of the Mi'kmaq and Maliseet nations in Atlantic Canada. Isabelle Knockwood, *Out of the Depths: The Experience of Mi-kmaw Children at the Indian Residential School at Shubenacadie, Nova Scotia* (Blackpoint, NS: Fernwood Publishing, 1992); Daniel N. Paul, *We Were Not Savages: First Nations History* (Blackpoint, NS: Fernwood Publishing, 2000).

12. See Wayne K. Spear, "Canada's Indian Residential School System," Posted March 10, 2010. http://waynekspear.wordpress.com/2010/03/10/ canada%E2%80%99s-indian-residential-school-system/. Accessed April 10, 2011.

13. In *Precarious Life*, Judith Butler (2004) advances a similar argument when she reconceives Levinas's notion of the relation between the self and the other in the context of contemporary political violence. Commenting on the human rights abuses in the American detention centers for "terrorist" suspects, she advocates for "a dimension of political life that has to do with exposure to violence and our complicity in it, with our vulnerability to loss and the task of mourning that follows, and with finding the basis for community in these conditions" (19). For Butler, politics must be reoriented based on "responsibility for the physical lives of one another" (30) and on the avowal of common human vulnerability that makes it possible for us to protect others from the kind of violence we have ourselves suffered or could suffer.

14. Adorno (1983) writes, "After Auschwitz, our feelings resist any claim of the positivity of existence as sanctimonious, as wronging the victims; they balk at squeezing any kind of sense, however bleached, out of victim's fate. And these feelings do have an objective side after events that make a mockery of the construction of immanence as endowed with a meaning radiated by an affirmatively posited transcendence" (361).

15. "Le travail de la mémoire ne consiste pas du tout à s'enfoncer dans le passé mais à renouveler le passé, par les nouvelles expériences, les nouvelles circonstances, les nouvelles merveilles ou horreurs de la vie vécue. Et dans ce sens-là, c'est l'avenir qui est important et non le pur passé. . . . Il est important de maintenir le pur souvenir des faits pour la vérité de la Shoah. Mais l'essentiel est de trouver toujours l'actualité des enseignements de la Shoah à partir de nos expériences nouvelles."

Abel, David. 2010. "A New Twist: The Misha Defonseca Story." *Globe and Mail* (Toronto, Canada). December 18.

Adelman, Gary. 2004. "Getting Started with Imre Kertész." *New England Review* 25:261–78.

Adorno, Theodor W. 1967. *Prisms*. Translated by Samuel Weber and Shierry Weber. London: Spearman.

———. 1983. *Negative Dialectics*. Translated by E. B. Ashton. New York: Continuum.

Agamben, Giorgio. 1999. *Remnants of Auschwitz: The Witness and the Archive*. Translated by Daniel Heller-Roazen. New York: Zone Books.

Améry, Jean. 1986. *At the Mind's Limits*. Translated by Sidney Rosenfeld and Stella P. Rosenfeld. New York: Schocken Books.

Amiel, Irit. 2008. *Podwójny krajobraz*. Warsaw: Prószyński i S-ka.

Amishai-Maisels, Ziva. 1993. *Depiction and Interpretation: The Influence of the Holocaust on Visual Arts*. Oxford: Pergamon Press.

———. 1995a. "Art Confronts the Holocaust." In *After Auschwitz: Responses to the Holocaust in Contemporary Art*, edited by Monica Bohm-Duchen, 47–77. Sunderland, UK: Northern Center for Contemporary Art, in association with Lund Humphires, London.

———. 1995b. "The Complexities of Witnessing." In *After Auschwitz: Responses to the Holocaust in Contemporary Art*, edited by Monica Bohm-Duchen, 24–48. Sunderland, UK: Northern Center for Contemporary Art, in association with Lund Humphires, London.

Arendt, Hannah. 1958. *The Origins of Totalitarianism*. New York: Meridian Books.

———. 1971. *The Life of the Mind*. San Diego: Harcourt Brace Janovich Publishers.

———. 2005. *Essays in Understanding, 1930–1954: Formation, Exile, and Totalitarianism*. Edited by Jerome Kohn. New York: Schocken Books.

Ball, Karyn. 2008. *Disciplining the Holocaust: Traumatic History as an Object of Enquiry and Desire.* Albany: SUNY Press.

Bauman, Zygmunt. 1989. *Modernity and the Holocaust.* Ithaca, NY: Cornell University Press.

Benjamin, Walter. 1969. *Illuminations.* Edited by Hannah Arendt. New York: Schocken.

———. 1986. *Reflections.* Translated by Edmund Jephcott. New York: Schocken Books.

Blanchot, Maurice. 1995. *The Writing of the Disaster.* Translated by Ann Smock. Lincoln: University of Nebraska Press.

Bohm-Duchen, Monica, ed. 1995a. *After Auschwitz: Responses to the Holocaust in Contemporary Art.* Sunderland, UK: Northern Center for Contemporary Art, in association with Lund Humphires, London.

———. 1995b. "Fifty Years On." In *After Auschwitz: Responses to the Holocaust in Contemporary Art,* edited by Monica Bohm-Duchen, 103–45. Sunderland, UK: Northern Center for Contemporary Art, in association with Lund Humphires, London.

Bojarska, Katarzyna. 2008. "Obecność zagłady w twórczości polskich artystów." Poznań, Poland: Instytut Adama Mickiewicza.

Boltanski, Christian, and Lynn Gumpert. 1994. *Christian Boltanski.* Paris: Flammarion.

Borowski, Tadeusz. 1976. *This Way for the Gas, Ladies and Gentlemen.* New York: Penguin Books.

Borradori, Giovanna. 2003. *Philosophy in the Times of Terror: Dialogues with Jürgen Habermas and Jacques Derrida.* Chicago: University of Chicago Press.

Buci-Glucksmann, Christine. 1996. "Bracha Lichtenberg Ettinger: Images of Absence in the Inner Space of Painting." In *Inside the Visible: An Elliptical Traverse of 20th Century Art in, of, and from the Feminine,* edited by M. Catherine de Zegher, 281–307. Boston: The MIT Press.

Butler, Judith. 2004. *Precarious Life: The Powers of Mourning and Violence.* New York: Verso.

Carroll, David. 1990. Foreword to *Heidegger and the 'Jews,"* by Jean-François Lyotard, "The Memory of Devastation and the Responsibilities of Thought: 'And Let's Not Talk about That,'" vii-xxix. Minneapolis: University of Minnesota Press.

———. 2000. "Memorial for the *Différend*: In Memory of Jean-François Lyotard." *Parallax* 6, no. 4:3–27.

Caruth, Cathy, ed. 1995. *Trauma: Explorations in Memory.* Baltimore, MD: Johns Hopkins University.

—. 1996. *Unclaimed Experience: Trauma, Narrative, and History.* Baltimore, MD: The Johns Hopkins University Press.

Caygill, Howard. 2002. *Levinas and the Political.* London: Routledge.

Célan, Paul. 1988. *Poems.* Translated by Michael Hamburger. New York: Persea Books.

—. 2001. *Selected Poems and Prose of Paul Célan.* Translated by John Felstiner. New York: W. W. Norton.

Chrisjohn, Roland, and Sherri Young. 1997. *The Circle Game: Shadows and Substance in the Indian Residential School Experience in Canada.* Penticton, BC: Theytus Books.

Cichowicz, Alicja. 2006. "Uobecnianie nieobecnego." *Obieg.* September 16. http//www.obieg.pl/recenzje/2621. Accessed July 24, 2009.

Cohen, Richard. 2004. Introduction to *Unforeseen History,* by Emmanuel Levinas, xi–xxv. Urbana, IL: University of Chicago Press.

Cole, Tim. 1999. *Selling the Holocaust.* New York: Routledge.

Congdon, Lee. 2003. "In the Key of Freedom: The Achievement of Imre Kertész." *The World and I* 18, no. 3:249–55.

Czarnecki, Joseph P. 1989. *Last Traces: The Lost Art of Auschwitz.* New York: Atheneum.

Deguy, Michel D. 1978. *Jumelages suivi de Made in USA.* Paris: Seuil.

DeKoven Ezrahi, Sidra. 1980. *By Words Alone: The Holocaust in Literature.* Chicago: University of Chicago Press.

Delbo, Charlotte. 1995. *Auschwitz and After.* Translated by Rosette C. Lamont. New Haven, CT: Yale University Press.

de Man, Paul. 1986. *The Resistance to Theory.* Minneapolis: Minnesota University Press.

Derrida, Jacques. 1976. *Of Grammatology.* Translated by Gayatri Chakravorty Spivak. Baltimore: The John Hopkins University Press.

—. 1978. *Writing and Difference.* Translated by Alan Bass. Chicago: University of Chicago Press.

—. 1985. "Des Tours de Babel." In *Difference in Translation,* edited by Joseph F. Graham, 165–248. Ithaca, NY: Cornell University Press.

—. 1986. "Racism's Last Word." In *Race, Writing and Difference,* edited by Henry Louis Gates, 329–38. Chicago: Chicago University Press.

—. 1988. *The Ear of the Other: Otobiography, Transference, Translation.* Translated by Peggy Kamuf. Lincoln: University of Nebraska Press.

—. 1989. *Of Spirit.* Translated by Geoffrey Bennington and Rachel Bowlby. Chicago: University of Chicago Press.

—. 1991. "At This Moment, in This Text, Here I Am." In *Re-Reading*

Levinas, edited by Robert Bernasconi and Simon Critchley, translated by Ruben Berezdivin, 1–48. Bloomington: Indiana University Press.

———. 1992a. *Acts of Literature.* Edited by Derek Attridge. New York: Routledge.

———. 1992b. *Given Time.* Translated by Peggy Kamuf. Chicago: University of Chicago Press.

———. 1996. *Archive Fever.* Translated by Eric Prenovitz. Chicago: University of Chicago Press.

———. 1998. *Monolingualism of the Other, or, The Prosthesis of Origin.* Translated by Patrick Mensah. Stanford: Stanford University Press.

———. 1999. *Adieu to Emmanuel Levinas.* Translated by Pascale-Anne Brault and Michael Naas. Stanford: Stanford University Press.

———. 2001. "Emmanuel Levinas." In *The Work of Mourning*, edited by Pascale-Anne Brault and Michael Naas, 197–209. Chicago: University of Chicago Press.

———. 2005. *Sovereignties in Question.* Edited by Thomas Dutoit and Outi Pasanaen. New York: Fordham University Press.

Des Pres, Terrence. 1976. *The Survivor: An Anatomy of Life in the Death Camps.* New York: Washington Square Press.

Didi-Huberman, Georges. 2008. *Images in Spite of All: Four Photographs from Auschwitz.* Translated by Shane B. Lillis. Chicago: University of Chicago Press.

Doerr, Karin. 2009. "Words of Fear, Fear of Words: Language Memories of Holocaust Survivors." *Explorations in Anthropology* 9, no. 1:47–57.

Dunn, Alan. 1993. "A Tyranny of Justice: The Ethics of Lyotard's Differend." *boundary 2* 20, no. 1:193–220.

Eaglestone, Robert. 2004. *The Holocaust and the Postmodern.* Oxford: Oxford University Press.

Engelking Boni, Barbara. 1994. *Zagłada i pamięć.* Warsaw: Wyd. IFiS PAN.

Epstein, Helen. 1979. *Children of the Holocaust: Conversations with Sons and Daughters of Survivors.* New York: Penguin Books.

Ettinger, Bracha L. 1993. *Matrix Halal(a)—Lapsus.* Oxford: Museum of Modern Art.

———. 1999. "Trauma and Beauty: Trans-subjectivity in Art." *Body, Space, Memory.* Special issue. *N. Paradoxa* 3:15–23.

———. 2001. "Wit(h)nessing Trauma and the Matrixial Gaze: From Phantasm to Trauma, from Phallic Structure to Matrixial Sphere." *Parallax* 7, no. 4:89–114.

Ettinger, Bracha L., and Emmanuel Levinas. 1997. "'Que dirait Eurydice?/ What would Eurydice say?' Emmanuel Levinas en/in conversation avec/

with Bracha Lichtenberg-Ettinger." In *Eurydice 1992–1996: Oeuvres de Bracha Lichtenberg-Ettinger,* edited by Bracha L. Ettinger, 21–32. Paris: BLE Atelier.

Fackenheim, Emil. 1994. *To Mend the World: Foundations of Post-Holocaust Jewish Thought.* Bloomington: Indiana University Press.

Farmulska, Karolina. 2006. "Budowanie tożsamości w utworach Idy Fink." *Zeszyt* 382:189–209. Toruń: Wydawnictwo Uniwersytetu Toruńskiego.

Faye, Esther. 2001. "Missing the 'Real' Trace of Trauma: How the Second Generation Remember the Holocaust." *American Imago* 58, no. 2:525–44.

Feinstein, Stephen C. 1998. "Mediums of Memory: Artistic Responses of the Second Generation." In *Breaking the Crystal: Writing and Memory after Auschwitz,* edited by Efraim Sicher, 201–51. Champaign: University of Illinois Press.

Ficowski, Jerzy. 1981. *A Reading of Ashes.* Translated by Keith Bosley and Krystyna Wandycz. London: The Menard Press.

———. 1988. *Odczytanie popiołów.* Warsaw: Iskry.

Fink, Ida. 1996. *A Scrap of Time.* Translated by Madeline Levine and Francine Prose. Evanston: Northwestern University Press.

———. 1998. *Traces.* Translated by Philip Boehm and Francine Prose. New York: Henry Holt and Company.

Friedlander, Saul. 1993. *Memory, History, and the Extermination of the Jews of Europe.* Bloomington: Indiana University Press.

Gasché, Rodolphe. 2007. *The Honor of Thinking: Critique, Theory, Philosophy.* Stanford: Stanford University Press.

Ginsberg, Terri. 2007. "St. Korczak of Warsaw." In *Imaginary Neighbors: Mediating Polish-Jewish Relations after the Holocaust,* edited by Dorota Glowacka and Joanna Zylinska, 110–34. Lincoln: Nebraska University Press.

Glowacka, Dorota, and Joanna Zylinska, eds. 2007. *Imaginary Neighbors: Mediating Polish-Jewish Relations after the Holocaust,* 110–34. Lincoln: Nebraska University Press.

Glowacka, Dorota, and Stephen Boos, eds. 2002. *Between Ethics and Aesthetics: Crossing the Boundaries.* Albany: SUNY Press.

Grimwood, Marita. 2007. *Holocaust Literature of the Second Generation.* New York: Palgrave Macmillan.

Hass, Aaron. 1990. *In the Shadow of the Holocaust: The Second Generation.* Ithaca, NY: Cornell University Press.

Hancock, Ian. 1996. "Responses to the Porrajmos: The Romani Holocaust." In *Is the Holocaust Unique?,* edited by Alan S. Rosenbaum, 39–64. Boulder, CO: Westview Press.

Hart, Kevin. 2005. "Ethics of the Image." In *Levinas Studies: An Annual Review 1*, edited by Jeffrey Bloechl and Jeffrey L. Kosky, 119–38. Pittsburgh, PA: Duquesne University Press.

Hartman, Geoffrey. 1992. "The Book of Destruction." In *Probing the Limits of Representation: Nazism and the "Final Solution*," edited by Saul Friedlander, 313–36. Cambridge, MA: Harvard University Press.

Hatley, James. 2000. *Suffering Witness: The Quandary of Responsibility after the Irreparable*. Albany: SUNY Press.

Hirsch, Marianne, and Leo Spitzer. 2007. "Gendered Translations: Claude Lanzmann's *Shoah*." In *Claude Lanzmann's Shoah: Key Essays*, edited by Stuart Liebman, 175–90. Oxford: Oxford University Press.

Hoffman, Eva. 2004. *After Such Knowledge: Memory, History, and the Legacy of the Holocaust*. New York: PublicAffairs.

Holy Bible. 1943. Philadelphia: National Bible Press.

Horowitz, Sara, R. 1997. *Voicing the Void: Muteness and Memory in Holocaust Fiction*. Albany: SUNY Press.

Huyssen, Andreas. 1995. *Twilight Memories: Marking Time in a Culture of Amnesia*. New York: Routledge.

Jacobs, Carol. 1975. "The Monstrosity of Translation." *MLN* 90:755–66.

Jagielski, Jan, and Tomasz Lec. 1997. *Nie zatarte ślady getta warszawskiego: The Remnants of the Warsaw Ghetto*. Warsaw: Jewish Historical Institute.

Kafka, Franz. 1971. *The Complete Stories*. Edited by N. Glatzer. New York: Schocken Books.

Kant, Immanuel. 1951. *Critique of Judgment*. Translated by J. H. Bernard. New York: Hafner Press.

Kaplan, Ashley Brett. 2007. *Unwanted Beauty: Aesthetic Pleasure in Holocaust Representation*. Chicago: University of Illinois Press.

Kashetsky, Herzl, and Tom Smart. 1997. *Herzl Kashetsky: A Prayer for the Dead*. Exhibition catalogue. Saint John, NB: New Brunswick Museum; Fredricton, NB: Beaverbrook Art Gallery.

Kearney, Richard. 2002. "Levinas and the Ethics of Imagining." In *Between Ethics and Aesthetics: Crossing the Boundaries*, edited by Dorota Glowacka and Stephen Boos, 85–96. Albany: SUNY Press.

Kertész, Imre. 1992. *Fateless*. Translated by Christopher C. Wilson and Katharina M. Wilson. Evanston: Northwestern University Press.

———. 1997. *Kaddish for a Child Not Born*. Translated by Christopher C. Wilson and Katharina M. Wilson. Evanston: Northwestern University Press.

———. 2004. *Język na wygnaniu*. Warsaw: Wydawnictwo WAB.

Kigel, Michael. 2006. "Translator's Notes." In *Emmanuel Levinas: His Life and Legacy*, by Salomon Malka, translated by Michael Kigel and Sonja M. Embree, xiii–xxxvii. Pittsburgh: Duquesne University Press.

Kleeblatt, Norman L., ed. 2002. *Mirroring Evil: Nazi Imagery/Recent Art*. New Brunswick: Rutgers University Press.

Klüger, Ruth. 1992. *weiter leben: Eine Jugend*. Göttingen, Germany: Wallstein Verlag.

Kluger, Ruth. 2001. *Still Alive: A Holocaust Girlhood Remembered*. New York: The Feminist Press at the City University of New York.

Koch, Gertrud. 2007. "The Aesthetic Transformation of the Image of the Unimaginable." In *Claude Lanzmann's Shoah: Key Essays*, edited by Stuart Liebman, 125–32. Oxford: Oxford University Press.

Krall, Hannah. 1996. "A Tale for Hallywood." In *The Eagle and the Crow*, edited by Teresa Halikowska and George Hyde. London: Serpent's Tale.

———. 2006. *Król kierowy znów na wylocie*. Warsaw: Świat Książki.

Kuhn, Anna K. 2003. "Still Alive: A Holocaust Girlhood Remembered," review of *Still Alive: A Holocaust Girlhood Remembered*, by Ruth Kluger. *World Literature Today* 77, no. 2 (July–September): 128–29.

Kuryluk, Ewa. 2004. *Goldi*. Warsaw: Twój Styl.

———. 2005. "Koszmar zaklęty w żółci." *Gazeta Wyborcza* 147:15.

LaCapra, Dominick. 1994. *Representing the Holocaust*. Ithaca, NY: Cornell University Press.

———. 1998. *History and Memory after Auschwitz*. Ithaca, NY: Cornell University Press.

———. 2001. *Writing History, Writing Trauma*. Baltimore, MD: The Johns Hopkins University Press.

———. 2004. *History in Transit: Experience, Identity, Critical Theory*. Ithaca, NY: Cornell University Press.

———. 2007a. "Resisting Apocalypse, Rethinking History." In *Manifestos for History*, edited by Keith Jenkins, Sue Morgan, and Alun Munslow, 160–75. New York: Routledge.

———. 2007b. "Lanzmann's *Shoah*: 'Here There Is No Why.'" In *Claude Lanzmann's Shoah: Key Essays*, edited by Stuart Liebman, 191–29. Oxford: Oxford University Press.

Lang, Berel. 1988. "Language and Genocide." In *Echoes from the Holocaust. Philosophical Reflections on a Dark Time*, edited by Alan Rosenberg and Gerald E. Myers, 341–64. Philadelphia: Temple University Press.

———. 1992. "The Representation of Limits." In *Probing the Limits of Representation*, edited by Saul Friedlander, 300–17. Cambridge, MA: Harvard University Press.

———. 1999. "Translating the Holocaust: For Whom Does One Write?" *Judaism* 48, no. 3:334–35.

Lanzmann, Claude, director. 1985. *Shoah: An Oral History of the Holocaust.*

———. 1995. *Shoah: The Complete Text of the Acclaimed Holocaust Film.* New York: Da Capo Press.

Laub, Dori, and Shoshana Felman. 1992. *Testimony: Crises of Witnessing in Literature, Psychoanalysis and History.* New York: Routledge.

Leitner, Isabella. 1978. *Fragments of Isabella: A Memoir of Auschwitz.* New York: Dell Publishing.

———. 1980. *Fragments of Isabella: A Memoir of Auschwitz.* London: New English Library.

Leitner, Isabella, and Irving A. Leitner. 1994. *Isabella: From Auschwitz to Freedom.* New York: Anchor Books.

Levi, Neil, and Michael Rothberg. 2003. *The Holocaust: Theoretical Readings.* New Brunswick: Rutgers University Press.

Levi, Primo. 1959. *If This Is a Man.* Translated by Stuart Woolf. New York: Orion Press.

———. 1979. *If This Is a Man and The Truce.* Translated by Stuart Woolf. New York: Penguin.

———. 1988. *The Drowned and the Saved.* Translated by Raymond Rosenthal. New York: Vintage Books.

———. 1993. *Survival in Auschwitz: The Nazi Assault on Humanity.* Translated by Stuart Woolf. New York: Collier Books.

Levinas, Emmanuel. 1969. *Totality and Infinity: An Essay on Exteriority.* Translated by Alphonso Lingis. Pittsburg: Duquesne University Press.

———. 1985. *Ethics and Infinity.* Translated by Richard A. Cohen. Pittsburgh: Duquesne University Press.

———. 1986. "The Trace of the Other." In *Deconstruction in Context,* edited by Mark C. Taylor, 345–59. Chicago: University of Chicago Press.

———. 1987a. *Collected Philosophical Papers.* Translated by Alphonso Lingis. Dordrecht, Netherlands: Martinus Nijihoff.

———. 1987b. "La mémoire d'un passé non révolu : Entretien avec Foulek." *Revue de l'Université de Bruxelles* 1–2:11–20.

———. 1989. "The Transcendence of Words." In *The Levinas Reader,* edited by Seán Hand, translated by Alphonso Lingis, 144–49. Oxford: Basil Blackwell.

———. 1990. "Signature." In *Difficult Freedom,* translated by Seán Hand, 291–95. Baltimore, MD: The Johns Hopkins University Press.

———. 1996. *Proper Names.* Edited by Michael Smith. Stanford: Stanford University Press.

———. 1998a. *Otherwise than Being, or Beyond Essence.* Translated by Alphonso Lingis. Pittsburgh: Duquesne University Press.

———. 1998b. "Useless Suffering." In *Entre Nous: Thinking-of-the-Other.* New York: Columbia University Press.

———. 1999. "Loving the Torah More than God." Afterward to "Yosl Rakover Talks to God," by Zvi Kolitz, 79–87. New York: Pantheon Books.

———. 2000. *God, Death, and Time.* Translated by Bettina Bergo. Stanford: Stanford University Press.

———. 2001. *Existence and Existents.* Translated by Alphonso Lingis. Pittsburgh: Duquesne University Press.

———. 2004. "Some Thoughts on the Philosophy of Hitlerism." In *Unforeseen History,* translated by Bettina Bergo, 13–21. Chicago: University of Chicago Press.

Liebman, Stuart, ed. 2007. *Claude Lanzmann's* Shoah: *Key Essays.* Oxford: Oxford University Press.

Liss, Andrea. 1998. *Trespassing Through Shadows: Memory, Photography, and the Holocaust.* Minneapolis: University of Minnesota Press.

Liss, Andrea, and Jill Snyder, 1994. Catalogue essay for *Impossible Evidence: Contemporary Artists View the Holocaust.* Curated by Jill Snyder. Reading, PA: Freedman Gallery, Albright College.

Lyotard, Jean-François. 1984. "Answering the Question: What Is Postmodernism?" Translated by Régis Durand. In *The Postmodern Condition: A Report on Knowledge,* translated by Geoff Bennington and Brian Massumi, 71–84. Minneapolis: University of Minnesota Press.

———. 1988. *The Differend: The Phrases in Dispute.* Translated by Georges Van Den Abbeele. Minneapolis: University of Minnesota Press.

———. 1989. *Just Gaming.* Translated by Wlad Godzich. Minneapolis: University of Minnesota Press.

———. 1990a. *Heidegger and the 'Jews.'* Translated by Andreas Michel and Mark S. Roberts. Minneapolis: University of Minnesota Press.

———. 1990b. "L'inarticulé ou le différend même." In *Figures et Conflits Rhétoriques,* edited by Michel Meyer and Alain Lempereur, 201–7. Brussels: Université de Bruxelles.

———. 1992. "Discussions or Phrasing 'After Auschwitz.'" In *The Lyotard Reader,* edited by Andrew Benjamin, 360–92. Oxford: Blackwell.

———. 1995a. "Diffracted Traces." In *Bracha Lichtenberg Ettinger: Halala-Autistwork,* catalogue essay, translated by Elodie Piquet and Joseph Simas, 21–31. Jerusalem: Israel Museum.

———. 1995b. "The Survivor." In *Toward the Postmodern,* edited by Robert Harvey and Mark S. Roberts, 144–63. Amherst, NY: Humanities Press.

MacAffee, Michelle. 2003. "Visitors Can 'Come without Fear.'" *Chronicle Herald*. May 23.

Malka, Salomon. 2006. *Emmanuel Levinas: His Life and Legacy*. Translated by Michael Kigel and Sonja M. Embree. Pittsburgh: Duquesne University Press.

Mandel, Naomi. 2006. *Against the Unspeakable: Complicity, the Holocaust and Slavery in America*. Charlottesville: University of Virginia Press.

Marcus, Amit. 2008. "Narrative Ethics and Incommensurable Discourses: Lyotard's *The Differend* and Fowles' *The Collector*." *Mosaic: A Journal for Interdisciplinary Study of Literature* 41, no. 4. http://umanitoba.ca/publications/mosaic/issues/getissue.php?vol=41&no=4. Accessed October 25, 2010.

Markiewicz, Lily. *Artist's Statement of Intent: Installations 1987–2001*. http://www.land2.uwe.ac.uk/lilymark.htm. Accessed December 12, 2010.

————. 1992. *The Price of Words: Places to Remember 1–26*. London: Book Works.

————. 2002. *Promise II*. Exhibition catalogue. Halifax: Mount Saint Vincent University.

McGlothlin, Erin. 2006. *Second-Generation Holocaust Literature: Legacies of Survival and Perpetration*. Rochester, NY: Camden House.

Michlic, Joanna B. 2006. *Poland's Threatening Other: The Image of the Jew from 1880 to the Present*. Lincoln: University of Nebraska Press.

Mills, Charles. 1997. *The Racial Contract*. Ithaca, NY: Cornell University Press.

Mole, Gary D. 1997. *Lévinas, Blanchot, Jabès: Figures of Estrangement*. Gainesville: University Press of Florida.

Morris, Leslie. 2001. "The Sound of Memory." *The German Quarterly* 74, no. 4:368–78.

Nancy, Jean-Luc. 1991a. "The Unsacrificeable." *Yale French Studies* 79:20–38.

————. 1991b. *The Inoperative Community*. Translated by Peter Connor et al. Minneapolis: University of Minnesota Press.

————. 1993. "The Sublime Offering." In *Of the Sublime: Presence in Question*, translated by Jeffrey S. Librett, 25–53. Albany: State University of New York.

Neumark, Devorah. 2001. "Between Terror and Belief." Catalogue essay. Leeds: The University of Leeds/Koffler Gallery.

Nora, Pierre. 1996. *Realms of Memory: The Construction of the French Past*. Translated by Arthur Goldhammer. New York: Columbia University Press.

Oliver, Kelly. 2001. *Witnessing: Beyond Recognition*. Minneapolis: University of Minnesota Press.

Orski, Mieczysław. 1994. "Dotrzeć do dna prawdy." *Dialog* 4:96–99.

Owen, Richard, and Gledhill, Ruth. 2009. "Pope Insists Bishop Richard Williamson Must Renounce Holocaust Denial." *The Times*, February 5. Accessed December 15, 2009. http://www.timesonline.co.uk/tol/comment/faith/article5663726.ece.

Patterson, David. 2006a. *Open Wounds: The Crisis of Jewish Thought in the Aftermath of Auschwitz*. Seattle: University of Washington Press.

———. 2006b. *Wrestling with the Angel: Toward a Jewish Understanding of the Nazi Assault on the Name*. St. Paul, MN: Paragon House.

Piersiak, Tadeusz. 2004. "An Interview with Irit Amiel." *Gazeta Wyborcza* (Częstochowa). April 24.

Plant, Bob. 2007. "On Testimony, Sincerity and Truth." *Paragraph* 30, no. 1:30–50.

Pollock, Griselda. 1995. "After the Reapers: Gleaning the Past, the Feminine and Another Future, from the Work of Bracha Lichtenberg Ettinger." In *Bracha Lichtenberg Ettinger: Halal-Autistwork*, catalogue essay, translated by Elodie Piquet and Joseph Simas, 129–54. Jerusalem: Israel Museum.

———. 2001a. "Catching and Losing the Sands of Time: The Dialectics of Place and No-Place in Jewish Being and Memory in the Work of Lily Markiewicz." Catalogue essay. Leeds: University of Leeds / Koffler Gallery.

———. 2001b. "From Trauma to Cultural Memory: The Second Generation and the Shoah." Lecture delivered at the conference "Revisioning the Shoah," University of Leeds, Centre CATH, April. www.leeds.ac.uk/cath/event/2001/0429/gp_address.html.

Potok, Chaim. 1989. Introduction to *Last Traces: The Lost Art of Auschwitz*, by Joseph P. Czarnecki, xi–xv. New York: Atheneum.

Pressburger, Chava, ed. 2007. *The Diary of Petr Ginz. 1941–1942*. New York: Grove Press.

Raczymow, Henri. 1985. *Un cri sans voix*. Paris: Éditions Gallimard.

———. 2003. "Memory Shot Through with Holes." In *The Holocaust: Theoretical Readings*, edited by Neil Levi and Michael Rothberg, 410–15. New Brunswick, NJ: Rutgers University Press.

Robbins, Jill. 1987. "Writing of the Holocaust: Claude Lanzmann's *Shoah*." *Prooftexts* 7:249–58.

———. 1995. "Aesthetic Totality and Ethical Infinity: Levinas on Art." *L'Esprit Créateur* 35, no. 3:66–79.

———. 1999. *Altered Readings: Levinas and Literature*. Chicago: University of Chicago Press.

————, ed. 2001. *Is It Righteous to Be? Interviews with Emmanuel Levinas*. Stanford: Stanford University Press.

Robin, Régine. 2002. "Les devoirs de mémoire et les problèmes de la transmission ou les dangers d'une mémoire sans transmission." In *Afterimages: Evocations of the Holocaust in Contemporary Canadian Arts and Literature*, edited by Loren Lerner, 128–47. Montréal: Concordia University Institute for Canadian Jewish Studies.

Ronell, Avital. 1989. "The Differends of Man." *Diacritics* 19, nos. 3–4:65–75.

Rosen, Alan. 2005. *Sounds of Defiance: The Holocaust, Multilingualism, and the Problem of English*. Lincoln: University of Nebraska Press.

Rosenbaum, Alan S. 1996. *Is the Holocaust Unique? Perspectives on Comparative Genocide*. Boulder, CO: Westview Press.

Rothberg, Michael. 2009. *Multidirectional Memory: Remembering the Holocaust in the Age of Decolonization*. Stanford, CA: Stanford University Press.

Rubinowicz, Dawid. 1981. *The Diary of Dawid Rubinowicz*. Translated by Derek Bowman. Edinburgh: William Blackwood.

Sabor, Agnieszka, and Jan Strzałka. 2003. "'Sztuka nie jest niewinna': Interview with Ewa Kuryluk." *Tygodnik Powszechny*, January 19.

Saltzman, Lisa. 2006. *Making Memory Matter: Strategies of Remembrance in Contemporary Art*. Chicago: University of Chicago Press.

Santner, Eric L. 1990. *Mourning, Memory and Film in Postwar Germany*. Ithaca, NY: Cornell University Press.

Schaumann, Caroline. 2004. "From *weiter leben* (1992) to *Still Alive* (2001): Ruth Kluger's Cultural Translation of Her 'German Book' for an American Audience." *The German Quarterly* 77, no. 3:324–39.

Schulte-Sasse, Linda. 2004. "'Living on' in the American Press: Ruth Kluger's *Still Alive* and Its Challenge to a Cherished Holocaust Paradigm." *German Studies Review* 27, no. 3:469–75.

Schwarz, R. Daniel. 1999. *Imagining the Holocaust*. New York: St. Martin's Press.

Semprún, Jorge. 1982. *What a Beautiful Sunday!* Translated by Alan Sheridan. San Diego: Harcourt Brace Jovanovich Publishers.

————. 1997. *Literature or Life*. Translated by Linda Coverdale. New York: Penguin Books.

————. 2005. *The Long Voyage*. Translated by Richard Searer. Woodstock: Overlook Press.

Sicher, Efraim. 1998. "'The Burden of Memory': The Writing of the Post-Holocaust Generation." In *Breaking the Crystal: Writing and Memory after Auschwitz*, edited by Efraim Sicher, 1–16. Chicago: University of Illinois Press.

Snyder, Jill. 1994. *Impossible Evidence: Contemporary Artists View the Holocaust*. Curated by Jill Snyder. Reading, PA: Freedman Gallery, Albright College.

Sobolewska, Justyna. 2003. "'Piszę szeptem'—rozmowa z Ida Fink." *Gazeta Wyborcza*. May 12. http://wyborcza.pl/1,75517,1472212.html.

Soussana, Gad. 2000. "Entre mémoire et archive: La langue de témoignage." In *Définitions de la culture visuelle IV: Mémoire et archive*, 131–37. Montreal: Musée d'art contemporain de Montréal.

Spargo, Clifton. 2006. *Vigilant Memory: Emmanuel Levinas, the Holocaust, and the Unjust Death*. Baltimore, MD: The Johns Hopkins University Press.

Spiegelman, Art. 1991. *Maus II: A Survivor's Tale: And Here My Troubles Began*. New York: Pantheon Books.

Spivak, Gayatri. 1996. "Echo." In *The Spivak Reader: Selected Works of Gayatri Spivak*, edited by Donna Landry and Gerald MacLean, 175–202. New York: Routledge.

Stryjkowski, Julian. 1980. *Wielki strach*. Warsaw: Czytelnik.

Suleiman, Susan Rubin. 1996. "Monuments in the Foreign Tongue: On Reading Holocaust Memoirs by Emigrants." *Poetics Today* 17, no. 4:639–57.

Szurek, Jean-Charles. 2007. "*Shoah*: From the Jewish Question to the Polish Question." In *Claude Lanzmann's* Shoah: *Key Essays*, edited by Stuart Liebman, 149–69. Oxford: Oxford University Press.

Trezise, Thomas. 2001. "Unspeakable." *The Yale Journal of Criticism* 14, no. 1:39–66.

van Alphen, Ernst. 1997. *Caught by History: Holocaust Effects in Contemporary Art, Literature, and Theory*. Stanford: Stanford University Press.

Vidal-Naquet, Pierre. 1992. *Assassins of Memory: Essays on the Denial of the Holocaust*. Translated by Jeffrey Mehlman. New York: Columbia University Press.

Wardi, Dina. 1992. *Memorial Candles*. Translated by Dina Wardi. New York: Routledge.

Weisel, Mindy. 2000. *Daughters of Absence: Transforming the Legacy of Loss*. Sterling, VA: Capital Books.

———. 2007. Artist's statement. Minneapolis: Center for Holocaust and Genocide Studies at the University of Minnesota. http://www.chgs.umn.edu/museum/exhibitions/witnessLeg/secondGen/weisel/. Accessed December 18, 2010.

Wiesel, Eli. 1966. *The Gates of the Forest*. Translated by Francis Frenaye. New York: Holt, Rinehart and Winston.

————. 1971. *One Generation After.* Translated by Lily Edelman and Elie Wiesel. London: Weidenfeld and Nicolson.

————. 1982. *Night.* Translated by Stella Rodway. New York: Bantam Books.

————. 1995. *Memoirs.* Vol. 1, *All Rivers Run to the Sea.* New York: Alfred A. Knopf.

————. 1999. *Memoirs.* Vol. 2, *And the Sea Is Never Full.* New York: Alfred A. Knopf.

Wieviorka, Annette. 2006. *The Era of the Witness.* Translated by Jared Stark. Ithaca, NY: Cornell University Press.

Wilczyński, Marek. 1994. "Trusting the Words: Paradoxes of Ida Fink." *Modern Language Studies* 24, no. 4:25–38.

Wirth, Andrzej. 2002. "Parachuting Sending Tremors." http://www.kuryluk .art.pl/index.php?option=com_content&task=view&id=132&Itemid =144&lang=en. Accessed December 18, 2010.

Wojdowski, Bogdan. 1997. *Bread for the Departed.* Translated by Madeline G. Levine. Evanston, WY: Northwestern University Press.

Wrobel, Eta. 2006. *My Life, My Way: The Extraordinary Memoir of a Jewish Partisan in WWII Poland.* New Milford, NJ: The Wordsmithy, LLC; New York: YIVO Institute for Jewish Research.

THE STEPHEN S. WEINSTEIN SERIES
IN POST-HOLOCAUST STUDIES

After-Words: Post-Holocaust Struggles with Forgiveness,
Reconciliation, Justice (2004)
Edited and Introduced by David Patterson and John K. Roth

Fire in the Ashes: God, Evil, and the Holocaust (2005)
Edited and Introduced by David Patterson and John K. Roth

Open Wounds: The Crisis of Jewish Thought in the Aftermath
of the Holocaust (2006)
by David Patterson

Testimony, Tensions, and Tikkun: *Reflections on Teaching*
the Holocaust in Colleges and Universities (2007)
Edited and Introduced by Myrna Goldenberg and Rochelle L. Millen

Disappearing Traces: Holocaust Testimonials, Ethics
and Aesthetics (2012)
by Dorota Glowacka

Encountering the Stranger: A Jewish-Christian-Muslim Trialogue (2012)
Edited and Introduced by Leonard Grob and John K. Roth